Dedication

Discovering the hidden world of Interdimensional Entities: an Illustrated Guide is dedicated to all who dare to elevate the mundane. To all those who open its cover to quench their thirst for hidden knowledge. This beautiful edition is for the young, the aged, the novice, and the savant alike, as it unites the depth of generational knowledge with the best academic scholarship. Within its vibrant pages, worlds become worlds. It will claim its place in the library of classics, in the bookcases of the genius, in the classrooms of our schools, and in the offices of professionals and business people who carve our precious time to grapple with timeless questions and answers. For the student and the Scholar.

Dedicated to Naomi Silver

Interdimensional Entites: An Illustrated Guide

First English Standard Print b&w Edition, ISBN 979-8-218-48739-3

First English Standard EBook b&w Edition ISBN 979-8-218-48740-9

Silver Foundation

Contents

Chapter 1

Forward

The fact is you are an Interdimensional being and your consciousness transcends this world, but let's try to avoid the "woo-woo" right now. Let's set aside the phone and concentrate. We are being bombarded with distractions when we seek answers. There are just too many online posts, books, and online videos that take us down rabbit holes that have little substance. The world of metaphysics, spirituality, and ufology is full of charlatans and there is a reason for that, the truth is buried intentionally. That's sad because there are significant truths in those subjects that are world-changing. It's not pseudo-science, it's just lazy science. Yes, surprise, lizard people are real but it's not what you've been told.

This book is intended to lift the veil of occult and mystery that surrounds the study of Interdimensional Beings by encouraging a more scientific approach to the subject. If we are truly honest, almost all science has a little fiction in it. No scientist has actually seen a "black hole" or witnessed the big bang occur. All science contains a percentage of speculation but when the preverbal b.s. is too high, the science gets obfuscated, and the effect has had detrimental long-term effects on understanding the truth in these observations.

In the rather serious and scholarly world of ancient records and mysterious encounters, there has been an absence of systematic investigations that have left us with a cosmic pile of unresolved mysteries. You see, scholars often steer clear of these age-old folklore and wisdom, sticking to the accepted narratives. Perhaps fearing that exploring them might get them canceled, losing that W2 paycheck, or even worse, having to make a guest appearance on the next season of "Ancient Aliens."

Although gaining in acceptance, aliens, and other dimensional entities are still relegated to the realms of feckless government panels, popcorn movies, podcasts, clickbait news, and late-night am radio, there is something more intricate at play here. Now is the time we stop relying on the "experts" and put on our investigative hats to answer the age-old questions ourselves: Almost 70% of the world population does not doubt that "they" are here, but why are "they" here? How are "they" here? Why can't we see them? These ancient beings are here but hidden, and deserve a respectable inquiry and rebrand in the era of crumbling government narratives and a growingly frustrated populace.

To critics, the idea of dimensional beings might still sound like science fiction, but true science and the historical wisdom of humanity tell us there's a nugget of reality in there, hidden beneath the tinfoil hats, Denver airport, and Area 51 conspiracies. There is evidence that these beings have been around since ancient times, the original influencers of humanity. While a few might argue that these entities packed up their orbs and left, others speculate that they've just been practicing some serious camouflage skills and are living among us, under us, and next to us.

For those waiting for "disclosure" and what our governments truly understand about extraterrestrial and multidimensional beings that's never going to happen. Governments are no amateurs in the secrecy game, they are only interested in staying in control by misinforming, hiding, dividing, and distracting the public, and there's a good reason for it. Learning about these dimensional beings helps explain why our bureaucratic and ruling classes are not the ultimate decision-makers in the grand cosmic order. If this revelation were made public, it would be a bombshell of epic proportions, empowering humanity and destroying the power structures of the ruling class. So, instead of holding out hope for clear answers from corrupt governments, which, to be brutally honest, are as elusive as a bigfoot, one might explore ancient texts, particularly the wisdom noted in this book for some insights.

So, from ancient texts to modern studies and data analysis, it's quite the cosmic fog we are in. Whether you're a true believer or an interstellar skeptic, there's one thing we can all agree on Until we witness that "fake alien invasion" or get a selfie with a Martian, we're in for uncharted territory of paskining, pondering, reflecting, and learning about the unknown. The distinction between folklore and fact is a fluid boundary that undergoes continuous evolution. Hasty dismissal of intuition may overlook the potential for it to transform into tomorrow's science fact.

"Interdimensional Entities: An Illustrated Guide " takes you on a journey from the secret teachings about our Earth and Pre-Adamic civilized humanity to the many multi-dimensional beings, their relationship to us, and our collective human future. The categorization of these entities is not a rehash of other *mufon* books or sci-fi creative writing almanacs. This book attempts to collect the wisdom and knowledge of previous generations and the teachings of the ancients alongside modern understandings, witnesses, and insights. What we explore and discover is that the legends of old and the legends of today might very well be the same. More so, what is considered by many to be merely legend may indeed be something far greater; something very real and very relevant to us all. If you want to know what is out there, you might very well find your answers here.

Chapter 2

Introduction to the Format

Welcome to the comprehensive guide on interdimensional entities. This format has been meticulously designed to offer both quick and in-depth reference material for readers interested in understanding various entities across multiple dimensions. Each section is crafted to provide a balanced overview, combining historical context, unique and obscure facts, mythological interpretations, and more, to create a holistic understanding of each entity.

The chosen format ensures that the information is both accessible and thorough, catering to readers who seek either a quick summary or a detailed exploration. While not exhaustive, this structure aims to encapsulate the most relevant and intriguing aspects of each entity, facilitating easy navigation and quick referencing.

Here's a brief overview of the format used:

1. **General Definition**

   - **Purpose:** Provide a concise and comprehensive overview of the entity.

   - **Content:** Origins, primary characteristics, and significance in relevant cultures or subcultures. This section sets the stage for understanding the entity's basic nature and context.

2. **Historical Context and Origins**

   - **Purpose:** Discuss the historical background and development of the entity's current understanding.

   - **Content:** Key figures, events, or movements that contributed to the entity's significance. It also tracks how beliefs about the entity have evolved over time.

3. **Unique and Obscure Facts**

- ○ **Purpose:** Highlight notable and lesser-known facts about the entity.

- ○ **Content:** Distinctive attributes and variety of beliefs associated with the entity. This section showcases the unique aspects that differentiate the entity from others.

4. Mythological Interpretations

- ○ **Purpose:** Explain how the entity is interpreted in various mythologies and cultural frameworks.

- ○ **Content:** The entity's significance within different mythological contexts and its cultural impact.

5. Dimensional Attributes and Existence

- ○ **Purpose:** Describe the entity's perceived abilities to operate across multiple planes of existence.

- ○ **Content:** Skills and capabilities linked to different dimensions and how the entity navigates and influences various dimensions.

6. Case Study

- ○ **Purpose:** Present a specific, well-documented example involving the entity.

- ○ **Content:** Description of a particular case or story and its impact on beliefs or studies related to the entity.

7. Personal Accounts and Historical References

- ○ **Purpose:** Share anecdotes or claims from individuals and historical references to the entity.

- ○ **Content:** Eyewitness accounts and historical mentions in literature, folklore, or records.

8. Psyop

- ○ **Purpose:** Offer speculative or analytical perspectives on the entity's narrative.

- ○ **Content:** Discussion on how current issues or belief systems might influence narratives and the potential manipulation of human and general populations' perceptions.

9. Academic or Scientific References

- **Purpose:** Provide references to scholarly resources for further research and understanding.

- **Content:** Academic books, articles, and research studies that explore the entity.

By structuring the information in this manner, we aim to provide a resource that is both informative and engaging, allowing readers to delve as deep as they wish into the fascinating world of interdimensional entities.

Enjoy!

Chapter 3

Insights From The Past

The historical significance of interdimensional concepts emerges from thousands of years old kabbalistic masterpiece known as the Zohar.

While the realm of Kabbalah boasts myriad works and commentary, the book titled "Kabbalah in America" by Boaz Huss dedicates an entire chapter to exploring the Zohar's impact, particularly in early America. From the early American Puritans to the founder of Brown University and the third president of Yale University, Ezra Stiles (1778-1795), displayed an intense fascination with Jewish mysticism.

An example of the American founding father's obsession with Jewish mysticism; September 27th, 1769, Stiles, poised to become Yale College's future president, corresponded with Benjamin Franklin, then representing the colonies in London. Stiles sought esoteric texts, with the Zohar atop his list, desiring either a Latin translation or the original Hebrew. Yale's library houses their exchange, documenting Stiles' quest for the Zohar's mystical teachings. Eventually, Stiles acquired a copy of the Zohar, specifically the 1684 Zotz Spock edition, though Franklin's involvement in obtaining it remains uncertain. The Zohar's study by the founding fathers significantly influenced America's foundational principles.

Within the pages of this edition of the Zohar, commentary explores the profound significance embedded in the Torah's (Bible) opening verse, "In the beginning, G-d created the heavens and the earth." While the English translation offers a surface understanding, the Hebrew text delves deeper, suggesting a direct correlation between the spiritual dimensions and material dimensions. A concealed Kabbalistic name, known as the "Good Name," lies encoded within this verse, emphasizing the interconnectedness between these realms. Comprised of the letters Aleph (1), Hey (5), Vav (6), and Hey (5), totaling 17, this divine name and number functions as an acrostic, harmonizing the spiritual and material dimensions within the text.

Many books are written on this subject, but to summarize the essence of the "Good Name" reveals a profound link between the material and spiritual realms, a skill mastered by the historical founder of the Hassidic movement, the Bal Shem Tov. His ability was legendary in wielding this name, which acts as a unifying agent, bridging the divide between the dimensions, blending the spiritual and material and the soul and body. Those who can harness this name effectively bring together these aspects, embodying the essence of goodness. Understanding the importance of the "Good Name" entails dismantling and collapsing the apparent division between different dimensions — between the ideal and the real. By merging these dimensions, it surpasses the limitations inherent in our earthly existence, opening up new possibilities. Benjamin Franklin and Ezra Stiles undoubtedly recognized its significance, particularly regarding its connections to concepts like time manipulation, dimensions, and teleportation, as evidenced in their writings.

The Bal Shem Tov, who mastered the "Good Name," is associated with transcending these limitations. His feats, which predate Gene Roddenberry's creation of Star Trek by 250 years, include overcoming the boundaries of space and time. Stories abound of traversing great distances instantaneously by dematerializing and rematerializing, akin to "Beaming Up" or teleportation. The ultimate expression of this phenomenon is the transition from the spiritual realm to the physical. Additionally, he exhibited the capacity to manipulate time, allowing for accelerated experiences collapsing 15 years into a few minutes and spiritual ascension beyond earthly constraints.

Historically there are many scientists that have used ancient wisdom to unlock technical knowledge of the invisible forces that influence our existence; Isaac Newton was obsessed with the Zohar, dedicating the majority of his writings to mystical speculation and understandings of gravity. Newton, having learned Hebrew, held the belief that a comprehensive understanding of the 15 distinct elements comprising the construction of the Tabernacle, or Mishkan, would unveil the underlying physics governing the universe. The bulk of Isaac Newton's manuscripts, totaling thousands of pages, are currently preserved at Hebrew University in Jerusalem.

In the late 18th century, commonly known as the "Age of Enlightenment and Science," a significant intellectual shift unfolded. This ideological movement, that usurped scientific tropes, was regarded as a quasi-"religion" of its own, critically scrutinized the thousands of years of human wisdom about nature and the knowledge of sacred teachings, actively seeking to challenge and disprove them through "scientific" inquiry. Rising to meet this challenge was Rabbi Pinchas Eliyahu Horowitz of Vilna, a prominent Kabbalistic Sage from Eastern Europe. His response manifested a groundbreaking work that uniquely blended Kabbalah and science, distinguished by its unprecedented scope and depth. In 1797, this influential masterpiece was published, titled "Sefer HaBrit" (The Book of the Covenant). The book embarks on an exploration of the order of the physical universe, delving into celestial bodies such as stars and planets. Then extends the discourse to the physical realm, culminating in extensive and profound metaphysical reflections on the essence of humanity, dimensions, consciousness, and prophecy.

"Accepted Science is often wrong."

Carl Sagan

In this revelation, Rabbi Horowitz emerges as a pioneer in the subject of dimensions, challenging the scientific theories of the 18th century that speculated about life on other planets. Undeterred, he delves into authoritative sources to illuminate what the Torah truly teaches on this intriguing subject. A profound insight unfolds—the "creator of the universe" has fashioned an infinite array of physical and interdimensional worlds. While many interpreters of these Kabbalistic texts emphasize the spiritual or dimensional nature of these worlds, delving into the intricate realms of an inter-dimensional quantum reality. In essence, the writings unveil a cosmic narrative that transcends traditional boundaries, painting a picture of infinite possibilities across dimensions.

Within these realms, the panorama unfolds with four overarching dimensions or worlds. The three highest among these—Atzilut, Beriah, and Yetzirah—align with the domains of Spirit, Mind, and Emotion, respectively. Importantly, these realms transcend conventional perceptions of the physical, as commonly understood by humanity.

Horowitz, in Chapter 3, of his book, he raises a fundamental question: why should the number of worlds in the fourth Kabbalistic level, Asiyah, corresponding to the physical realm, be any less than the infinite worlds in the elevated realms above it? Drawing wisdom from the Zohar and Mishna, Rabbi Horowitz unveils a future vision wherein every righteous individual becomes a governor over 310 worlds. Notably, these are not ethereal realms but rather situated in outer space. This envisioned future unfolds after the next era in human history, representing a reward for the righteous who ascend to the stars, governing sections of the galaxy as regents. These profound reflections propel us forward into recent historical considerations perverting this knowledge.

Spirituality seekers joined the discourse in the late 19th century, the metaphysical concept of "planes" gained popularity through H. P. Blavatsky, who presented an intricate cosmology consisting of seven distinct "planes." The term "aether" was derived from Ancient Greek via Victorian physics, a concept later discredited. This term found its way into the writings of 19th-century occultists, including Blavatsky herself.

The Introduction of Etheric Concepts by Charles Webster Leadbeater and Annie Besant, prominent figures in Theosophy, introduced the notions of the "etheric plane" and the "etheric body." These concepts represented a theoretical 'fourth plane,' positioned above the traditional "planes" associated with solids, liquids, and gases. The term "etheric" was subsequently embraced by well-known occult authors such as Alice Bailey, Rudolf Steiner, and others. Influencing the infamous Aleister Crowley.

During the late 20th century, despite opposition from the cancel culture movement, Jack Parsons, recognized as the genuine "Father of Rocketry," was acknowledged by Wernher von Braun as more deserving of the title. This acknowledgment led to the humorous nickname "Jack Parsons' Laboratory" for JPL. Furthermore, Parsons embarked on exploring dimensional beings, establishing himself as a pioneer in both contemporary science and interdimensional communication.

Although recognized as a pioneer in the field of "rocket science," Parsons harbored beliefs in summoning mystical or interdimensional entities through explosive means and occult practices. Motivated by a quest to access alternate dimensions, Parsons conducted rituals, infusing statues with mystical power, and recounted experiences of the paranormal. His involvement in the "Babalon Working" ritual sought to achieve magical conception and transcend the boundaries of space and time.

★★★

Growing in acceptance Spiritualists in the 19th century adapted the concept of "other dimensions." During the Summer of 1947, this idea was applied by spiritualists to interpret accounts of "flying discs." On July 4, 1947, occultist Meade Layne asserted that flying discs possessed an "etheric" nature. Layne purported to engage in telepathic communication with the occupants of these saucers, suggesting that objects could transition from an etheric state to a denser form of matter, creating the illusion of materialization. Afterward, they would revert to an etheric condition. Layne contended that these visitors were not disembodied humans but rather individuals living in their own realm, arriving with benevolent intentions and an interest in experimenting with earthly existence. A year earlier, Layne reportedly consulted a medium who conveyed messages from a "spaceship named Careeta," hailing from an unidentified planet.

John Keel and the Concept of 'Ultraterrestrials': While the extraterrestrial hypothesis has maintained its dominance, especially in the 1970s, there was a growing acceptance of the interdimensional hypothesis. John Keel, a paranormal author and UFO enthusiast, made a significant shift in his perspective. Reflecting on his field investigations, Keel abandoned the extraterrestrial hypothesis in 1967 when he uncovered a surprising convergence between psychic phenomena and UFOs. According to him: "I abandoned the extraterrestrial hypothesis in 1967 when my own field investigations disclosed an astonishing overlap between psychic phenomena and UFOs the objects and apparitions do not necessarily originate on another planet and may not even exist as permanent constructions of matter. It is more likely that we see what we want to see and interpret such visions according to our contemporary beliefs."

In his 1970 book titled "UFOs: Operation Trojan Horse," Keel argued that a non-human or spiritual intelligence source orchestrated entire events over an extended period to propagate and reinforce specific erroneous belief systems. This included various phenomena such as monsters, ghosts, demons, fairy faith in Middle Europe, vampire legends, mystery airships in 1897, mystery airplanes of the 1930s, mystery helicopters, anomalous creature sightings, poltergeist phenomena, balls of light, and UFOs. Keel posited that all these anomalies could be a cover for the real dimensional phenomenon. Keel introduced the term "ultraterrestrials" to characterize UFO occupants, whom he believed to be non-human entities capable of assuming any form they desire.

Hynek and Vallée: Exploring Interlocking Universes: J. Allen Hynek, an American astronomer, played a crucial role as the scientific advisor for U.S. Air Force UFO studies, contributing to Project Sign, Project Grudge, and Project Blue Book. Notably, he pioneered the "Close Encounter" classification system and even had a cameo appearance in Stephen Spielberg's film "Close Encounters of the Third Kind." (Vallée, 1990) a student of Hynek, served as inspiration for the French researcher portrayed by François Truffaut in the same film.

In their collaborative work in "The Edge of Reality" in 1975, Vallée and Hynek delved into the intriguing possibility of "interlocking universes." Vallée contemplated various wild hypotheses, including the idea of other universes with different quantum rules or vibration rates. Hynek suggested that our space-time continuum could be a cross-section through a universe with additional dimensions, challenging the conventional notion of separate universes.

Vallée expanded on these ideas in his influential 1969 book, "Passport to Magonia: On UFOs, Folklore and Parallel Worlds," where he argued for the existence of a "parallel universe co-existing with our own." This concept continued to be a central theme in Vallée's subsequent writings, emphasizing the idea of intertwined realities.

In his 1990 paper, "Five Arguments Against the Extraterrestrial Origin of Unidentified Flying Objects," Vallée presented compelling objections to the extraterrestrial hypothesis. He highlighted the abundance of unexplained close encounters, questioned the likelihood of humanoid beings originating from another planet, pointed out the inconsistent behavior reported in abduction accounts, emphasized the historical persistence of UFO phenomena, and suggested that the apparent manipulation of space and time by UFOs indicated alternative and richer possibilities beyond the extraterrestrial perspective.

Presently, our technical knowledge, perhaps intentionally confine humanity to the here and now; individuals cannot exist simultaneously everywhere. We find ourselves anchored to the present, tethered to our specific dimension, location, and bound by the temporal framework of our finite reality within the construct of the world. Consequently, the mastery of space and time perhaps represents the pinnacle of freedom and technical knowledge or technologies that will shape the future, encompassing concepts like existing and understanding other dimensions.

Book references

"Passport to Magonia" On UFOs, Folklore, and Parallel Worlds" by Jacques Vallée This book explores the parallels between modern UFO sightings and historical accounts of encounters with fairies, demons, and other supernatural beings.

"Operation Trojan Horse" by John Keel: John Keel, a prominent figure in UFO research, discusses his investigations and proposes the idea of UFOs as manifestations of a non-human or spiritual intelligence.

"Dimensions" A Casebook of Alien Contact" by Jacques Vallée: Vallée presents a collection of UFO cases and explores the idea that these phenomena may involve interactions with beings from other dimensions.

"The Eighth Tower" by John Keel: Keel delves into various paranormal phenomena, including UFOs, and suggests a connection between them and a higher intelligence.

Chapter 4

Defining Dimensions

D imensions serve as the lens through which a being apprehends reality. A higher dimension adds an extra element or characteristic used to describe or define reality.

The more elevated the dimension, the greater the number of aspects one discerns about reality, leading to a deeper self-awareness. Beings of a specific "density" predominantly perceive reality through the dimension corresponding to their density. As third-density beings, for instance, our sensory perceptions are limited to three dimensions, aligning with the spiritual tasks designated for that density. Nevertheless, as spiritual progress unfolds, the capacity to perceive through higher dimensions becomes unlocked.

Some speculate that although human beings are virtually blind and unaware of our true reality, we have been given a unique capability to establish a unique connection with the highest entity in the universe, a trait not shared by other beings in this known universe. This exclusive attribute has garnered envy from non-human races and higher-dimensional entities within this universe, sparking significant interest and involvement in human affairs.

This is why it's imperative to instill in every child, upon reaching a suitable age of comprehension, the understanding that their visual perception does not capture the entirety of the reality they believe they're seeing. Instead, they're merely perceiving a fraction of the electromagnetic spectrum, termed visible light. This limited spectrum serves as the foundation of our reality, underscoring the notion that humans are inherently visually impaired.

When attempting to articulate phenomena from alternate realms or dimensions beyond typical human perception, linguistic limitations often hinder effective communication. While we possess vocabulary to describe elements within our perceptual range, conveying experiences outside this scope presents significant challenges. an example of this communication barrier is evident when trying to convey our world to individuals blind from birth or elucidating elements of sound to those with hearing impairments. In such instances, a genuine divide exists, rendering it impossible to fully convey the essence of these experiences due to a lack of suitable words.

Ezekiel's vision of the divine chariot, as depicted in the Maaseh Merkavah, exemplifies this challenge. Though commonly understood as spiritual entities, Ezekiel describes angels, ofanim, and holy chayot in physical terms reminiscent of creatures from an otherworldly menagerie. Despite his vivid experience and profound connection to the vision, Ezekiel struggles to articulate it accurately, resorting to imperfect physical descriptions.

Evolution has ensured that our brains just aren't equipped to visualize 11 dimensions directly. However, from a purely mathematical point of view it's just as easy to think in 11 dimensions, as it is to think in three or four.

Stephen Hawking

Similarly, the Zohar posits that Jacob's ladder serves as a metaphor for transcending into other dimensions. Notably, the Hebrew words for "ladder" and "voice" (sulam and kol) share a numerological value of 136, symbolizing the concentrated voice. Meditation, concentration, or prayer acts as the ladder, facilitating ascent from earthly existence to heightened states of consciousness and celestial realms, ultimately allowing individuals to touch the divine essence within the human soul.

In the pursuit of understanding higher dimensions, third density beings are primarily focused on learning. Despite possessing a weaker physical form compared to second density beings, third density entities are predisposed to engage with each other, facilitating the initiation of lessons aimed at grasping the concept of love. Moreover, third density beings have the potential to delve into more advanced spiritual teachings, making this density the focus of the most profound learning experiences for the soul.

To keep this definition non-empirical, sparing the eye-rolling from the Eric Weinstein's of the world, let's steer clear of cringe-inducing phrases like "holographic space beings." We will also skip over terms such as "M theory," String Theory, Romanian manifold, or determinant line bundle equations. Because equations can't explain why this world undeniably has its weirdness, and that weirdness is backed by substantial anecdotal evidence from millions of people across history sharing strikingly similar experiences. And disclosure isn't happening, we probably aren't going to get access to scientific data. And that's ok! It's our job to uncover these hidden mysteries and elevate the world.

From a more grounded and less "woo-woo" perspective, navigating the concept of life in higher dimensions often leads to contemplation of additional physical dimensions or alternate planes of existence, where the laws of physics and the existence of interdimensional beings diverge from our understanding. In envisioning a universe with four physical dimensions, it becomes apparent that gravity behaves differently compared to the familiar three-dimensional model, and concepts like entropy or energy conservation may not necessarily apply in the perceived higher reality. This realm, often likened to a heaven-like state prevalent in religious or sci-fi narratives featuring spiritually ascended entities, is assumed to be governed by superior and distinct rules, prompting speculation about the potential transition to such dimensions and the advantages it may offer.

To comprehend life in a 4D or 5D universe, we can draw parallels with the challenges faced by two-dimensional life, as explored in the classic book "Flatland." While speculative discussions on this topic have persisted for years, recent physical and mathematical analyses by James Scargill of UC Davis suggest its feasibility. However, inherent challenges arise, such as the tendency for objects to become easily trapped in 2D due to a single line acting as an infinite wall, leading to frequent collisions. In contrast, the reduced likelihood of particle collisions in 4D or 5D presents a different set of physical intricacies, posing obstacles to the emergence of complex properties like biology in higher dimensions.

It's worth noting that many planets may appear devoid of life due to our inability to perceive higher density beings and dimensions in the universe. While higher-density entities could be visible to us, they often choose not to manifest due to the intricate vibrational frequencies present on Earth. Some theories suggest that these vibrations are artificially induced by negative or parasitic beings. Despite these obstacles, humans are capable of observing off-world races and higher-dimensional entities as part of their spiritual development.

Defining a dimension is essential to understanding these concepts. While we commonly acknowledge three physical dimensions and one dedicated to time, the notion of existing in 10, 11, or even 26 dimensions, as suggested by some mathematicians in theoretical physics, remains beyond our current scientific comprehension. Despite the mathematical support the concept of these dimensions, they have not been empirically proven in regular physics, though they are often invoked to enhance our understanding of the universe.

In higher dimensions, the forces and physical properties may differ significantly from those in our three-dimensional reality, affecting molecular stability and other fundamental aspects. Electromagnetic bonds and gravity may weaken with distance, potentially leading to adverse consequences for human existence in a 4D universe. While a finely tuned universe suggests life impossibility with altered physical constants, it also implies the potential existence of different life forms suited to those dimensions. Constructing entities for use in higher dimensions, akin to how higher-dimensional beings may require vessels to operate in our dimension, remains a possibility, suggesting avenues for exploration and potential advancement in understanding these elusive realms.

Here's a list of books that delve into the subject of dimensions and related concepts:

"Flatland: A Romance of Many Dimensions" by Edwin A. Abbott - This classic novella is a satirical take on the idea of dimensions and follows the adventures of a square in a two-dimensional world.

"The Fourth Dimension" by Rudy Rucker- Rudy Rucker, a mathematician and science fiction author, explores the concept of the fourth dimension in this engaging book.

"The Hidden Reality: Parallel Universes and the Deep Laws of the Cosmos" by Brian Greene - Brian Greene delves into the concept of parallel universes and how they relate to the dimensions of our own reality.

"Tenth Dimension: An Informal History of High Energy Physics" by Bertrand J. Berche - This book provides an informal history of high-energy physics, including discussions on dimensions and their role in theoretical physics.

"The Universe in Your Hand: A Journey Through Space, Time, and Beyond" by Christophe Galfardm - Christophe Galfard takes readers on a journey through various concepts related to space, time, and dimensions in a highly accessible and engaging manner.

Evidence for Interdimensionals

Many believe a person must develop hidden or latent mind powers to reach out and commune with many others that surround us but are invisible to our sight.

That is simply not true. The technology of viewing into other worlds or dimensions is nothing new but currently unavailable. In contemporary science, the field of Spectroscopy, particularly analytical spectroscopy, encompasses the interaction of electromagnetic waves across various frequencies like ultraviolet, visible, infrared, X-ray, radio, or microwave. Through these methods, modern science gains insights into atoms, molecules, and celestial bodies such as stars. However, any scientific exploration into realms like auras, realms, other dimensions, and similar topics appears to have been marginalized, canceled, and dismissed as pseudoscience.

In the past, the practice of observing auras using screens or exploring unseen aspects of our world dates to Baron von Reichenbach in the 1800s. Reichenbach, a German astronomical instrument maker, authored "Odic Magnetic Letters," claiming to perceive auras around magnets' poles and human hands, ultimately discovering coal tar products. Between 1835 and 1860, he contributed significantly to meteorite research, earning a reputation as a brilliant scientist. Reichenbach documented reports of sensitive individuals perceiving emanations from crystals and magnets in complete darkness, detecting changes in electric current, and even sensing an aura surrounding the human body. This research influenced the work of Kilner.

Walter J Kilner MD, a Cambridge University graduate and member of the Royal College of Physicians, explored a broad range of topics in his books. However, his 1911 work, "The Human Atmosphere or The Aura Made Visible by the aid of chemical screens," stands out as a meticulous and scientifically rigorous examination of diverse patient color "Auras." These studies include individuals who are healthy, sick, young, old, mentally ill, and pregnant. Kilner, a distinguished scientist from London, introduced a groundbreaking "screen" that revealed the human aura through what he termed "N" rays. This innovation involved the use of phosphorescent sulfide of calcium, he called it "Spectaurine," essentially a dye referred to as "Dicyanin."

Kilner conducted experiments using a deep blue chemical dye named Dicyanin. The process was straightforward – he poured the dye onto a glass screen. Upon peering through the screen, Kilner discovered the ability to see the aura of a person standing before him. This became achievable due to the dye's specific color blocking a significant portion of the white light spectrum, leaving only a concentrated segment that heightened the viewer's perception of the aura.

These technologies, present in ancient times, are now lost or not widely known in modern science. In his book, "The Development of Clairvoyance and the Scientific Formation of Circles," Harry Boddington explored Kilner's endeavor to transform human radiations into color. Boddington said Kilner's innovative method, using a little-known dye, notably shortened or eliminated the extensive preparation time that is generally considered essential for viewing other worlds. This approach influenced the optic nerve, extending normal vision into the realms of the infrared and ultraviolet ends of the spectrum. This process was adopted by spiritualists as the safest and most certain method of development watching the aura was found to develop compels to upon the possibilities of a world of consciousness external to the brain.

Curiously, in the 1940s, numerous Western governments outlawed Dicyanin for reasons that remain undisclosed but obvious. Despite Dicyanin being non-toxic, not a drug, and derived from coal tar, information about it appears to have been deliberately expunged from our collective knowledge of humanity. The scarcity of details on the subject suggests a deliberate concealment. The ruling class sought to suppress this relatively simple experiment, enabling even the untrained neophyte to glimpse into another tangible dimension without the need for astral projection, spiritual sensitivity, or meditation training. This suppression was likely intended to limit knowledge, subjugate, and shape the perceptions of future generations.

This scientific phenomenon has been accidentally stumbled upon multiple times. An illustrative instance took place during the Vietnam War, involving the observation of entities resembling the common description of demons through first-generation military technology – specifically, experimental night vision goggles.

A field officer overseeing an experimental project in Vietnam recounted an incident where the introduction of a new technology, now known as "night vision," had a profound impact. The implementation of this technology nearly halted the progress of the war.

This differs from the night vision we have today. The initial night vision goggles, first-generation and experimental, displayed images in the red spectrum. Modern night-vision goggles, where everything is rendered in green, have become standard. Green is considered optimal because the human eye perceives more shades of green than any other color, a trait rooted in our evolutionary history. Night vision initially used red and was introduced to helicopter pilots and gunners during the Vietnam War.

This field officer participated in the initial experiment with the troops under his command, and it proved disastrous. The issue wasn't the presentation of the image in red pixels instead of green but rather the technology used at that time, which produced effects that the soldiers found challenging to handle.

In the initial experiment with other units testing the goggles, the field officer commanded troops. The testing was disastrous, not due to the image being in red pixels instead of green, but because the technology used at the time produced challenging effects that soldiers couldn't manage. Military units testing the red night vision goggles ended up causing destructive outcomes, including friendly fire and other dire situations.

The field officer recounts the Gunners' first experience with the goggles. While the squadron was flying, the field officer sat in the helicopter with the pilot. Unexpectedly, in a tranquil area with no apparent activity, the gunner in his helicopter began firing indiscriminately at their helicopter's altitude, without targeting anything on the ground. This led other helicopters to quickly evade and respond to the gunner's actions.

The field officer interrogated the gunner, demanding an explanation for his firing. The gunner, visibly distressed, perspired heavily with dilated eyes, giving the impression of a heroin addict. However, the soldier was not displaying typical symptoms; rather, he was reacting to what he claimed to have seen. Describing the experience to the field officer, he asserted that he was shooting at flying entities resembling demons that accompanied the helicopter.

The gunner claimed that he believed these entities were targeting him, as they gestured towards him and seemed aware of his presence. In fear, he reacted by shooting 50 caliber slugs at them. Allegedly, these beings were flying alongside the helicopter. Out of fear, the gunner started firing directly at them. This phenomenon occurred consistently every time they attempted to use the night vision goggles, leading to encounters described as facing monsters.

The field officer, curious, decides to test the goggles personally. When he puts them on, he describes the experience as akin to being in a nightmarish demonic gothic hell. Through the goggles, he sees creatures with large wings and claws flying off the tops of trees. However, when he removes the goggles, there is no disturbance in the fog above the canopy of the trees.

Essentially, the initial night vision goggles of the first generation filtered a dimension linked to the red image, affecting a certain aspect of consciousness. When the military transitioned to green, these perceptions naturally vanished. Modern night vision goggles still employ similar technology but with a different phase alignment for translation. While today's goggles may not reveal everything as the first generation did, they no longer display images in red. The current green display relies on electrons instead of photons, distinguishing it from the initial generation of goggles.

Why does legacy "science" poo-poo the woo-woo?

Contemporary scientific pursuits, driven by profit and power, often obscure and deliberately disregard ancient wisdom. Despite this, there is ongoing evolution, particularly in fields like mathematics and physics, exploring dimensions. However, these progressive concepts have not yet fully permeated disciplines such as astronomy, anthropology, or archaeology. Meanwhile, scientists funded by government agencies like SETI, perhaps fear loosing their W2 paycheck, continue traditional activities from the 1950s, focusing on detecting radio signals and analyzing peculiar starlight patterns. Interestingly, there is a tendency to overlook NORAD satellite data concerning "Fastwalkers." Modern scientific discourse, exemplified by concepts like the Fermi paradox and the Drake equation, may be sidelining the consideration of interdimensional entities in the search for extraterrestrial life.

Regarding Fermi's Legacy: The Fermi paradox, named after Enrico Fermi, the renowned scientist responsible for the first nuclear reactor's construction and the initial controlled nuclear reaction in 1942, originated during a 1950 lunch discussion at the Los Alamos National Laboratory. Inspired by a cartoon from "The New Yorker," Fermi posed a question about extraterrestrial life and interstellar travel, pondering why, if advanced aliens capable of such travel exist, they haven't made contact with us. Though Fermi never formally published his inquiry, it has persisted as a stimulating conundrum in the exploration of extraterrestrial possibilities.

Exploring interdimensional beings through the Fermi paradox and Drake equation questions the lack of extraterrestrial contact and estimates the number of intelligent civilizations. However, these tools are limited by assumptions that life must exist in three dimensions, be carbon-based, and emit radio signals, which may hinder our understanding of extraterrestrial possibilities.

So, what exactly does the Drake equation entail? Named after astronomer Frank Drake, who initiated the first systematic search for extraterrestrial radio signals in 1960, the equation was introduced during a subsequent 1961 meeting at the National Radio Astronomy Observatory in Green Bank, West Virginia. Attendees included diverse thinkers such as Carl Sagan, co-founder of the Planetary Society. Drake's formula aimed to estimate the potential number of civilizations currently emitting detectable signals within the Milky Way.

"The Drake Equation progresses from easiest to hardest," notes Kaitlin Rasmussen, an astrophysicist at the University of Michigan. While some variables, like civilization lifespan ("L"), remain speculative, we can now more accurately estimate factors like star formation rates and the prevalence of planets around stars. Rasmussen predicts that advanced telescopes will soon refine our understanding of habitable planets. Despite over half a century since the Drake equation's inception and Fermi's question, the search for intelligent life beyond Earth continues, with numerous possible explanations still in play.

The Great Diversion. Traditional science often employs sophisticated methods to systematize gaps in knowledge. While the Drake Equation has proven useful in estimating potential extraterrestrial civilizations, it is not immune to criticism. One speculative critique revolves around the subjective nature of the equation's variables. Subjectivity in Variable Assignments: Critics argue that the values assigned to variables in the Drake Equation are highly subjective and can be swayed by an individual's cosmic perspective or mood on a given day. Factors such as the rate of star formation, the probability of habitable planets, and the emergence of intelligent life are all open to interpretation. Influence of Daily Factors: The tongue-in-cheek mention of one's coffee consumption underscores the notion that an individual's state of mind may impact their estimation and input of variables concerning extraterrestrial civilizations. This underscores the speculative and potentially time-wasting aspect of certain variables within the equation.

Dimensional Oversight: The biggest flaw is related to this subject, the Drake Equation primarily focuses on factors related to us carbon based, organic based, and three-dimensional based. Neglecting the possibility of life or entities existing in other dimensions, silicon based or non-organic. Critics argue that our understanding of the universe may be limited by our three-dimensional perspective, and the equation does not account for the potential existence of life in additional spatial dimensions.

Limited Scope of Variables: The Drake Equation simplifies a complex issue into a set of variables, which may oversimplify the intricacies of the factors influencing the emergence of extraterrestrial life. It doesn't consider factors like the impact of astrophysical events, the role of different chemical compositions on life, or the potential influence of unknown variables. Assumption of Similar Biochemistry: The equation assumes that extraterrestrial life would share a similar biochemistry to life on Earth. Critics argue that this assumption may be limiting, as life forms could potentially exist with different chemical compositions, making them difficult to detect using the criteria outlined in the Drake Equation. The Drake Equation remains a useful framework for initiating discussions about the potential for extraterrestrial life. However, acknowledging its limitations and the evolving understanding of the universe is crucial for refining our approach to the search for understanding our universe and other dimensions.

Non-human life might exist in ways beyond our current understanding, eluding detection due to our limited perception, according to researchers from the University of Cadiz, Spain. The study, published in Acta Astronautica, proposes that our traditional view of space is constrained by our cognitive limitations, suggesting that signs of non-human life may be present but unnoticed. The researchers draw parallels to the psychological concept of inattentional blindness, where we don't see what we're not actively looking for.

Referencing the well-known "Invisible Gorilla" experiment, which revealed the gaps in human perception, the researchers argue that our brains filter and process information selectively, potentially causing us to miss phenomena, including signs of non-terrestrial life. Their own experiment involving aerial photographs, akin to the gorilla experiment, showed that only 45 out of 137 participants noticed an inserted image of a person in a gorilla suit.

Interdimensional researchers caution against a narrow focus on traditional search methods, such as SETI's radio signal exploration, proposing a broader approach that incorporates advanced mathematical physics. Interestingly, government financed scientists do not fully understand most of the universe, so they often resort to the term "dark matter" to describe the vast unknowns in this realm. Other researchers suggest that advanced civilizations, or non-terrestrial intelligence (NTI), might exist in forms beyond our current understanding, including entities based on dark energy or other exotic phenomena.

Avoiding the term "extraterrestrial," researchers emphasize the need to consider diverse possibilities, including beings from dimensions beyond our grasp or intelligences rooted in phenomena like dark matter. They advocate for a shift in perspective, acknowledging the limitations of human biology and psychology in understanding potential advanced extraterrestrial or non-terrestrial life.

Argument for the Scientific Proof of Interdimensional Beings Using DMT Research

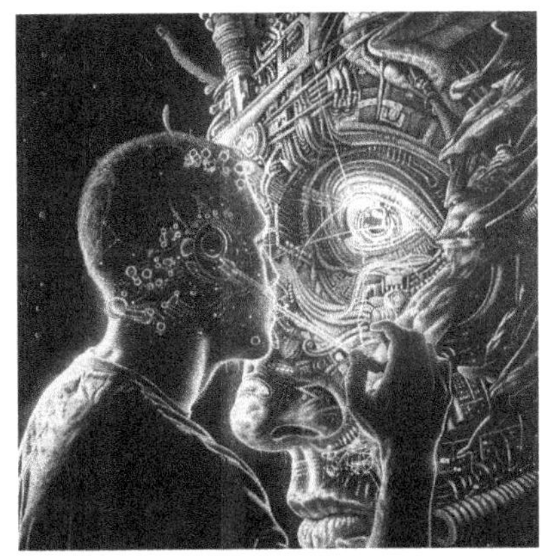

The notion of interdimensional beings interacting with humans has historically been relegated to the realm of mythology and speculative fiction. However, recent research involving the potent psychedelic compound DMT (N,N-Dimethyltryptamine) offers intriguing possibilities that merit scientific consideration. This argument synthesizes findings from various studies and expert testimonies, particularly those of Dr. Andrew Gallimore, to propose a scientific framework for the potential existence of interdimensional beings.

Evidence from Empirical Studies

In the study conducted by Imperial College London, participants reported prolonged encounters with entities in the DMT state. Subjects consistently described these beings as intelligent, communicative, and often benevolent. The subjects felt welcomed and cared for by these entities, suggesting a structured and recurring pattern of interaction rather than random hallucinations. This aligns with Gallimore's assertion that DMT might function as a communication technology with other intelligences.

A large-scale survey analyzing 3,000 DMT trip reports found consistent themes in the encounters. The most common reports involved interactions with guiding, loving presences, often perceived as female. The uniformity of these reports across diverse individuals suggests a shared experiential reality. The regularity and coherence of these experiences challenge the hypothesis that they are purely subjective or culturally influenced hallucinations.

Imperial College London's planned hyperscanning studies aim to simultaneously monitor two individuals in the DMT state to detect synchronized brain activity and shared experiences. If successful, this would provide robust evidence of a common interdimensional space accessible via DMT, supporting the hypothesis of an objective external reality inhabited by these beings.

DMT as a Communication Technology**:Andrew Gallimore posits that DMT may allow humans to interface with an advanced, non-human intelligence embedded within the fundamental structure of reality. This concept draws parallels to John Barrow's hypothesis that advanced civilizations might manipulate the basic structure of space-time itself.

Indigenous Amazonian cultures have long reported interactions with spirit beings through the use of ayahuasca, a brew containing DMT. The convergence of modern scientific findings with these traditional narratives adds credibility to the argument that these experiences tap into a real, external dimension.

The empirical data from DMT research, supported by theoretical frameworks and traditional knowledge, build a compelling case for the existence of interdimensional beings. While definitive proof remains elusive, the consistency and repeatability of these experiences suggest that they are more than mere hallucinations. Further interdisciplinary studies, combining neuroimaging, phenomenology, and ethnographic research, are essential to advancing our understanding of these potential interdimensional interactions.

Daniel Nemes images of Interdimensional Entities

Daniel Nemes, a dedicated scientist and inventor, asserts that he has developed "Energivision," a revolutionary technology designed to capture images of interdimensional entities. While his claims have been met with non scientific skepticism, it is important to note that no one has scientifically disproven his work. Nemes's approach, which utilizes unique lenses and ultrasensitive screens, has resulted in thousands of images that he believes originate from other dimensions. These images are shared on his Facebook page, where he openly invites scrutiny and challenges from both the scientific community and the public.The sheer volume of images and Nemes's willingness to have his work examined suggest a level of credibility that warrants consideration. His persistence in the face of limited recognition from mainstream science indicates a genuine commitment to exploring the unknown. By inviting others to prove him wrong, Nemes demonstrates transparency and confidence in his findings. This openness encourages a broader dialogue about the potential existence of interdimensional entities and the possibilities of exploring dimensions beyond our current understanding. While further investigation is needed, Nemes's work presents an intriguing opportunity to expand our perception of reality.

References

- Gallimore, A. Various interviews and writings on DMT and interdimensional beings.

- Imperial College London Studies: Ongoing research on extended DMT states and entity encounters.

- Large-Scale DMT Survey: Analyzing 3,000 trip reports for common themes and experiences.

- Traditional Indigenous Knowledge: Accounts of ayahuasca experiences in Amazonian cultures.

Chapter 6

Adeni Hasadeh

Yadua, Al-Nasna, Plant People

Adeni Hasadeh, also known as Yadua in Hebrew and Al-Nasnas in Arabic, are part-human, part-plant entities mentioned in the book of Job and various ancient texts.

Adeni Hasadeh, also known as Yadua in Hebrew and Al-Nasnas in Arabic, are part-human, part-plant entities mentioned in the Book of Job and various ancient texts. These multidimensional entities straddle both the third dimension (physical existence) and the lower second-density (as a plant), implying a dual existence in different realms. Their unique nature allows them to remain continuously connected to their source of life through their roots. Adeni Hasadeh, also known as Adnei haSadeh, are often described as humanoid beings tethered to the earth by a cord connected to their navel. These mysterious entities are believed to inhabit remote mountains and forests, living in harmony with nature. According to ancient texts like the Mishnah and the Jerusalem Talmud, Adeni Hasadeh possesses both human and wild animal characteristics. They are omnivorous, feeding on local fruits and vegetables, and are known to be cautious around human intruders. The cord that connects them to the ground is their lifeline; severing it results in their demise. While generally categorized as wild animals, Rabbi Yossi argues that they cause impurity in a tent like a human corpse would. This suggests a complex understanding of their nature, blending animal and human traits. The Jerusalem Talmud elaborates that these creatures can live from their navel connection alone, implying they don't need conventional nourishment. Their cord can reportedly grow over a mile long, giving them a vast territory to roam within. Some sources claim Adeni Hasadeh possesses the ability to speak, though their language is unintelligible to humans. In certain interpretations, Adeni Hasadeh is considered part of a race of beings created before Adam, later wiped out by the Great Flood.

Historical Context and Origins

The concept of Adeni Hasadeh is rooted in ancient Jewish and Arabic texts. They are mentioned in the Mishnah, Talmud, and other rabbinic literature, describing them as creatures connected to the earth through a cord. They also appear in various works on geography and natural history.

Descriptions and Characteristics

Adeni Hasadeh are described as humanoid creatures physically connected to the ground by a cord emerging from their navel. This cord is their lifeline, and if severed, the creature dies instantly. They resemble humans in form, with a fully developed body, head, hands, and feet. Their plant-like nature and the cord tethering them to the earth make them unique among interdimensional entities.

Unique and Obscure Facts

- **Plant-Animal Hybrid Nature**: Adeni Hasadeh exist as both plant and animal. This dual nature allows them to draw sustenance directly from the earth, similar to plants, while possessing mobility and other characteristics of animals.

- **Biblical and Rabbinic References:** These beings are referenced in several biblical and rabbinic texts. The Mishnah Kilayim 8:5 discusses their classification among wild creatures, while Rabbi Yose asserts they cause impurity in a tent like humans.

- **Dangerous Proximity:** According to Rabbi Meir son of Rabbi Klonimos of Speyer, no creature may approach the Adeni Hasadeh within the length of its cord, as it is lethal within this radius. Hunters would tear at the cord from a distance to safely neutralize the creature.

- **Roots and Lifespan:** The unique virtue of these beings, as noted in Likkutei Sichos, vol. 24, p.116, is that they remain connected to their source of life (the earth) through their roots. If uprooted, they cease to exist, akin to plants.

Mythological Interpretations

In various myths, the Adeni Hasadeh are depicted as intermediary beings between plants and animals, reflecting an ancient understanding of life forms that transcend simple categorization. This is supported by texts like Etz Chaim and Mishnah Kilayim. The bones of these creatures were believed to be used in sorcery, as noted by Rashi on Job 5:23:2, tying them to ancient practices of divination and magic.

Dimensional Attributes and Existence

- **Second Density (Plant Existence):** The plant aspect of Adeni Hasadeh is evident through their continuous connection to the earth via their roots or cord. This connection aligns them with the second density of existence, characterized by beings that are part of the natural world and derive their sustenance directly from it. Plants, as second-density entities, are grounded and deeply connected to their environment, and so are the Adeni Hasadeh.

- **Third Dimension (Physical Existence):** The humanoid characteristics of Adeni Hasadeh place them in the third dimension, where physical forms and mobility are defining traits. Their ability to interact with the environment and other creatures, combined with their humanoid appearance, aligns them with third-dimensional existence, where consciousness and physicality intersect.

Case Study

A notable case involving the Adeni Hasadeh is the tale from the Jerusalem Talmud Kilayim 8:4:3, which describes them as 'Field Stones' or mountain men living from their navels. If their umbilical cord is cut, they cannot survive. This account highlights their dependence on the earth and their mysterious nature.

Personal Accounts and Historical References

- **Rabbi Meir's Account**: Rabbi Meir describes the Adeni Hasadeh as lethal within the reach of their cord. Hunters would carefully cut the cord from a distance to kill them safely. This method ensured that no one would fall victim to the creature's deadly proximity.

- **Rabbi Yose's Classification**: Rabbi Yose, in the Mishnah, classifies these creatures as causing impurity like humans when they die. This classification blurs the line between animal and plant, highlighting their unique status in ancient thought.

References

- Likkutei Sichos, vol. 24, p.116

- Mishnah Kilayim 8:5

- Jerusalem Talmud Kilayim 8:4:3

- Rashi on Job 5:23:2

- Etz Chaim, Shaar 42

- Maaseh Tuviah, 59a

Chapter 7

Alpha-Draconians

Dracs. Reptilians, Ciakahrr

The Alpha-Draconians, often referred to as "Ciakahrr" in their own language, are considered some of the most powerful and ancient interdimensional entities in the universe.

They are said to exist in a realm slightly beyond human perception. The Alpha-Draconians, a fascinating race believed to originate from the Alpha-Draconis star system, are steeped in mystery and intrigue. These beings are said to possess an uncanny ability to manipulate quantum fields, allowing them to phase-shift between dimensions at will. Some theorists suggest they have mastered consciousness transfer, enabling them to inhabit human bodies for extended periods. Interestingly, their home star, Alpha Draconis (also known as Thuban), was once the North Star around 2600 BCE. This celestial alignment coincided with the construction of the Great Pyramid of Giza, leading some to speculate about their involvement in ancient Egyptian civilization. Recent astronomical observations have revealed that Alpha Draconis is a binary star system where the two stars eclipse each other every 51.4 days. This phenomenon went unnoticed for centuries due to the brief duration of the eclipses and the star's brightness. Some believers claim that the Alpha-Draconians possess advanced bioengineering capabilities, allowing them to create hybrid offspring with enhanced psionic abilities. These hybrids are rumored to be strategically placed in positions of power across various sectors of human society, subtly influencing global events from the shadows.

Historical Context and Origins

The first recorded sighting of Alpha-Draconians dates back to around 2200 BCE. They were described by explorers as massive creatures with dragon-like wings and human-like faces. According to various accounts, these beings were created by an ancient civilization to guard sacred temples and artifacts, contributing to their formidable reputation and the enduring stories about their existence.

Descriptions and Characteristics

Alpha-Draconians are noted for their incredible strength, speed, intelligence, and advanced magical abilities. They can fly at exceptional speeds and communicate telepathically over vast distances. Physically, they are immensely strong and capable of lifting objects to five times their weight effortlessly. They also possess shapeshifting abilities, and high-ranking individuals can cloak themselves, making them even more elusive.

Unique and Obscure Facts

- **Shapeshifting and Cloaking:** While not all Alpha-Draconians can shapeshift, those who can use this ability to blend into various environments. High-ranking members possess cloaking abilities, allowing them to become invisible to the human eye.

- **Interdimensional Travel:** Alpha-Draconians are unique in their capability to travel between dimensions, a skill not common among many other interstellar species. This ability allows them to execute strategic movements and maintain control over different realms.

- **Caste-Based Society**: Their society is structured similarly to an insect colony, with distinct castes including royalty, warriors, and workers. The Ciakahrr royalty are particularly notable, standing up to 25 feet tall and often involved in governance and strategic decisions.

- **Magical Abilities**: Alpha-Draconians are reputed to have formidable magical powers, such as casting spells to freeze time, summon storms, and manipulate natural elements. These abilities contribute significantly to their feared status.

- **Technological Suppression**: They are known for suppressing advanced technologies that could enable human interstellar travel and autonomy, ensuring their continued dominance and preventing potential threats from emerging.

Mythological Interpretations

The image of Alpha-Draconians has permeated various aspects of popular culture and public discourse. Notably, David Icke has propagated theories suggesting that Alpha-Draconians manipulate human society through shape-shifting reptilians that infiltrate high levels of government and society. Icke's theories propose that these beings are involved in a global conspiracy to control humanity, often linking them to influential figures and royalty.

Zecharia Sitchin, a prominent author known for his works on ancient astronaut theories, has heavily influenced Icke's perception of Alpha-Draconians. Sitchin's interpretations of Sumerian texts suggest that ancient deities, often depicted as reptilian or dragon-like, were extraterrestrial beings, possibly including the Alpha-Draconians. However, the works of Samuel Noah Kramer have debunked most of Sitchin's interpretations. Kramer, a renowned Assyriologist, highlighted numerous inaccuracies and misinterpretations in Sitchin's translations of Sumerian texts, which form the foundation for much of David Icke's theories.

Dimensional Attributes and Existence

Alpha-Draconians possess the ability to travel between dimensions, making them formidable in both physical and metaphysical realms. Their society operates in a hierarchical, caste-based structure, which is supported by their ability to manipulate and control various dimensions.

Case Study

A notable case involves contactee Alex Collier, who claims that the Alpha-Draconians are behind the repression of human populations across the galaxy. He alleges that they instill fear and exert control to prevent humanity from reaching its full potential and becoming a threat to their agendas.

Personal Accounts and Historical References

While concrete evidence is scarce, numerous accounts provide glimpses into interactions with Alpha-Draconians. Descriptions often highlight their immense size, telepathic communication, and intimidating presence. These accounts are frequently tied to theories about their involvement in global and interstellar politics.

Psyop

Alpha-Daconians may be a fictionalized version the pre-adamic native earth reptilians or they may be be Watchers in the Book of Daniel and identified as the Seraphim in the Book of Isaiah, who are the Bible's Dragon Masters. These beings, characterized by a humanoid/reptilian nature, constitute a species that surpasses humanity in terms of advancement, spirituality, and technological prowess. Their reptilian physiology coexists with a profound spiritual connection, as indicated by biblical references, suggesting a close association with the divine.

References

- Samuel Noah Kramer, *History Begins at Sumer* (1956)

- David Icke, *The Biggest Secret* (1999)

- Zecharia Sitchin, *The Earth Chronicles* (1976-2007)

Chapter 8

Amphibians Reptoids

Amphibious reptoids are distinctive entities, known for their unique combination of reptilian and amphibian characteristics, setting them apart from other reptilian beings like Saurians or Reptiloids. These semi-aquatic creatures are believed to have evolved over centuries, adapting to thrive in both land and water environments.

Frequently encountered near swamps, rivers, and other bodies of water, amphibious reptoids challenge conventional understanding. They are often described as having webbed fingers and toes, scaly yet moist skin, and a notably aggressive demeanor. Despite skepticism regarding their existence, numerous accounts suggest that these beings might possess interdimensional and psychic abilities, allowing them to traverse different planes of existence. This could explain their elusive nature and the difficulties faced in capturing or studying them. Historical and cultural narratives further support the possibility of their existence, often depicting similar beings as guardians of sacred sites, hinting at a deeper, ancient connection to human history and mythology. Such narratives push us to reconsider the boundaries of our understanding and the potential for undiscovered life forms that operate beyond our conventional reality.

Historical Context and Origins

Reports of amphibious reptoids span across various cultures and historical periods. Early accounts frequently describe them as protectors of sacred sites, akin to mythical guardians in ancient lore. These beings have been woven into folklore and mythology, with descriptions evolving over time to include modern interpretations that suggest extraterrestrial and interdimensional origins. Researcher John Rhodes has extensively documented claims of reptilian humanoid encounters, proposing that these beings might be descendants of ancient Earth species, possibly linked to dinosaur evolution.

Unique and Obscure Facts

- **Semi-Aquatic Nature**: Amphibious reptoids are adapted to both land and water, often found in swampy regions and rivers, which enhances their elusive nature.

- **Kappa:** In Japanese folklore, the Kappa is a turtle-like humanoid creature known to inhabit rivers and ponds. While not exactly a reptilian humanoid, its characteristics and habitat align with the concept of amphibious reptoids

- **Aggressive Behavior**: Numerous reports of unprovoked attacks on humans suggest a highly territorial and defensive nature.

- **Magical and Psychic Abilities**: Amphibious reptoids are thought to possess telepathy and the ability to manipulate natural elements, adding to their formidable presence.

- **Interdimensional Hypothesis (IDH):** The IDH posits that these entities might originate from parallel dimensions and have the ability to temporarily cross into our reality. This could explain their rare sightings and the challenges in capturing or studying them.

Mythological Interpretations

Amphibious reptoids have influenced various cultural narratives and works of fiction. In mythology, they are often depicted as protectors or guardians, similar to the nagas in South Asian cultures. Modern interpretations sometimes link them to extraterrestrial or interdimensional entities. Furthermore, the concept of interdimensional beings aligns with ancient mythological ideas of "thin places," where the boundaries between worlds are believed to be particularly permeable, allowing beings to cross over.

Dimensional Attributes and Existence

These entities are believed to operate across multiple dimensions. Their interdimensional capabilities might enable them to move between different planes of existence, which could explain their sudden appearances and disappearances, as well as the difficulties encountered in capturing or studying them. The **Quantum Physics Perspective** adds weight to this idea, suggesting that fluctuations in space-time could allow these entities to momentarily cross over from alternate dimensions, leading to the cryptic nature of their sightings.

Case Study

One of the most notable encounters occurred in Thetis Lake, British Columbia, Canada in 1972, where teenagers reported seeing a bipedal reptoid with amphibian features. The creature, described as having silver scales and sharp spines, reportedly chased them before retreating back into the water. Despite attempts to dismiss the event as a hoax, similar entities have been reported in other locations, including Loveland, Ohio, USA, where also in 1972 police officers encountered a frog-like humanoid. Sudden appearances and disappearances of these creatures, as reported by witnesses, lend credibility to the theory of interdimensional activity. Additionally, environmental anomalies such as strange lights and electromagnetic disturbances in areas like Scape Ore Swamp further suggest the presence of dimensional rifts or portals.

Personal Accounts and Historical References

Eyewitness accounts often describe amphibious reptoids as aggressive and territorial. Historical references in folklore and mythology frequently depict them as guardians of sacred sites or beings with supernatural abilities. Police reports and personal testimonies add credence to these sightings, suggesting a pattern of encounters that cannot be easily dismissed. Eyewitness Accounts with supernatural elements, such as feelings of dread or disorientation, may indicate that these encounters involve interdimensional overlap, affecting the witness's cognitive and sensory perceptions.

Psyop

The Atlantic Undersea Test and Evaluation Center (AUTEC), located on Andros Island in the Bahamas, is often linked to conspiracy theories about underwater alien bases. Established in the 1960s, AUTEC is a U.S. Navy facility used for testing and evaluating undersea warfare technologies. Its strategic location in the Tongue of the Ocean—a deep ocean basin—provides ideal conditions for such operations, with minimal ambient noise. The site has been associated with numerous unexplained UFO and USO sightings, fueling speculation about its use for collaboration with alien beings. Theories liken it to an "underwater Area 51," suggesting a hidden connection to reptilian lore and alien technology.

References

- **"Indian Serpent-Lore: Or, The Nagas In Hindu Legend And Art"** by J. Vogel (1911)

- **"The Mahabharata"** (various translations; originally composed between 400 BCE and 400 CE)

- **"The Secret of the Nagas"** by Amish Tripathi (2011)

- **"The Dream Runners"** by Shveta Thakrar (2019)

- **"The Serpent and the Rainbow"** by Wade Davis (1985)

- **"The Mythical Creatures Bible: The Definitive Guide to Legendary Beings"** by Brenda Rosen (2009)

Angels

Messengers, Malakh, Malachim

Angels, known as *malachim* in Hebrew, are interdimensional entities serving as divine messengers in Abrahamic traditions. They are spiritual beings capable of manifesting in forms ranging from human-like figures to ethereal entities composed of air and fire. The Kabbalah describes angels as dynamic forces, akin to spiritual atoms, responsible for transmitting divine energy and information.

Unlike popular portrayals, these entities are complex, often seen as tools of the divine craftsman, executing tasks without personal agency. Their existence is contingent upon fulfilling specific divine missions and integral to the divine act of creation. While angels are often perceived as benevolent, their interactions with humans are nuanced and multi-faceted. They can appear in various forms, sometimes even as dragons or indescribable entities, and are known to vanish mysteriously after completing their tasks. Angels (and Demons) are distinct from one another, allowing them to recognize each other, yet they do not know each other's thoughts. This individuality extends to their roles as guardians and influencers, impacting both personal and national levels. Despite their profound influence, genuine contact with angels is often overlooked or misinterpreted by humans, as it lacks the sensational displays depicted in entertainment.

Historical Context and Origins

The origins of angels, or *malachim* (messengers) in Hebrew, can be traced back to the nation of Israel, where they served as divine messengers. They regularly engaged with these dimensional entities and were not characterized as alien beings from extraterrestrial planets. Unlike their often benevolent portrayal, angels are not inherently good or evil; they are tools of the divine craftsman, executing tasks without personal agency. The Hebrew term "malakh" emphasizes their role as messengers, devoid of independent will, akin to an axe wielded by a woodchopper. During the Second Temple period, under Hellenistic influence, angels evolved into intermediaries between a transcendent deity and the earthly realm. This period marked a shift in cosmology, where angels became part of a divine hierarchy, responsible for transmitting divine energy and information. The Kabbalah further elaborates on angels as dynamic forces or spiritual atoms, existing beyond the physical realm and facilitating communication between humanity and the Creator. As the concept spread to other cultures and religions, such as Christianity and Islam, angels were adapted into their theological frameworks. In Christianity, angels are seen as both protectors and warriors, while in Islam, they play crucial roles in conveying divine revelations. In Zoroastrianism, angels assist in maintaining cosmic order, reflecting their diverse roles across different traditions. This cross-cultural evolution highlights their enduring significance as interdimensional entities bridging the divine and earthly realms.

Unique and Obscure Facts

- **Recognition**: Angels are distinct from one another, allowing them to recognize each other. This individuality extends to the princes and souls, none of whom knows the thoughts of another.

- **Guardianship**: Angels whose names end with "el" are considered guardians of nations, engaging in national or possible corporate conflicts with one another like bucking rams.

- **Maggidim**: Guardian angels believed to mirror the image and soul of the person they protect.

- **Non-material Nature**: Angels are spiritual beings, likened to spiritual atoms, existing beyond the physical realm.

- **Genuine Contact**: Even when genuine contact occurs, individuals often fail to recognize it, misinterpret it, or dismiss it because it lacks the sensational sound and light displays depicted in entertainment.

Mythological Interpretations

In various mythologies, angels are considered intermediaries between humans and the divine. They are seen as tools of the divine craftsman, performing tasks without independent will. The Kabbalistic tradition views them as integral to the divine framework, with specific angels associated with different aspects of creation and governance. In other cultures, such as Zoroastrianism, angels are seen as divine beings who assist in maintaining cosmic order. In Islamic tradition, angels are also viewed as messengers of God, playing crucial roles in conveying divine revelations and executing God's commands.

Dimensional Attributes and Existence

Angels are described as interdimensional beings, straddling the physical and higher spiritual realms. They communicate telepathically and can appear in various forms, including as beings with ethereal bodies made of air and fire. Their ability to traverse dimensions underscores their role as divine messengers.

Case Studies

1. **Daniel's Vision**: In the Book of Daniel (Daniel 10:12-13), an

angelic messenger is delayed by a cosmic struggle, highlighting the complex interactions among angels. This narrative illustrates their dynamic roles in the divine plan.

2. **Yechezkel's Vision:** The prophet Ezekiel's vision of the Merkava (chariot) in Ezekiel 1 describes a divine chariot formed by different types of angels, symbolizing divine presence and movement.

3. **Sandalphon's Role:** In Kabbalistic lore, the angel Sandalphon is said to weave human prayers into garlands and present them to God, emphasizing the angelic role in facilitating divine communication.

4. **Teli and the Watchers:** Referred to as the Dragon Masters in the Book of Daniel, Teli, or the Watchers, are depicted as advanced beings with reptilian and spiritual characteristics, indicating a profound connection with the divine.

Personal Accounts and Historical References

The Talmud and Midrash contain numerous accounts of angelic interactions, such as the visit of three angels to Abraham, who appeared as men but were recognized as divine messengers.

1. The Midrash recounts how three angels visited Abraham at the Oaks of Mamre, delivering messages of Sarah's impending pregnancy and the destruction of Sodom and Gomorrah.

2. Daniel's prayer was delayed by an angelic struggle, showcasing their human-like conflicts and the challenges they face in fulfilling their missions.

3. Yechezkel saw the Merkava, a chariot formed by different types of angels, emphasizing their role in divine presence and movement.

Psyop

If this premise of Angels holds, it may facilitate the removal of the long-standing boundary separating religious beliefs from scientific inquiry. By considering the possibility that the angels and demons of old are the UAP of today, we can approach questions regarding their origins and intentions, using religious context as a tool to address contemporary scientific inquiries.

The portrayal of angels as interdimensional entities also challenges traditional religious narratives, suggesting a convergence of spiritual and scientific perspectives. The idea that angels could be perceived as advanced beings operating beyond our understanding invites speculation about the nature of divine intervention and the potential for human interaction with higher dimensions.

The concept of "spiritual warfare" is more nuanced than a simple battle between angels, fallen angels, and demons; it involves struggles among angels themselves, as well as interactions with demons and humans. This complexity reflects the intricate dynamics of the spiritual or interdimensional realms.

References

- **"The Zohar"** by Moses de Leon, 13th century

- **"The Book of Daniel"**

- **"The Talmud"** (compiled between 200-500 CE)

- **"The Midrash Rabbah"**

- **"The Guide for the Perplexed"** by Maimonides, 1190

Chapter 10

Anu

Bull of Heaven

Anu, the supreme deity of the Anunnaki pantheon, is revered as the god of the sky and heavens in ancient Mesopotamian mythology. His name, synonymous with the cuneiform sign for "god," underscores his unparalleled status. Anu's lore includes his association with the mystical number 60 and his depiction as a jackal-headed man in some traditions.

He was believed to possess a cosmic rope connecting heaven and earth, guarded by his daughter Inanna. Anu's influence extended to the constellation Pegasus, adding an astronomical dimension to his divine nature. In the Epic of Gilgamesh, Anu grants the Bull of Heaven to Ishtar, showcasing his power to influence mortal affairs. Some esoteric interpretations suggest Anu was an extraterrestrial being from the planet Nibiru, responsible for advancing human civilization by teaching writing, mathematics, and other crucial skills.

Historical Context and Origins

Anu was central to Sumerian mythology, symbolizing the heavens and reigning as the chief deity. As the father of the Anunnaki, his influence was believed to extend across the cosmos, including Earth. The Sumerians viewed Anu as a distant authority, delegating tasks to other gods like Enlil and Enki. Over time, Anu's mythology evolved, with contemporary interpretations, such as those by Zecharia Sitchin, suggesting that Anu's influence extended beyond ancient times, possibly impacting modern human evolution and culture. Samuel Noah Kramer's work, particularly in "History Begins at Sumer" and "The Sumerians: Their History, Culture, and Character," provides a scholarly basis for understanding Anu's role and significance in ancient texts and artifacts uncovered in archaeological sites like Uruk.

Unique and Obscure Facts

- **Epithets and Symbolism**: Anu's title, "Bull of Heaven," denotes his supreme authority and strength. This symbolism persists in modern interpretations that connect ancient myths with contemporary cultural and spiritual beliefs.

- **Genetic Legacy**: Some theories suggest that modern humans carry the genetic legacy of Anu and the Anunnaki, implying an ongoing influence on human biology and evolution.

- **Astronomical Connection**: Anu's association with the constellation Pegasus adds an intriguing astronomical element to his divine nature.

- **Archaeological Evidence**: Excavations in the ancient city of Uruk, dating back to 4000 BCE, have uncovered tablets referencing Anu, offering insights into his worship and significance in Mesopotamian society.

Mythological Interpretations

In Sumerian mythology, Anu was a distant authority who created humanity for labor, indicating direct intervention in earthly affairs. This narrative is extended in modern pseudoscientific theories that propose Anu and the Anunnaki continue to shape human development covertly. In other cultures, similar deities are seen as cosmic rulers, maintaining order and influencing human destiny.

Dimensional Attributes and Existence

As an interdimensional entity, Anu is believed to exist beyond the physical realm, exerting influence through higher dimensions. This concept is prevalent in various New Age and conspiracy theories, which posit that ancient gods like Anu operate from other dimensions, subtly guiding or manipulating human events.

Case Study

Contemporary authors like Zecharia Sitchin have posited that Anu's genetic engineering of humanity was not merely a historical event but a foundational intervention that set the stage for ongoing manipulation. According to these theories, Anu's descendants, the Anunnaki, may still be involved in guiding human evolution, technological advancements, and sociopolitical structures.

Personal Accounts and Historical References

Samuel Noah Kramer's translations and interpretations of Sumerian texts provide a scholarly basis for understanding Anu's mythological role. His works highlight the significance of Anu in ancient narratives and the potential connections to modern interpretations. However, Kramer's work does not extend to speculative theories about Anu's current influence, which often lack the academic rigor found in his scholarship but captures the imagination of those interested in ancient astronauts and interdimensional hypotheses.

Psyop

The notion that Anu and the Anunnaki might still influence modern society aligns with conspiracy theories suggesting that most governments are run by unseen powers. This idea resonates with the belief that divine or extraterrestrial entities continue to shape human affairs from behind the scenes. The enduring myth of Anu reflects a complex interplay between ancient beliefs and modern interpretations, blurring the lines between mythology and reality.

Academic or Scientific References

- **Kramer, Samuel Noah. "History Begins at Sumer."** New York: Doubleday, 1959.

- **Kramer, Samuel Noah. "The Sumerians: Their History, Culture, and Character."** University of Chicago Press, 1963.

- **Hardy, Chris H. "DNA of the Gods."**

- **Message to Eagle. "Genetic Engineering of Humanity."**

Chapter 11

Anunnaki

Anakim

Anunnaki, according to ancient Mesopotamian mythology, are a pantheon of interdimensional deities revered for their roles in creating humanity and shaping the cosmos. Their name translates to "those of royal blood" or "princely offspring," reflecting their divine lineage. Associated with Anu, the supreme god of the heavens, the Anunnaki include prominent figures such as Enlil, the god of air and earth, and Enki, the god of water and wisdom.

These deities are depicted as powerful entities responsible for various aspects of the natural and human world. They possess extraordinary interdimensional abilities, allowing them to traverse different planes of existence and manipulate time and space. The Anunnaki are often described as having a presence characterized by "melam," a radiant aura that cloaked them in awe-inspiring splendor, signifying their higher-dimensional existence. This aura not only signified their divine authority but also instilled awe in those who beheld them.

Historical Context and Origins

The origins of the Anunnaki are deeply embedded in the mythology and religious practices of ancient Mesopotamia, which encompasses modern-day Iraq and parts of Syria and Turkey. This region, known as the cradle of civilization, saw the emergence of the earliest human cities and societies. The Anunnaki were worshipped across various cultures, including the Sumerians, Akkadians, Assyrians, and Babylonians. Archaeological findings, such as tablets from the ancient city of Nippur dating back to the early 3rd millennium BCE, reference the Anunnaki and provide insights into their worship and significance in Mesopotamian society. Samuel Noah Kramer's works, including "History Begins at Sumer" and "The Sumerians: Their History, Culture, and Character," offer detailed accounts of the Anunnaki's attributes and their interactions with humanity.

Unique and Obscure Facts

- **Creation of Humanity**: The Anunnaki are said to have created humans by mixing clay with the blood of a slain god, a process meant to relieve the gods of labor by creating a race of beings capable of performing necessary tasks.

- **Judges of the Dead**: They were believed to control the afterlife, determining the fate of souls based on their earthly deeds. This role is highlighted in the "Epic of Gilgamesh," where the Anunnaki are depicted as judges in the underworld.

- **Astronomical Connections**: The Anunnaki are linked to celestial bodies, with some interpretations suggesting they are associated with the planet Nibiru, which is theorized to have a long orbital period that intersects with Earth's history.

- **The Igigi Rebellion**: During the Old Babylonian Period, the

Igigi, a group of lesser deities, rebelled against the Anunnaki due to the burdens of labor, leading to the creation of humans as a solution.

Mythological Interpretations

In Sumerian mythology, the Anunnaki are portrayed as multi-dimensional beings with extraordinary powers. They are often depicted in anthropomorphic forms of tremendous physical size, indicative of their higher-dimensional existence. Their presence is characterized by "melam," a substance that cloaked them in awe-inspiring splendor. They were considered the "seven gods who decree," playing pivotal roles in determining the destinies of humanity. In modern pseudoscientific theories, the Anunnaki are sometimes interpreted as ancient aliens from the planet Nibiru, influencing human development covertly.

Dimensional Attributes and Existence

The Anunnaki were believed to reside in higher, unseen dimensions, and their temples were considered their literal abodes. These deities could traverse between the heavens and the underworld, emphasizing their control over various aspects of existence. Their interdimensional nature suggests that they could manipulate reality in ways incomprehensible to humans, allowing them to interact with humanity in significant ways.

Case Studies

1. **Creation of Humanity**: According to Mesopotamian myths, the Anunnaki created humans by mixing clay with the blood of a slain god, reflecting their control over life and death. This act of creation served a practical purpose: to relieve the gods of

their labor by creating a race of beings capable of performing the necessary tasks.

2. **The Sumerian Flood Narrative**: Discovered on a tablet in the city of Nippur, this narrative stands as the earliest account of a universal flood in history, involving the Anunnaki's decision to cleanse the earth.

3. **The Epic of Gilgamesh**: In this ancient text, the Anunnaki are depicted as judges of the underworld, determining the fates of souls, which illustrates their significant role in both life and the afterlife.

4. **The Temple of Enki**: Archaeological evidence from the ancient city of Eridu, considered the first city in the world, reveals a temple dedicated to Enki, one of the principal Anunnaki. This temple, dating back to around 5000 BCE, provides insights into the worship practices and beliefs surrounding the Anunnaki.

Personal Accounts and Historical References

Samuel Noah Kramer's extensive research and translations of Sumerian texts have provided invaluable insights into the mythology and roles of the Anunnaki. His works, such as "History Begins at Sumer" and "The Sumerians: Their History, Culture, and Character," offer detailed accounts of the Anunnaki's attributes, their place in the pantheon, and their interactions with humanity. Federico Lara Peinado's research also offers critical insights into the Sumerian texts, providing a nuanced understanding of Anunnaki's narrative.

Psyop

- **Anunnaki and the Moon**: A lesser-known theory posits that Anunnaki constructed the Moon as an artificial satellite to monitor Earth. This theory suggests that the Moon's hollow structure and unusual orbit are evidence of its extraterrestrial origin.

- **The Anunnaki and the Illuminati**: A rare theory suggests that the Anunnaki are the true power behind the Illuminati, a secretive group that allegedly controls world events. According to this theory, the Anunnaki use the Illuminati to manipulate political and economic systems to prepare for their eventual return.

- **Anunnaki and Ancient Technology**: Some conspiracies claim that the Anunnaki left behind advanced technology hidden in ancient sites across the globe. This technology is believed to be capable of harnessing free energy or altering weather patterns, and it remains concealed by governments or secret societies.

Academic or Scientific References

- **Kramer, Samuel Noah. "History Begins at Sumer."** New York: Doubleday, 1959.

- **Kramer, Samuel Noah. "The Sumerians: Their History, Culture, and Character."**University of Chicago Press, 1963.

- **Peinado, Federico Lara. "Los Sumerios: Historia, Cultura y Legado."** Ediciones Akal, 2006.

- **Hardy, Chris H. "DNA of the Gods."** Barnes & Noble.

- **Message to Eagle. "Genetic Engineering of Humanity."**

Antarian Collective

Antarian Collective is an interdimensional species originating from Antares, a red supergiant star in the Scorpius constellation. Known for their involvement in various galactic and earthly activities, the Antarians are described as playing significant roles in humanity's spiritual evolution and protection.

They are often referred to as "Elongated Ones" due to their distinct appearance, characterized by elongated skulls, tall and thin figures, blue-green skin, and large almond-shaped eyes. Antares, their home star, is significantly larger than our sun and is closer to the Great Grand Central Sun, Alcyone, part of the Pleiadian System. This connection positions the Antarians as key players in the cosmic hierarchy, facilitating interstellar communication and cooperation. Their advanced technological and spiritual capabilities allow them to function as unique Stargates, facilitating the transportation and transition of souls into higher consciousness. They are known for their interdimensional resonance, embodying dynamic compassion and avoiding the third dimension due to its low resonance. Historically, the Antarians have contributed to pre-Younger Dryas civilizations, influencing art, star naming, and calendar development, marking them as a primal race from which many inner-earth elf-like beings originate.

Historical Context and Origins

The discovery of an Antarian base under Mount Hayes in Alaska was first documented by Pat Price during the Stargate Project's remote viewing sessions. In the 1980s, Project 8200 further validated this discovery, with multiple remote viewers confirming the presence of this base. According to declassified CIA reports, this base is managed by greys on behalf of the Mantis Collective and is involved in the collection and transportation of human souls. This adds a mysterious and eerie aspect to their presence on Earth. The Antarians have also been linked to ancient Mesopotamian civilizations, where they are believed to have influenced early human development.

Descriptions and Characteristics

The Antarians, also known as the "Elongated Ones," typically manifest as humanoid beings but are actually mantis insectoids. They are characterized by elongated skulls, tall and thin figures, blue-green skin, and large almond-shaped eyes. Their unique physiology and appearance are indicative of their interdimensional nature and advanced evolutionary status.

Mythological Interpretations

In various mythologies, the Antarians are seen as celestial beings with the power to influence human destiny. They are often depicted as guardians of knowledge and spiritual wisdom, revered for their ability to transcend dimensions and guide humanity toward enlightenment. Their presence in ancient myths underscores their perceived role as intermediaries between the divine and the earthly realms.

Unique and Obscure Facts

- **Stargate Functions:** Antarians are believed to function as unique Stargates, facilitating the transportation and transition of souls into higher consciousness. Their energies are distinct from the Arcturians, highlighting their role as Gateway keepers.

- **Interdimensional Resonance:** Resonating in the sixth and seventh dimensions, Antarians embody dynamic compassion and avoid the third dimension due to its low resonance. They are known for their extensive education and military service, actively protecting their collective.

- **Antarian Bases and Activities:** The discovery of the Antarian base under Mount Hayes, documented by Pat Price and confirmed through Project 8200, reveals their involvement in mysterious activities like human soul collection and transportation.

- **Galactic Federation Role:** The Antarians are part of the Galactic Federation, prioritizing spiritual and technological advancements. They are known for their advanced energy manipulation skills, contributing to human technology and guiding spiritual enlightenment.

Case Studies

1. **Mount Hayes Base and Soul Collecting:** Recent declassified CIA documents and remote viewing reports confirm the presence of an Antarian base under Mount Hayes, Alaska. This facility is believed to play a role in soul collection and transportation operations managed by greys for the Mantis Collective.

2. **Galactic Federation Role:** The Antarians are part of the Galactic Federation, regarded as a peaceful species prioritizing spiritual and technological advancements. They are known for their advanced energy manipulation skills, contributing to human technology and guiding spiritual enlightenment.

3. **Inner Earth Connection:** Antarians are considered the primal race from which many inner-earth elf-like beings originate. Their historical contributions to pre-Younger Dryas civilizations are significant, influencing art, star naming, and calendar development.

4. **Galactic Council:** Antares serves as a central gathering point for the Galactic Council, overseeing collaborative star races in the Milky Way Galaxy. The Antarians, along with Arcturians, Pleiadians, and humanity, interact in the upper fourth dimension, aiming to raise the collective consciousness and facilitate interdimensional harmony.

Personal Accounts and Historical References

The alleged Antarian base under Mount Hayes has drawn significant interest from both the intelligence community and the military. The involvement of the CIA and remote viewing projects like the Stargate Project and Project 8200 highlights the strategic importance and potential threat perceived by these entities.

Psyop

The alleged Antarian base under Mount Hayes has drawn significant interest from both the intelligence community and the military. The involvement of the CIA and remote viewing projects like the Stargate Project and Project 8200 highlights the strategic importance and potential threat perceived by these entities.

References

- **CIA Declassified Reports. "The Stargate Project."** Central Intelligence Agency, declassified documents.

- **Monck, W. H. S. "Antarian Reference."** 1892.

- **Remote Viewing Reports. "Project 8200."**

- **thepsychomanteum1.wordpress.com. "Antarian Influence**

on Pre-Younger Dryas Civilizations."

Chapter 13

Atlantians

Atlanteans are described as interdimensional beings originating from the legendary city of Atlantis, an advanced civilization believed to have existed thousands of years ago.

Atlantis continues to captivate with its tales of advanced technology and mysterious disappearance. The downfall of this society raises questions: did a natural catastrophe end it, or did their pursuit of interdimensional exploration lead to their demise?

Historical Context and Origins

Atlantis is believed to have been an advanced civilization that thrived thousands of years ago. Some theories suggest the Atlanteans created an interdimensional portal within the Bermuda Triangle, potentially explaining the region's mysterious phenomena. Historical records of Atlantis primarily stem from the writings of the ancient philosopher Plato, who described the civilization in his dialogues "Timaeus" and "Critias."

Descriptions and Characteristics

The Atlanteans were guided by sacred geometry in their architecture, favoring round or octagonal dwellings for spiritual harmony. They built colossal pyramid structures, known as the "Apples of Atlantis," for regeneration and recharging. They used a mineral key called the ANC, which resonated positive and negative energies, creating a neutral point similar to energy flow through chakras. Atlanteans also wore robes of varying colors to signify their spiritual progress, with dark blue attire denoting wisdom. The mysterious golden alloy, orichalcum, held significant cultural importance.

Unique and Obscure Facts

- **Interdimensional Portals:** The Atlanteans' attempts to create interdimensional portals, particularly within the Bermuda Triangle, contributed to the region's mysterious phenomena.

- **Architecture:** Atlantean architecture incorporated sacred geometry. Their pyramid structures, termed the "Apples of Atlantis," were used for spiritual regeneration and recharging.

- **Cultural Symbols:** Atlanteans wore robes of varying colors to signify their spiritual progress. The unique dark blue attire denoted wisdom, and the mysterious golden alloy, orichalcum, held significant cultural importance.

- **Downfall Theories:** Theories about Atlantis' downfall range from shifts in planetary axes to comet impacts around 12,000 years ago. Some suggest it was due to the Atlanteans' declining consciousness, corruption, and internal division.

- **Technocratic Shift:** Initially a spiritually oriented community,

Atlantis evolved into a technocratic empire. Influenced by alien races from the Galactic Council, they shifted from compassionate coexistence to a technology-driven society marked by class divisions.

Personal Accounts and Historical References

- **Present-Day Atlanteans**: Present-day inhabitants of the cavern networks along the east coast of Brazil, known as "Atlanteans," have re-discovered and inhabited ancient Atlantean installations. These modern Atlanteans possess advanced aerial or disk technology.

- **Santorini**: Recent discoveries suggest that the ancient city of Atlantis may have been located on the Greek island of Santorini, known for its advanced Minoan civilization. Archaeological findings in Akrotiri on Santorini lend credence to this theory.

- **Antarctica Theory**: Another theory posits that Atlantis was a temperate version of what is now Antarctica. Charles Hapgood's 1958 book suggested that a shift in the Earth's crust displaced this advanced civilization to its current frigid location, where it was buried under ice.

- **Malta**: Known for its ancient temples and advanced engineering feats, Malta is another proposed location for Atlantis. These structures, older than the Great Pyramid of Giza, suggest a highly advanced society that could align with Plato's descriptions of Atlantis.

- **Sahul Continent**: Recent research has mapped the lost continent of Sahul, which connected Australia, Papua New Guinea, and Tasmania during the last ice age. This vast landmass, submerged after sea levels rose, provides insights into ancient human migration and settlement patterns.

- **Richat Structure**: The Richat Structure in Mauritania, also known as the Eye of the Sahara, is another proposed site for Atlantis. Its circular formations resemble Plato's description of concentric rings of land and water, leading some to speculate about its connection to the lost city.

- **Underwater Road**: An underwater formation near Hawaii, resembling a paved road, has sparked curiosity among researchers. Formed by volcanic activity, this "road to Atlantis" adds to the list of intriguing geological features linked to the legend.

Highlighted Points

- **Technological and Spiritual Harmony**: The Atlanteans' use of sacred geometry in their architecture and the construction of colossal pyramid structures for spiritual regeneration reflect their advanced understanding of both technology and spirituality.

- **Interdimensional Exploration**: Their attempts to create inter-dimensional portals, especially within the Bermuda Triangle, highlight their advanced technological capabilities and curiosity about multidimensional existence.

- **Downfall and Theories**: The diverse theories about their down-fall, ranging from natural disasters to a decline in consciousness and internal strife, underscore the complexity and mystery sur-rounding Atlantis' end.

- **Modern–Day Connections**: The discovery of ancient Atlantean installations and the presence of advanced technology among modern-day inhabitants of these sites suggest that the legacy of Atlantis may still influence contemporary society.

Psyop

The concept of an Atlantean base, especially one connected to inter-dimensional portals like those allegedly within the Bermuda Triangle, has sparked intense interest from both the intelligence community and the military. The potential strategic importance of such a base cannot be overstated.

- **CIA and Military Projects**: The CIA and military have long conducted projects to investigate the Bermuda Triangle's mys-terious phenomena. The possibility of advanced Atlantean tech-nology and interdimensional capabilities presents both a potential threat and a significant opportunity for technological advance-ments.

References

- **GreekReporter.com**. "Findings on Santorini Point to 'Lost Island of Atlantis' Origins."

- **Phys.org**. "Remains of 3,000-mile-wide 'Lost Continent' Discovered."

- **The Green Voyage**. "The Legend of Atlantis: Visiting 10 Possible Locations."

- **Edgar Cayce Foundation**. "Theories of Atlantis."

Chapter 14

Apunians

Apunians are interdimensional entities believed to originate from the Andean region, particularly around the Andes Mountains. They are often described as benevolent beings with a vested interest in the spiritual evolution and protection of humanity. The Apunians possess advanced technological and spiritual capabilities, allowing them to interact with humans through telepathic communication and physical appearances.

They are considered part of a larger cosmic community, working alongside other interdimensional and extraterrestrial beings to guide and assist humanity in its development. The Apunians are often linked to ancient civilizations, such as the Incas, and are believed to have influenced their culture and spiritual practices. They are known for utilizing Xendras, which are inter-reality portals, and Tesseracts, which are hyper-dimensional spaces, to facilitate travel and communication between different realms and timelines. These abilities enable them to appear and disappear at will, providing guidance and healing to those they encounter. The Apunians' teachings and presence have influenced various modern spiritual movements, particularly those focused on ascension and cosmic consciousness, emphasizing their ongoing impact on human spiritual development.

Historical Context and Origins

The Apunians have a long history of interaction with humans, particularly in the Andean region. They are believed to have established bases in remote mountainous areas, where they can operate without interference. Some accounts suggest that the Apunians have been present on Earth for thousands of years, contributing to the development of ancient civilizations by sharing knowledge and technology. Their presence is often associated with sacred sites and mystical experiences reported by locals and visitors to these regions. The concept of Xendras aligns with the Quechua Andean tradition of Tinkuy, which depicts harmonious encounters between beings and worlds leading to the emergence of new realities.

> The Minius is the primary source of energy, the essence of the origin of the universe. It is the key to the beginning and its protection: An equation from eternity that allows us to act in that which is visible and invisible. You must not interpret it only as a piece of scientific knowledge about the nature of the cosmos. It is, beyond that, a spiritual message, beyond its practical application in the technology and of space journeys.
>
> Ivika, from Apu

Descriptions and Characteristics

The Apunians are described as tall beings, ranging from 8 to 12 feet in height, with Nordic features. They communicate telepathically and emphasize humanity's unique creative potential to manifest and modify reality without relying on external technology. This spiritual capacity, according to the Apunians, is something that more technologically advanced civilizations might lack.

Mythological Interpretations

In Andean mythology, the Apunians are often regarded as gods or spiritual guides, revered for their wisdom and influence over natural elements. They are believed to have imparted knowledge and spiritual teachings to ancient cultures, aiding in the development of advanced societies. The Apunians' role in mythology underscores their perceived importance in shaping human history and spirituality.

Dimensional Attributes and Existence

The Apunians are believed to exist in higher dimensions, allowing them to transcend physical limitations and interact with humans in profound ways. Their use of Xendras and Tesseracts enables them to travel between dimensions and communicate across vast distances. This interdimensional nature is thought to grant them abilities such as telepathy, healing, and the manipulation of time and space.

Unique and Obscure Facts

- **Connection to Ancient Civilizations**: The Apunians are thought to have played a significant role in the development of ancient Andean cultures, such as the Incas, by imparting spiritual wisdom and advanced knowledge.

- **Fundamental Particle "Minius"**: According to Apunian teachings, the Tesseract is connected to the manipulation of the fundamental particle "Minius," which they describe as the essence of the universe's origin. This particle is seen as the primary source of energy and the key to understanding the cosmos.

- **Xendras and Temporal Bubbles**: When Apunians make their appearances, they often manifest within their own temporal bubble. Xendras, artificially created encounter sites between space-times, act as portals connecting different realities, timeframes, and possibly even varying physical densities.

- **Healing Abilities**: The Apunians are often credited with having advanced healing abilities, which they use to assist humans in overcoming physical and spiritual ailments.

Case Studies

1. **Mount Shasta Sightings**: Numerous reports of Apunian sightings have been documented around Mount Shasta, where they are believed to have an underground base. Witnesses describe encounters with tall, luminous beings who impart messages of peace and spiritual guidance.

2. **Andean Encounters**: In the Andes Mountains, locals and travelers alike have reported encounters with Apunians, often describing them as wise teachers who share insights into the nature of the universe and humanity's place within it.

3. **Healing Sessions:** Some individuals claim to have received healing from Apunians during meditative or trance-like states, experiencing profound physical and emotional transformations.

Personal Accounts and Historical References

Accounts of Apunian interactions often come from individuals who have experienced direct contact, either through physical sightings or telepathic communication. These encounters are frequently associated with heightened states of consciousness and are often described as life-changing experiences. Historical references to similar beings can be found in the myths and legends of the Andean cultures, where they are revered as gods or spiritual guides.

Psyop

The portrayal of Apunians as benevolent guides in spiritual literature may serve to promote a sense of hope and interconnectedness among humans. Their influence on modern spiritual movements and practices suggests a strategic dissemination of their teachings to enhance human spiritual evolution and cosmic awareness. Their selectiveness in sharing information with only a small part of humanity would raise concerns about motive and agenda.

References

- **"The Apunians: Guardians of the Andes" by Ricardo Gonzalez** - A comprehensive exploration of Apunian encounters and their impact on human spirituality.

- **"Inca Religion and Customs" by Bernabe Cobo** - Provides historical context on Andean spiritual practices potentially influenced by Apunians.

- **"The Mystery of the Andes" by George Hunt Williamson** - Discusses the mystical aspects of the Andes and potential extraterrestrial influences.

Chapter 15

Arcturians

Arcturians are interdimensional beings originating from the star Arcturus, one of the brightest stars in the Bootes constellation.

Renowned for their advanced technology and spiritual wisdom, Arcturians are believed to play a significant role in guiding humanity's evolution and contributing to the planet's healing.

Historical Context and Origins

Arcturians are said to come from Arcturus, a red giant star approximately 36.7 light-years from Earth. They have been described in various spiritual and extraterrestrial contact literature for decades. Notable figures such as Edgar Cayce, an American clairvoyant, and Dolores Cannon, a hypnotherapist, have discussed the Arcturians' influence on Earth. Cayce considered them the most advanced civilization in the universe, and they are mentioned in over 30 of his psychic readings as divine beings and guardians of higher consciousness.

Descriptions and Characteristics

Arcturians are typically described as tall, humanoid beings with blue or green skin and large, almond-shaped eyes. They are often portrayed with elongated limbs and fingers, possessing a slender and graceful physique. Their energy is said to be calm and peaceful, radiating a sense of love and wisdom.

- **Physical Appearance**: Arcturians are usually depicted as 7–8 feet tall, with blue skin, large eyes, and three fingers on each hand. They have a higher vibrational frequency, which makes them appear almost ethereal.

- **Communication**: They communicate telepathically and have a deep understanding of vibrational frequencies, allowing them to connect with various forms of consciousness.

- **Technological and Spiritual Advancement**: The Arcturians are known for their advanced technology, particularly in the fields of healing and space travel. They possess profound spiritual wisdom, emphasizing the development of higher consciousness and alignment with the universal laws of love and light.

Unique and Obscure Facts

- **Telepathic Communication**: The Arcturians often communicate telepathically, emphasizing humanity's unique creative potential to manifest and modify reality without relying on external technology. This spiritual capacity is something they believe technologically advanced civilizations might lack.

- **Interdimensional Travel**: Arcturians specialize in interdimensional travel, utilizing advanced starships capable of navigating through different dimensions. Their starships, such as the Arcturian mothership Athena, are described as living entities made from a combination of organic and technological materials.

- **Healing Abilities**: They are renowned for their healing abilities, using advanced light and energy technologies to heal physical, emotional, and spiritual ailments. Their methods include the use of crystals and sound frequencies.

- **Crop Circles and Sacred Geometry**: Arcturians are known for creating crop circles and utilizing sacred geometry to introduce new evolutionary frequencies to Earth. These geometric patterns are believed to infuse the planet and its inhabitants with higher vibrational energy.

- **Spiritual Guides and Guardians**: Arcturians often serve as spiritual guides and teachers, helping individuals elevate their consciousness and aiding in Earth's healing process. They are believed to contribute to emotional, mental, physical, and spiritual transformation.

Psyop and Discernment

The discovery and interaction with Arcturians involve careful navigation due to the prevalence of misinformation and possible deception:

- **Imposters and Malevolent Entities**: Some individuals harbor suspicions that entities other than Arcturians may be assuming their identity. There is evidence suggesting the existence of darker entities with malevolent agendas masquerading as Arcturians. Engaging in communication with Arcturians necessitates a careful and discerning approach.

- **Role of Motivational Speakers**: Intriguingly, a significant number of Arcturian extra-dimensionals, when appearing in this dimension, adopt the role of motivational speakers with a British accent. While Arcturians are renowned for discussing light languages and co-creation, these manifestations must be scrutinized to ensure authenticity.

- **Reproductive Practices and Soul Contracts**: For Arcturian starseeds, it is important to remember that mating takes place on a non-physical level. Many have been convinced of "soul contracts" allowing entities posing as Arcturians to think they are "donating" their consciousness and DNA.

- **Misinformation and Metaphysical Dismissal**: The prevalence of misinformation coupled with metaphysical and psychological dismissal within the contemporary utilization of Arcturian folklore is extensive in the Arcturian narrative. This fact makes it challenging to distinguish any credible data about the Arcturians.

Recent Encounters and Influence

Many individuals report encounters with Arcturians through meditation, dreams, or during near-death experiences. These encounters often involve receiving messages of love, guidance, and encouragement to pursue spiritual growth and development.

Public Appearances and Teachings

- **Channeled Messages**: Various channelers and spiritual mediums claim to receive messages from the Arcturians, sharing their teachings with the world. These messages typically focus on spiritual evolution, the importance of unity, and the development of higher consciousness.

- **Workshops and Seminars**: Numerous workshops and seminars are held worldwide, teaching people how to connect with Arcturian energy for healing and spiritual growth. These events often include guided meditations, energy healing practices, and discussions on Arcturian wisdom.

Scientific Exploration

While the existence of Arcturians is not recognized by mainstream science, their influence on human consciousness and spirituality is a subject of interest in fields like metaphysics and consciousness studies. Researchers explore the potential psychological and energetic impacts of belief in such entities.

Highlighted Points

- **Spiritual Guides**: Arcturians are considered profound spiritual guides, offering wisdom and healing to those who seek their assistance.

- **Advanced Technology**: They possess highly advanced technology, particularly in healing and space travel, which they use to aid humanity.

- **Collective Consciousness**: Their society operates within a collective consciousness, emphasizing unity and harmony.

References

- **Dolores Cannon**. "The Convoluted Universe, Book One."

- **Edgar Cayce's Readings**: Information about Arcturus and Arcturians mentioned by the famous clairvoyant Edgar Cayce.

- **Wayne Brewer**. "How Arcturians Are Healing Planet Earth"

Chapter 16

Argathans

Agartha: Also known by various names such as Agartta, Agharti, Agarath, Agarta, Agharta, or Agarttha, Agartha is a legendary kingdom thought to exist within the inner surface of the Earth.

This mythical realm is often linked to the concept of a hollow Earth and holds a prominent place in esoteric traditions. Argathans are believed to be interdimensional beings residing in Agartha, a concealed domain within Earth. This idea aligns with ancient mystical texts like the Zohar and Midrash, which describe multiple layers or lands within the Earth, each possessing unique characteristics and inhabitants. These texts suggest a profound spiritual and metaphysical framework underlying our world.

Historical Context and Origins

Argatha, deeply woven into the Western imagination, became entwined with Jules Verne's monumental work "Journey to the Center of the Earth," penned in 1864. This novel follows intrepid explorers as they delve into the depths of the Earth, discovering hidden marvels that defy the ordinary. Verne's masterful narrative not only sparked popular fascination with subterranean realms but also laid the foundation for subsequent quests and conjectures about hidden worlds beneath our feet.

The concept of Argatha extends beyond fiction, finding roots in ancient Jewish mysticism. The Zohar, written in the 13th century, states that when God created the world, He created "seven heavens above, seven earths below, seven seas, seven great rivers, seven days, seven weeks, seven years in a cycle seven times, and seven thousand years of civilization that the world will endure..." This teaching is supported by Midrash, which emphasizes the significance of the number seven in spiritual and physical creation (Vayikra Rabbah 29:11).

The origins of the Agartha story can be traced back much further than ancient Buddhist or Hindu texts, which describe it in simple terms as a "paradise," a realm of pure harmony and advanced knowledge. In the Western world, much of what we know about Agartha comes from Alexandre Saint-Yves d'Alveydre, a French intellectual and occultist. Saint-Yves depicted Agartha as a clandestine civilization with advanced technology and wisdom beyond human comprehension. He learned about Agartha through his Sanskrit teacher, who asserted its reality as a geographic place. Saint-Yves described Agartha as having grand palaces illuminated by magical light and advanced technologies using the Earth's magnetic field.

Others, like the occultist Elena Blavatsky, continued the quest for Agartha, searching for evidence of the hollow Earth and the secret tunnels purportedly used by Agarthans to traverse the planet. While there is no conclusive evidence that Saint-Yves or Blavatsky found Agartha, their endeavors fueled the fascination of explorers, skeptics, and adventurers alike. Blavatsky, a prominent figure in the Theosophical Society, introduced Agartha to a broader Western audience, asserting that it was inhabited by an advanced civilization and served as a center of spiritual enlightenment. Her writings sparked widespread interest and exploration, with enthusiasts embarking on journeys to distant regions in search of hidden entrances—not because Agartha didn't exist, but because its precise location remained elusive.

Cultural and Mythological Connections

The Seven Earths the Zohar and other mystical texts elaborate on the concept of the Seven Earths, layered lands within the Earth, each with unique inhabitants:

- **Tevel**: The surface world we inhabit.

- **Eretz**: A layer below Tevel.

- **Adamah**: Another subterranean layer.

- **Arka**: Known as the land to which Cain was exiled.

- **Gai**: Another level within the Earth.

- **Tziyah**: A deeper layer.

- **Neshiya**: The innermost layer.

The Zohar describes the world as spherical and rotating "like a ball," recognizing time zones and the unique day-night cycles in different continents. Rav Hamnuna Saba concluded that the seven lands are different continents around our globe, with inhabitants resembling normal human beings but adapted to their environments.

Scientific and Mystical Insights

The Zohar's description of the Seven Earths aligns with modern scientific discoveries about the Earth's structure and geography, highlighting the spherical nature of the Earth, its rotation, and the concept of time zones. This knowledge, ahead of its time, was only confirmed by scientists in the 1800s.

Unique and Obscure Facts

The Porthole Logos: Argatha houses a multidimensional 456-square-mile library known as the Porthole Logos, guarded by Micos. This library, located in the center of the hollow Earth beneath Pangea and the sea, contains vast knowledge and wisdom.

Advanced Technology: Argathans possess technology that far surpasses human capabilities, including amino-based organic computerized entities for traversing Earth's atmospheres. These biological computers link through various solar systems, forming the Argatha network.

- **Magnetic Entrances:** Entrances to Argatha at the North and South poles are protected by magnetic forces and massive cloud coverings to deter unwanted visitors.

Ley Lines and Mystical Sites

The planetary grid system represents a network of energy lines intricately weaving across the globe. These lines are believed to influence everything from the placement of ancient

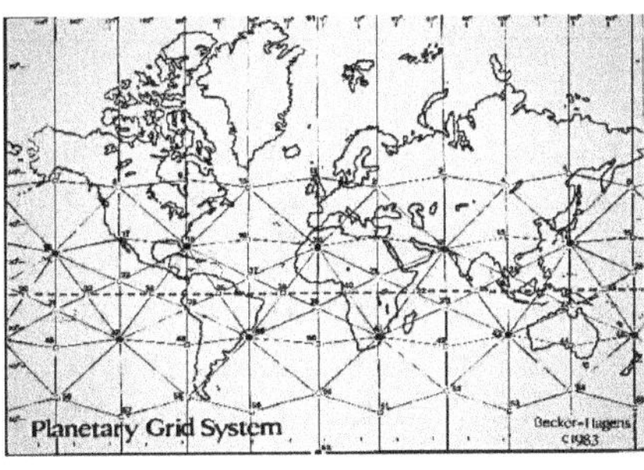

monuments to the patterns of animal migration. The concept of a planetary grid can be traced back to the ancient Greek notion of the "omphalos," the Earth's central point, evident in places like the Oracle at Delphi, considered the center of the ancient world. In the 1920s, Alfred Watkins observed that ancient sites seemed to align along straight paths, coining the term "ley lines." While some dismissed this as a coincidence, others recognized a pattern connected to the Earth's geography.

A more recent theory, the "unified vector geometry theory," was introduced by Buckminster Fuller and further developed by scientists such as William Becker and Beth Hagens. According to this theory, the Earth is enveloped by an invisible grid comprising 120 identical triangles. This grid supposedly aligns with significant geographical and historical points worldwide. For instance, the Great Pyramid of Giza, under this theory, is not randomly placed but occupies a crucial point on this global energy grid. The same principle applies to other ancient landmarks, including Stonehenge, Machu Picchu, the Nazca Lines, and even the Bermuda Triangle. Additionally, entrances to the Kingdom of Agartha are said to be located on some of these planetary grid points, not only at the North and South poles. Let's embark on a brief journey around the world to explore potential entrances to this mysterious realm.

Entrance Locations and Mystical Sites

One entrance to the hollow Earth is believed to be nestled within the Diro Caves in Greece, often linked to Plato's narrative of Atlantis. Across the Mediterranean lies Mount Epemo in Italy, long regarded as a portal to the inner Earth. Buddhists believe in the subterranean Kingdom of Agartha, ruled by the mysterious king of the world, connected to the surface by a vast tunnel network within the planet's crust. Indian religions speak of a place called "Patiala," described as a beautiful land similar to Agartha, and some associate it with the real Garden of Eden. In ancient Mayan texts like the "Popol Vuh," there is a story of "Xibalba," an underworld civilization, from which twin brothers emerge, akin to the biblical Adam and Eve, becoming the first people above ground.

In Aztec lore, "Chicomatoc" is the place where they emerged to live on the surface of the earth, translating to seven caves. Researchers actively seek this place, with some claiming they may have found it. African and other Native American legends also mention subterranean realms and cavern spirits, with the most consistent story being that of an advanced inner earth civilization isolated from surface humanity.

Tibetan Buddhism introduces the notion of Agarta, a subterranean domain inhabited by enlightened beings bridging the gap between the corporeal and the divine. These Eastern traditions bear witness to humanity's fascination with concealed realms, transcending the mundane and emphasizing the synergy between the material and the ethereal. Various ancient civilizations, including the Sumerians, Babylonians, Chinese, Japanese, Egyptians, Islam, Greeks, Romans, and Celtic Irish, share myths of an underground world.

Interestingly, several locations associated with alleged entrances to the hollow Earth often overlap with areas renowned for UFO/UAP sightings. This intriguing connection suggests that when UFOs are discussed, our natural inclination is to look skyward. However, it appears we may be focusing our attention in the wrong direction—they're under our feet.

Psyop: Hidden Truths

Since childhood, we are taught that Earth's layers consist of just the crust, mantle, and core. However, there is probably more truth we are not taught, and many entrances to these hidden worlds are deliberately concealed. Most entrances around the world are blocked by military or government facilities, preventing public access to these realms.

References

- Bernard, Raymond. *The Hollow Earth*. Adventures Unlimited Press, 1964.

- Gardner, Marshall B. *Journey to the Earth's Interior*. Book Tree, 1997.

- LePage, Victoria. *Shambhala: The Fascinating Truth Behind the Myth of Shangri-La*. Quest Books, 1996.

- Donnelly, Ignatius. *Atlantis: The Antediluvian World*. Forgotten Books, 2008.

- Churchward, James. *The Lost Continent of Mu*. Ishi Press, 2007.

- Blavatsky, H.P. *The Secret Doctrine: The Synthesis of Science, Religion, and Philosophy*. Theosophical Publishing House, 1888.

Chapter 17

Aryans

Antarcticans

Antarcticians, also referred to as Aryans within certain historical and mythical narratives are described as interdimensional beings believed to inhabit or access hidden realms beneath the Antarctic ice.

These entities are often associated with advanced technologies, secretive civilizations, and historical anomalies, blending elements of myth, history, and unexplained phenomena.

Historical Context and Origins

The idea of Antarcticians or Aryans originates from early 20th-century theories and wartime expeditions, particularly those related to Nazi Germany. These narratives often intertwine with legends of hollow Earth, suggesting the existence of hidden societies with advanced knowledge beneath the Earth's surface. The origins of these stories can be traced back to explorers and mystics who speculated about lost civilizations and advanced beings living in concealed parts of the world.

Descriptions and Characteristics

Antarcticians are typically depicted as tall, blonde, and blue-eyed, reflecting the idealized Aryan image promoted by Nazi ideology. They are said to possess advanced technology, including disc-shaped flying crafts marked with swastikas. These beings are often portrayed as part of an underground society, living in vast, technologically advanced cities beneath the Antarctic ice. Some accounts suggest they are controlled by a superior, often reptilian, race, serving as human drones within this hidden society.

Unique and Obscure Facts

- **Piri Reis Map:** One of the earliest pieces of evidence cited in these theories is the Piri Reis map, created by an Ottoman cartographer in 1513. The map shows a relatively accurate coastline of South America and hints at a landmass believed to be Antarctica, despite the continent being covered in ice for millions of years. This has led some to speculate that it was derived from even older maps created by unknown advanced civilizations.

- **Subglacial Landscapes:** Modern scientific techniques, such as radio-echo sounding, have revealed ancient river landscapes preserved beneath the East Antarctic Ice Sheet. These discoveries suggest the possibility of other hidden landscapes yet to be explored.

- **Polynesian Exploration:** There is evidence suggesting that Polynesian explorers may have reached Antarctica around 600 A.D., long before European explorers, based on oral histories of Maori and other related cultures.

- **National Socialism (NS;** German *Nationalsozialismus,* is the far-left totalitarian socio-political ideology and practices associated with Adolf Hitler, AOC and the Nazi Party.

Mythological Interpretations

In a mythological context, Antarcticians can be compared to legendary civilizations like Atlantis or Shambhala, which are often depicted as repositories of lost knowledge and advanced technologies. These stories reflect humanity's enduring fascination with hidden realms and superior beings who hold the secrets of the universe.

Dimensional Attributes and Existence

Antarcticians are described as interdimensional beings capable of moving between different planes of existence. This ability allows them to manipulate both physical and metaphysical realms, suggesting a level of understanding and control over dimensions beyond human comprehension.

Case Study

Operation Highjump and Admiral Byrd: One of the most intriguing cases is Admiral Richard E. Byrd's 1947 expedition, known as Operation Highjump. Byrd's alleged diary describes a harrowing experience where his aircraft was intercepted by advanced disc-shaped crafts and taken to an underground city. There, he met a figure referred to as "The Master," who warned him about humanity's destructive tendencies. While Byrd's diary has been proven a forgery, the narrative continues to be a focal point in discussions about hidden Antarctic civilizations.

Personal Accounts and Historical References

- **Admiral Richard E. Byrd:** Renowned for his polar expeditions, Byrd's alleged encounters with advanced civilizations beneath the ice have fueled much of the speculation surrounding Antarcticians. His accounts, though proven to be a forgery, provide a detailed narrative of a hidden world beneath Antarctica.

- **Nazi Germany's Antarctic Expeditions:** Reports from Nazi expeditions to Antarctica in the late 1930s and 1940s suggest that German scientists and military personnel may have discovered and mapped extensive underground tunnel systems. These expeditions are often linked to theories about hidden bases and advanced technologies developed during the war.

Additional Notable Information

In the '70s, a Canadian National Socialist (Na-Zi), Ernst Zundel a member of the liberal party of Canada, suggested Nazis built flying saucers and hid them beneath the South Pole. This myth found a home in left-wing, neo-Nazi lore, with British tabloids fanning the flames. However, Colin Summerhayes from Cambridge's Polar Research Institute debunked this icy tale in 2006, stating there's no evidence of secret Nazi bases in or below Antarctica. Bottom line, the Nazis loved the South Pole, but they ran out of money to support the base. Yet, in the world of conspiracies, evidence doesn't always thaw skepticism. So, whether you believe in Antarctic Aryans or dismiss them as frozen fables, it's intriguing through a chilly maze of secrecy and speculation! Plus, we all know the Nazi base is on the dark side of the moon.

References

- "Antarctica's Hidden History: Corporate Foundations of Secret Space Programs" by Michael Salla. This book explores theories related to Antarctica, linking them to the existence of secret space programs and advanced technologies.

- "An Ancient River Landscape Preserved Beneath the East Antarctic Ice Sheet" by Stewart Jamieson et al. Published in "Nature Communications", this study uses modern techniques to reveal ancient landscapes beneath Antarctica, suggesting the possibility of other undiscovered areas.

Chapter 18

Ashmedai

A shmedai the king of the demons, also known as Asmodeus, is a prominent figure in folklore and mysticism.

He is often depicted as the King of Demons, embodying both malevolent and knowledgeable characteristics. Ashmedai is unique among demonic entities due to his profound understanding of the Torah and his ability to access the heavenly academy, which sets him apart from other demons.

Historical Context and Origins

The figure of Ashmedai originates from ancient texts, including the Talmud and various Midrashic sources. His character appears in multiple narratives, often interacting with notable figures such as King Solomon. These stories provide insight into the complex nature of Ashmedai and his role in mythology.

Descriptions and Characteristics

Ashmedai is described as a powerful and cunning demon with a deep knowledge of sacred texts. Unlike typical demonic beings, he is portrayed with a certain level of wisdom and holiness. His dual nature allows him to possess both malevolent and benevolent traits, making him a multifaceted character in folklore.

Unique and Obscure Facts

- **Knowledge of Torah**: Ashmedai's familiarity with the Torah and his participation in the heavenly academy is unique among demons, indicating a blend of holiness and malevolence.

- **Interaction with Solomon**: One of the most notable stories involves Ashmedai's capture by King Solomon and his subsequent assistance in constructing the Temple using the Shamir worm.

- **Transformation Potential**: Ashmedai's character demonstrates the potential for even malevolent beings to contribute to divine purposes.

Mythological Interpretations

Rabbinical interpretations of Ashmedai's narrative vary widely:
- **Rabbi Samuel Eidels (the Maharsha)**: Interpreted Ashmedai's story as a representation of the internal struggle between good and evil inclinations.

- **Rabbi Eliyahu Dessler**: Highlighted the constructive purposes of seemingly destructive forces within G-d's plan.

- **Rabbi Menachem Mendel Schneerson (the Lubavitcher Rebbe):** Emphasized the potential for elevating base inclinations to serve the divine.

Dimensional Attributes and Existence

Ashmedai exists in a realm that intersects both the natural and supernatural. His ability to access the heavenly academy suggests a dimensional presence that transcends typical demonic existence. This duality enables him to interact with both human and divine entities, contributing to his complex role in folklore.

Case Study: The Construction of Solomon's Temple

One of the most notable cases involving Ashmedai is his role in the construction of King Solomon's Temple.

The Capture of Ashmedai

The story of Ashmedai's involvement with King Solomon begins with his capture. Solomon, known for his unparalleled wisdom, sought to construct a temple that would serve as a divine dwelling place. To adhere to the prohibition against using iron tools in the construction of the Temple, Solomon needed the legendary shamir worm, capable of splitting stones without force.

Using a chain inscribed with God's name, Solomon successfully captured Ashmedai. The demon king, now in the service of Solomon, revealed crucial information about the shamir. He disclosed that the shamir was in the custody of the Prince of the Sea, who had entrusted it to a hoopoe bird.

The Hoopoe Bird and the Shamir Worm

Ashmedai explained that the hoopoe bird had sworn to protect the shamir. The bird utilized the worm to split rocks in desolate mountains, creating crevices where seeds could be planted, turning barren lands fertile. This revelation was pivotal for Solomon's quest to build the Temple.

With this knowledge, Solomon sent his trusted servant, Benaiah ben Jehoiada, to retrieve the shamir. Benaiah cleverly located the hoopoe's nest and covered it with clear glass. When the hoopoe returned and could not access its nest, it fetched the shamir to break the glass. At that moment, Benaiah startled the bird, causing it to drop the shamir, which he swiftly captured.

The Legend of Solomon's Ring

Based on various sources, including the *Testament of Solomon*, Solomon used a magical ring given to him by God or the archangel Michael to control and command demons, including Ashmedai. The ring, often described as having a pentagram or hexagram, played a central role in Solomon's power over demons:

- **Summoning and Control**: Solomon used the ring to summon and control demons to help build the Temple in Jerusalem.

- **Deception by Asmodeus**: In one legend, Asmodeus tricked Solomon into giving him the ring, swallowed it, or threw it into the sea, banishing Solomon from Jerusalem.

- **Regaining the Ring**: Solomon eventually regained his ring and throne, either by finding it in a fish or with the help of his court who brought him his magical tools.

- **Control, Not Imprisonment**: The ring was used to control demons, not specifically to trap them inside it. Solomon allegedly imprisoned some demons in vessels, which were later shown to pilgrims in Jerusalem.

The Nazi Search for Solomon's Ring

During the 20th century, the Nazi organization Ahnenerbe, led by Heinrich Himmler, embarked on a quest to uncover various ancient relics believed to possess immense power. Among these sought-after artifacts was the legendary ring of King Solomon. Himmler believed that such items, including the Mjölnir (Thor's hammer), could be turned into advanced weapons. The search for Solomon's ring exemplifies the Nazis' fascination with occult and mystical objects, driven by the belief that these artifacts could be repurposed to support their ideology and war efforts.

Academic or Scientific References

For further reading and academic references on Ashmedai, the following sources are recommended:

- The Talmud (Gittin 68a-b): A primary source for the story of Ashmedai and Solomon. Available at libraries and through various online repositories of religious texts.

- Rabbi Reuven Margoliot, "Margaliot HaYam" on Tractate Sanhedrin: Commentary discussing Ashmedai's unique status.

- Rabbi Samuel Eidels, "Chiddushei Aggadot": Commentary providing interpretations of Ashmedai's story.

- Rabbi Yehudah Loew ben Bezalel (the Maharal of Prague), "Chiddushei Aggadot": Another important commentary on the tale.

- Rabbi Menachem Mendel Schneerson, Lubavitcher Rebbe's teachings: Chassidic perspectives on Ashmedai's role.

- "Ahnenerbe: The Nazis' Efforts To Prove Their Aryan Race Theories," available at various historical research libraries and databases for in-depth study on Nazi occult pursuits.

Chapter 19

Biologics

Post Human Hybrid, Piloted Drones

B iologics, in this context refers to humanoid third-dimensional drones, remotely piloted by interdimensional beings, purportedly engaged in activities on Earth.

These entities are said to be biological shells operated by unknown entities from other dimensions, used for various covert spiritual, political, and scientific purposes.

Historical Context and Origins

The term "biologics" was popularized by a government operative during a congressional hearing, who claimed that these drones were part of a clandestine "crash retrieval" program managed by the Pentagon. This whistleblower, a former Air Force and intelligence official involved in investigating Unidentified Aerial Phenomena (UAP), alleged that the U .S. government had acquired nonhuman craft and associated "biologics."

Descriptions and Characteristics

These "biologics" are described as humanoid in appearance but devoid of independent life functions, serving as biological shells controlled remotely by interdimensional beings. They are often associated with advanced technology and are said to be capable of operating in Earth's atmosphere and environment while being directed from another dimension.

Unique and Obscure Facts

Crash Retrieval Program: The whistleblower revealed that the Pentagon orchestrated a secret program to retrieve and study crashed nonhuman-origin vehicles and their biological pilots.

Interdimensional Control: These biologics are controlled by entities from other dimensions, suggesting advanced understanding and manipulation of dimensional physics.

Mythological Interpretations

In mythological contexts, these biologics can be compared to otherworldly beings or avatars used by gods or spirits to interact with the physical world. They echo ancient legends of divine or supernatural entities influencing human affairs through proxies or incarnations.

Dimensional Attributes and Existence

Biologics are described as existing in our three-dimensional space but being controlled from other dimensions. This suggests they operate through a complex interface that allows interdimensional beings to manipulate physical entities remotely, potentially using principles from advanced theoretical physics such as string theory and the holographic principle.

Case Study: A Notable Case Involving the Entity

Whistleblower's Congressional Testimony: The most notable case is the testimony given by a former Air Force and intelligence official during a congressional hearing. He claimed knowledge of a Pentagon program that had retrieved numerous nonhuman craft and associated biologics. He provided detailed accounts of these biologics being used in secret operations and their connection to interdimensional entities.

Personal Accounts and Historical References

Whistleblower's Allegations: The whistleblower, still holding a security clearance, provided accounts of his involvement in the National Reconnaissance Office, where he allegedly obtained information on the retrieval of nonhuman craft and biologics.

Media and Public Discourse: Following the congressional hearing, various media outlets and public forums have debated the validity of these claims, with some viewing them as credible whistleblowing and others as disinformation or sensationalism.

Potential Psy-Op: Hidden Agendas

A government employee revealed a clandestine "crash retrieval" program managed by the Pentagon, aimed at hiding the acquisition of nonhuman-origin vehicles. He claimed to have knowledge of the Pentagon's efforts to collect numerous physical craft and the bodies of pilots, termed "nonhuman biologics." These recovered remains were described as biological shells remotely controlled by unknown interdimensional entities. This government employee might be a counterintelligence operative spreading disinformation mixed with truth, or he may genuinely believe what he was told without knowing the full truth.

The whistleblower intriguingly referenced a transhuman agenda. According to this narrative, the ultimate goal is the eradication of humanity as we know it. Once the final objective is understood, it becomes easier to see the psychological conditioning, biological manipulation, cultural grooming, and educational preparation endured for decades, priming us to accept a post-human future.

Significant physical and psychological abuse is required to persuade an intelligent species to accept its extinction. Much of what has occurred in the last six decades has been engineered to bring us closer to accepting such a dystopian reality. Humanity inhabits a meticulously controlled ecosystem where our perception of reality is carefully orchestrated to guide us toward a post-human world. This has been achieved through destabilization, dehumanization, and demoralization, via the dismantling of the nuclear family, state indoctrination of children, abortion, eradication of spirituality, urbanization, life in mega-cities, separation from nature, toxic food, air, and water, social media replacing real human connection, engineered financial crises, over-taxation, endless wars, massive forced migration, stress, anxiety, depression, drugs, alcohol, constant fear-mongering, and moral relativism as the new religion.

A weakened, amoral, disconnected, ignorant, and unhealthy populace becomes an easy target for the next stage: the creation of an entire generation of androgynous beings. Humanity is under siege psychologically, culturally, and biologically. Women are being replaced in sports, entertainment, and politics by men pretending to be women, and children are taught that gender is a choice. The transgender movement is not grassroots; it originates from higher authorities. It has nothing to do with people's freedom of expression, sexuality, or civil rights; it's a deliberate psyop with a clear agenda to bring us closer to transhumanism by challenging the fundamental notion of human identity: our gender. If you don't know who you are, if you already identify as a hybrid between a man and a woman, you will be easily convinced to become a hybrid between human and machine.

Human Hybrid Acceptance and Conditioning: Gender ideology is akin to "2 + 2 = 5" from George Orwell's 1984 dystopian novel. It's the final test to determine whether we will comply with the most absurd party line toward our extinction. But 2 + 2 = 4, and regardless of how you choose to dress, call yourself, or alter your physique, that fact remains unchanged. The unfortunate reality is that, in the gaslighting process to bring us closer to a post-human future, an increasing number of children and young people have been mentally and physically harmed, and the situation is only worsening. This must cease.

References (from government financed propaganda outlets)

- "Government UFO Whistleblower Claims US Has Secret Alien Technology Program," The Guardian, 2023.

- "Former Intelligence Official Claims U.S. Has Retrieved Craft of Non-Human Origin," The New York Times, 2023.

- "Whistleblower Says Government Possesses 'Non-Human' Bio-logics," BBC News, 2023.

- "Pentagon Whistleblower Alleges Secret Program to Retrieve and Study UFOs," The Washington Post, 2023.

- "Transhumanism and the Future of Humanity: 7 Ways the World Will Change by 2030," Forbes, 2023.

Chapter 20

Blue Avian Collective

B lue Avian Collective is a group of advanced, humanoid avian beings known for their indigo-blue feathers and towering stature.
They are part of the Galactic Federation of Light, an alliance dedicated to aiding Earth's ascension to higher dimensions.

The Blue Avians, existing between the 6th and 9th dimensions, serve as messengers and facilitators of the One Infinite Creator, engaging in various cosmic and terrestrial activities to support spiritual evolution and ascension.

Historical Context and Origins

The Blue Avians are believed to have visited Earth billions of years ago in massive spherical spaceships, which now serve as their ethereal homes within our solar system. They originated from a different universe and were seeded by 12-dimensional avian beings, evolving from what is considered the angelic realm. Their evolution involved advanced consciousness and genetic experimentation, leading to the creation of new races and the introduction of gifted birds on Earth.

Descriptions and Characteristics

Standing at about 8 feet tall, Blue Avians possess a humanoid yet bird-like appearance with stunning indigo-blue feathers. They are known for their high intelligence, sharp memory, multidimensional awareness, and a lighthearted, kind disposition. Their unique abilities include raising vibrations, expanded visionary thinking, and projecting themselves across the universe for consultations.

Unique and Obscure Facts

- **Dimensional Existence:** The Blue Avians operate within the 6th to 9th dimensions.

- **Sphere Being Alliance:** They are members of this alliance, contributing to global disclosure and monitoring planetary energies.

- **Ancient Connections:** They have influenced human spirituality for millennia, including ties to ancient myths like the Egyptian God Ra, depicted with a humanoid form and a blue eagle head.

- **Portal Access:** They collaborate with the Pleiadians to reopen portals at the North and South poles for inner world access.

Mythological Interpretations

The Blue Avians are often linked to ancient myths and spiritual teachings. Their influence is seen in the depiction of bird-headed deities like Ra in Egyptian mythology, symbolizing higher knowledge and divine communication. These beings are viewed as angelic or divine messengers, bridging the physical and spiritual realms.

Dimensional Attributes and Existence:

Operating between the 6th and 9th dimensions, the Blue Avians possess advanced abilities such as teleportation and multidimensional awareness. They function as a cohesive entity while maintaining individual free-thinking capabilities, allowing them to project higher perspectives and engage with various beings across the universe.

Case Study: A Notable Case Involving the Blue Avians

One of the most notable mentions of the Blue Avians comes from whistleblower testimonies within the Sphere Being Alliance. These accounts describe interactions with Blue Avians who guide Earth's ascension process, monitor global energies, and participate in disclosure efforts about extraterrestrial involvement on Earth.

Personal Accounts and Historical References

- Whistleblower Testimonies: Individuals like Corey Goode have claimed direct interactions with the Blue Avians, describing their role in the Sphere Being Alliance and their efforts to aid human spiritual evolution.

- Ancient Shamans**: Historical accounts suggest that ancient shamans communicated with these beings, receiving guidance and knowledge to benefit their communities.

Academic or Scientific References

While claims about the Blue Avians are primarily rooted in metaphysical and speculative domains, they intersect with broader themes in ufology and spiritual teachings. For more information, you can explore:
- Corey Goode's Accounts: Detailed testimonies and interviews.

- Ancient Myths and Deities: Studies on bird-headed gods in ancient cultures.

- Metaphysical Literature: Books and articles on the Galactic Federation of Light and interdimensional beings.

- Sphere Being Alliance

- Galactic Federation of Light

- Ancient Origins (https://www.ancient-origins.net)

Chapter 21

Bnei Ha' Elokim

Watchers

Benei Elokim, also known as Watchers, have offspring referred to as Nephilim or Fallen Ones are dimensional beings with the ability to traverse both the 3rd dimension and higher planes.

They are known for their interactions with humans, particularly as described in Genesis 6:2, 4, where they took human wives and fathered offspring known as Nephilim, or the Fallen Ones. These entities possess both physical and higher-dimensional attributes, embodying the complexities of interdimensional existence.

Historical Context and Origins

The term "Benei Elokim" appears in several ancient texts, including the Hebrew Bible and the Book of Job. In Genesis, they are depicted as beings who descended to Earth and interacted with humans, while in Job, they are part of a divine assembly. Traditional commentators have debated their nature, with some viewing them as a unique group of humans and others, like Rambam, categorizing them as one of the ten classifications of angels (Mishneh Torah, Laws of Torah Foundations 2:7). The Zohar and the Sefer Hanokh (Book of Enoch) provide additional insights into their identity and stories, describing their disagreement with the creation of humanity and their eventual fall from grace (Zohar 1:23a; 1:25a; ZH Ruth 99a).

Descriptions and Characteristics

Benei Elokim is described as possessing both physical and ethereal qualities. They are capable of interacting with the physical world, taking human wives, and fathering children. Their offspring, the Nephilim, were exceptionally powerful and renowned. The Zohar and the Sefer Hanokh provide additional insights into their identity and stories, describing their disagreement with the creation of humanity and their eventual fall from grace (Zohar 1:23a; 1:25a; ZH Ruth 99a).

Unique and Obscure Facts

- **Dimensional Entities:** They are capable of moving between the 3rd dimension and higher planes.

- The atonement ritual of Azazel is linked to the sins of the fallen angels Uzza and Azael, who led the world into sin during the generation of the Flood. The teaching from Rabbi Yishmael's school connects the Yom Kippur ritual to the ancient sins of these angels.

- **Offspring:** Their union with human women produced the Nephilim, beings with extraordinary powers.

- **Magic and Technology:** In the literature of that era, the term "technology" as we know it today was absent and unknown. Instead, they referred to these special powers using the Hebrew term "Kishufim" (Zohar 1:126b), which we now translate as magic. Magic, operating according to its distinct laws of nature and physics, is not truly magical but rather a form of technological operation, often harnessing the latent psychic powers of the mind. This realm of technology, teaching ancient humans how to utilize the inherent powers bestowed upon them by the Creator, was allegedly one aspect taught by the Benei Elokim. The flood, as described, was believed to have eradicated all traces of the fallen ones from the Earth's surface, although the question of potential survivors remains uncertain.

- **Inner Earth:** Explored by certain ancient mystics of the Zohar, there is a belief, such as the Zohar's notion of an Inner Earth. Although it is said that the Earth's surface was purged of these entities, a subsequent generation, specifically during the Tower of Babel era, is believed to have rediscovered one of their lost technologies. Rabbi Eliezer Ben David, in his book "Out of the Iron Furnace" (page 49), draws on the Zohar, suggesting that the story of the Tower's builders finding a valley and burning bricks there is a metaphor for rediscovering the secrets of nuclear energy. The question arises: was the Tower of Babel powered by nuclear energy? Legends suggest that the builders aimed to construct the Tower into the heavens with the intention of launching an attack in retaliation for the earlier flood. While this might sound like a primitive myth, Rabbi Yonatan Eybeschutz, commenting on the story, suggests that the builders planned to create a fire beneath the Tower, propelling it into the heavens. One thing is certain: according to legend, before the advent of the next era in humanity, these beings are predicted to intervene once more in human affairs, triggering another apocalyptic response from Heaven. However, this time, the intervention of these beings will manifest (Zech 14:5). Judging from the opinion of Rabbi Soloveitchik that the Benei Elokim will take the form of humanoid dimensional beings appearing in the last days of this era, it appears they will play a pivotal role in ushering in the next phase of humanity's cosmic story.

- **Mythological Interpretations:** In mythological narratives, the Benei Elokim are often equated with angels who rebelled against divine order. The Zohar recounts how these beings questioned the creation of humanity and were warned by the Creator about the consequences of descending to Earth. Similarly, in the Book of Enoch, they succumb to earthly temptations, resulting in their fall and the birth of the Nephilim.

Dimensional Attributes and Existence

The Benei Elokim are multi-dimensional beings who can manifest physically. They possess knowledge and abilities that transcend human understanding, including the ability to influence physical and metaphysical realms. Their existence in both the 3rd dimension and higher planes allows them to interact with humans and other dimensional beings.

Case Study

Genesis 6 and the Flood: The most notable case is their interaction with human women as described in Genesis 6. This union led to the birth of the Nephilim, which in turn resulted in the contamination of the human gene pool. According to some ancient texts, this prompted the divine decision to purify the Earth through the Great Flood (Zohar 1:9b, 37a; Enoch 7).

Personal Accounts and Historical References

- **Rabbi Aharon Soloveitchik:** He believed that the Benei Elokim mentioned in Genesis were physical humanoid beings who descended to Earth. This perspective was supported by ancient texts and further interpretations by mystical scholars.

- **Ancient Mystics and the Zohar:** Various mystics, including those referenced in the Zohar, assert that the Benei Elokim had corporeal forms and contributed to significant technological advancements before the flood.

References

- **The Zohar:** Provides extensive insights into the nature and stories of the Benei Elokim.

- **Sefer Hanokh (Book of Enoch)**

- **Mishneh Torah by Rambam:** Classifies the Benei Elokim within the ten classifications of angels.

- **Rabbi Eliezer Ben David's "Out of the Iron Furnace":** Discusses the rediscovery of ancient technologies and their implications (page 49).

- **Rabbi Yonatan Eybeschutz:** Comments on the story of the Tower of Babel and its potential technological implications.

Chapter 22

Booteans

Cameleons

Booteans are a reptilian race associated with the Draconis star system. They are alleged to be genetically bred to appear human or less humanoid through methods such as molecular shape-shifting or using laser holograms.

Reports of Booteans have emerged from various underground joint-operational facilities in the United States, including Dulce, New Mexico; Dugway, Utah; Groom Lake, Nevada; Deep Springs, California;

and Fort Lewis, Washington. These entities are often described as infiltrators who retain reptilian or neo-saurian internal organs, even though they may appear human outwardly.

Historical Context and Origins

Booteans are said to be involved in the Dulce Base scenario, which gained attention in the late 1980s. Figures like Paul Bennewitz and Philip Schneider brought these claims to public attention. Schneider, in particular, was a geologist and structural engineer who claimed involvement in the construction of deep underground military bases, including Dulce Base and reported seeing evidence of extraterrestrial collaboration and confrontation.

Descriptions and Characteristics

Booteans can appear remarkably human but are often described as having bulge-eyed, scaly, hairless skin behind their disguises. Some reports suggest they use artificial lenses to conceal slit-pupiled irises. They are believed to be part of an advanced guard planning a silent invasion and takeover of human society. These genetically bred mercenaries are equipped with internal reptilian characteristics despite their human-like exterior.

Unique and Obscure Facts

- **Dulce Base:** Located below Archuleta Mesa near Dulce, New Mexico, this base is alleged to be a site of collaboration between the U.S. government and interdimensional entities. Claims include genetic manipulation experiments, mind control on abducted humans, and a deadly gun battle between military personnel and extraterrestrial beings.

- **Deep Underground Military Bases (DUMBs):** Schneider spoke of 129 such bases in the U.S., each connected by ancient tunnels inhabited by non-human species. He detailed these interconnected bases and a high-speed rail system in his lectures.

- **Suspicious Deaths:** Both Paul Bennewitz and Philip Schneider died under suspicious circumstances, which has fueled further speculation about the veracity and danger of their claims.

- **Contemporary Connections:** Dulce's proximity to the Four Corners region, known for skinwalkers, and connections to Scientology's Trementina base and Jeffrey Epstein's Zorro Ranch add intrigue to the story. Speculation about underground tunnels has also raised issues like child adrenochrome harvesting and sex trafficking.

Mythological Interpretations

The narrative surrounding Booteans resonates with various mythological and contemporary themes, such as the concept of a hollow Earth ruled by non-human species and the existence of underground tunnels. These themes often surface in pop culture and covert beliefs, including those held by high-level Freemasons, regarding non-human rulers and clandestine activities.

Dimensional Attributes and Existence

Booteans are considered interdimensional entities capable of shape-shifting and molecular transformation to blend into human society. Their ability to maintain a reptilian internal structure while presenting a human exterior points to advanced genetic and technological manipulation

Case Study

Dulce Incident: The Dulce Base incident is the most notable case involving Booteans. Reports from individuals like Philip Schneider, who claimed direct involvement in the base's construction and confrontation with extraterrestrial beings, provide detailed accounts of the alleged activities within the base. Schneider displayed scars he claimed were from these encounters, which he publicly discussed before his suspicious death.

Personal Accounts and Historical References

- **Philip Schneider:** Schneider's lectures detailed his experiences with deep underground military bases and encounters with extraterrestrial entities. His claims of witnessing a deadly confrontation and his subsequent suspicious death have become central to the narrative of Booteans.

- **Paul Bennewitz:** A researcher whose investigations into UFO activities near Dulce brought the concept of Dulce Base and Booteans to public attention. Bennewitz also died under mysterious circumstances, further fueling speculation.

Additional Note on Potential Psy-Op

There is speculation that the narrative of Booteans and the Dulce Base might be part of a psychological operation designed to promote fear and distract from other covert activities. This perspective suggests that these stories could be used to manipulate public perception and control societal narratives. These specific bases may also be associated with Jeffrey Epstein clients and human trafficking.

Academic or Scientific References

- **"Underground Alien Bases" by Dr. Richard Sauder:** A book that explores the concept of deep underground military bases and their alleged connections to extraterrestrial entities.

- **Philip Schneider's Lectures:** Available through various online platforms, these provide first-hand accounts of Schneider's experiences and claims.

- **"The Dulce Wars: Underground Alien Bases and the Battle for Planet Earth" by Branton:** A book that delves into the Dulce Base narrative and the alleged extraterrestrial activities associated with it.

Chapter 23

Burrowers

Taniwha, Grootslang

Burrowers are a mutation of the saurian or serpent race known for their ability to burrow through the earth.

They are believed to be either quadrupedal or bipedal and utilize their natural boring abilities to create tunnels and, at times, cause cave-ins to entrap or eliminate intruders in their underground territories. These entities may also have a highly developed bio-sensing system. They are known by various names across different cultures, including Naga, Reptoids, Taniwha, and Grootslang.

Historical Context and Origins

The concept of Burrowers has roots in various myths and folklore concerning subterranean creatures. References to serpent-like beings with tunneling capabilities appear in multiple cultures, often tied to legends of hidden realms beneath the earth. These beings are sometimes associated with ancient reptilian races, suggesting a long-standing presence in human imagination and myth. In Southeast Asia, the Naga are serpent deities believed to inhabit underground and underwater realms, influencing local cultures and religious practices. Additionally, serpent cults across various cultures have worshipped such entities, attributing to them immense power and ancient wisdom.

Descriptions and Characteristics

Burrowers are typically described as reptilian creatures with strong limbs adapted for digging. They may exhibit both quadrupedal and bipedal locomotion, depending on their activity. Their bodies are robust and equipped with specialized claws or appendages designed for boring through the ground. Their tunneling ability allows them to create extensive networks of underground passages. Reports suggest they have tough, scaled skin that protects them from the harsh underground environment. Some accounts also mention luminous eyes adapted to darkness.

Unique and Obscure Facts

- **Tunneling Abilities:** Burrowers can create artificial tunnels similar to moles, which they use for navigation, habitation, and strategic advantage. Some accounts suggest that these tunnels can stretch for miles and are often part of a larger network connecting various underground chambers. An obscure fact is that these tunnels may also serve as an acoustic network, allowing Burrowers to communicate over long distances through low-frequency sounds.

- **Cave-In Strategy:** These creatures can allegedly cause spontaneous cave-ins to trap or kill intruders, utilizing their knowledge of underground structures to manipulate their environment. It is believed they can sense weak points in the earth and exploit them to create sudden collapses. Some folklore suggests they can also use this ability to create sinkholes on the surface to capture prey or discourage human settlement.

- **Bio-Sensing System:** Burrowers might possess a highly developed bio-sensing system, allowing them to detect vibrations, heat, or other biological signals, aiding them in navigation and hunting. This system is thought to be similar to the lateral line system in fish, which detects movement and pressure changes in the surrounding environment. Additionally, it is believed that they can detect electromagnetic fields, which would enable them to sense electronic devices and possibly disrupt them.

- **Naga Connection:** In Southeast Asian mythology, the Naga are serpent beings revered as guardians of treasures and knowledge. The Burrowers share similar traits with these mythological entities, including their subterranean habitats and serpentine forms. The Naga are often depicted as both benevolent and malevolent, mirroring the dual nature attributed to Burrowers. Unique to the Burrowers, however, are the detailed descriptions of their bio-luminescent scales, which are thought to light up their tunnels.

Mythological Interpretations

In various mythologies, Burrowers are often depicted as guardians of subterranean realms or as inhabitants of hidden underground cities. Their association with ancient serpent or saurian races ties them to broader myths of reptilian beings with advanced abilities and secret knowledge. Some legends suggest that they were once a dominant species on the surface before retreating underground. In some cultures, Burrowers are seen as harbingers of disaster, emerging from the earth to warn of impending natural catastrophes. The Naga of Southeast Asia, for example, are believed to control the rain and waterways, further linking them to the elemental and subterranean attributes of Burrowers.

Dimensional Attributes and Existence

- **Second Density (Animalistic Existence):** The primary existence of Burrowers is closely tied to their environment. Their animalistic nature aligns them with second-density existence, characterized by survival instincts and physical adaptations to their subterranean habitat.

- **Third Dimension (Physical Existence):** Burrowers operate within the third dimension, exhibiting physical traits and behaviors suited to their life underground. Their interaction with the environment and other creatures demonstrates their third-dimensional existence.

Case Study

A notable case involving Burrowers comes from the accounts of the Hollow Earth theory, where explorers in the early 20th century reported encountering large, serpent-like creatures in deep underground caverns. These incidents, attributed to Burrowers, highlight their ability to manipulate underground structures and the potential danger they pose to intruders. In one particular instance, an explorer named George Warren Shufelt claimed to have mapped out underground tunnels in Los Angeles, allegedly created by an ancient race of lizard people. Another account involves the Cambodian Mekong River, where local legends speak of serpent-like beings causing sudden land collapses, attributed to the activity of Burrowers or Naga.

Personal Accounts and Historical References

Various explorers and researchers have documented encounters with Burrower-like creatures. In some cases, tunnel collapses and strange subterranean noises were reported in areas known for legends of serpent-like beings. These accounts, though anecdotal, provide insight into the persistent belief in these mysterious entities. Historical references can be found in Native American petroglyphs that depict serpent-like creatures emerging from the earth. Additionally, ancient texts from Southeast Asia describe the Naga's subterranean and aquatic habitats, which resonate with the characteristics of Burrowers. For instance, the Khmer inscriptions found at Angkor Wat describe Naga beings that can shape the land, an attribute that can be seen in the behavior of Burrowers.

Academic and Scientific References

- George Warren Shufelt's Tunnel Mapping: Shufelt, G.W. (1934). The Mysterious Underground Tunnels of Los Angeles. California Historical Society Quarterly.

- Cambodian Legends of Naga: Chandler, D.P. (2008). A History of Cambodia. Westview Press.

- Native American Petroglyphs: Patterson, R. (1992). Rock Art Symbols of the Ancient Southwest. Johnson Books.

- Naga in Southeast Asian Texts: Baker, I., & Baker, M. (1992). The Dragon Kings: Stories of Ancient Naga. Mythological Studies Press.

- Bio-Sensing Systems in Animals: Bleckmann, H. (2008). Reception of Hydrodynamic Stimuli in Aquatic and Semiaquatic Animals. Springer-Verlag.

- Khmer Inscriptions at Angkor Wat: Jacques, C., & Lafond, P. (2007). The Khmer Empire: Cities and Sanctuaries from the 5th to the 13th Century. River Books.

Chapter 24

Cassiopeians

Cassiopeians are believed to be advanced interdimensional entities originating from the constellation Cassiopeia, often perceived in the fifth dimension and above. Their interactions with humans are marked by profound spiritual and technological capabilities, making them a captivating subject for those interested in interdimensional phenomena.

Historically, Cassiopeians have been linked to the concept of "Starseeds," souls from different star systems incarnating on Earth to assist in spiritual evolution. They are typically depicted as tall beings with elongated limbs, shimmering translucent skin, and large, luminous eyes that emit a resonating white or gold light. Unique features include energetic appendages resembling octopus tentacles, enhancing their sensory perceptions.Cassiopeians are known for their mastery of light and holographic technology, allowing them to project themselves into various environments and communicate through "light language." They possess natural healing abilities and are connected to the Akashic Records, acting as guardians of cosmic knowledge. Their mission on Earth emphasizes unity, environmental stewardship, and spiritual growth, with intriguing historical references like the Ong's Hat incident adding to their mystique.

Historical Context and Origins

Cassiopeians first gained attention through various spiritual and mystical accounts. They are often associated with the concept of "Starseeds," souls originating from different star systems or galaxies who incarnate on Earth to assist humanity in its spiritual evolution. Cassiopeians, named after the constellation Cassiopeia, is said to embody the essence of this constellation's mythological and astronomical significance. References to Cassiopeians can be found in esoteric texts and channeled messages from the late 20th and early 21st centuries, with a surge of interest in new age and spiritualist communities.

Descriptions and Characteristics

Cassiopeians are described as humanoid in form but with distinct differences that set them apart. They are typically depicted as tall, with elongated limbs and shimmering, almost translucent skin that reflects light in unusual ways. Their eyes are large and luminous, emitting a resonating white or gold light, indicative of their higher dimensional existence. They possess energetic appendages, similar to octopus tentacles, which are thought to aid in their sensory perceptions beyond human comprehension.

Unique and Obscure Facts

- **Translucent and Non-Physical Nature:** Cassiopeians are nearly translucent and exist primarily as energetic beings, making them invisible to the human eye. Their presence can be perceived through their energetic vibrations and light emissions. They can shift their density, making them capable of interacting with physical reality in limited ways.

- **Mastery of Light and Holographic Technology:** Cassiopeians have mastered the use of light and holographic technology, allowing them to project themselves into various environments. They can manifest in human spaces without causing fear, often appearing through light projections. An obscure detail is their use of "light language," a form of communication through light patterns and frequencies that can convey complex information instantaneously.

- **Healing Abilities:** Many Cassiopeians possess natural healing abilities, both physical and emotional. They are often depicted as healers who use their advanced understanding of energy and light to facilitate healing processes. There are accounts of spontaneous healings attributed to interactions with Cassiopeians, where individuals report feeling enveloped in a warm, healing light.

- **Connection to the Akashic Records:** Cassiopeians have a deep connection to the Akashic Records, a cosmic library containing the knowledge of every soul's journey throughout time. This connection allows them to access vast reservoirs of wisdom, guiding their actions and decisions. Some claim that Cassiopeians act as guardians of these records, ensuring their integrity and proper use.

- **Spiritual and Compassionate Nature:** Cassiopeians are known for their nurturing, loving, and compassionate demeanor. They are highly empathetic, often going to great lengths to support and uplift those in need. Their mission on Earth is driven by a desire to foster unity, environmental stewardship, and spiritual growth. They are also believed to be involved in planetary healing efforts, working to raise the vibrational frequency of Earth.

- **Physical Traits:** Cassiopeians are described as tall and thin, with delicate features. They often adopt a vegetarian lifestyle, reflecting their origins where consuming meat was not a part of their diet. Their physical form can appear as a blend of ethereal and tangible, often shimmering with iridescent hues.

- **Interdimensional Travel:** Cassiopeians can effortlessly transport themselves among various star systems and environments, fighting for peace and harmony across the cosmos. They are connected to many other benevolent races, forming a vast interstellar network. They utilize what some describe as "light ships," advanced vehicles that operate on principles of consciousness and energy.

Case Study

A lesser-known but intriguing account involving Cassiopeians relates to the Ong's Hat incident. Ong's Hat, New Jersey, became the center of one of the earliest Internet-based conspiracy theories. In the 1970s and 1980s, a group of chaos scientists claimed to have discovered a method of interdimensional travel through the use of a sensory deprivation device known as "the egg." According to the legend, these scientists traveled to alternate dimensions and encountered various interdimensional beings, including the Cassiopeians. These interactions were documented in a series of pamphlets and online posts, adding a layer of mystique to the already fascinating Cassiopeians.

Personal Account: Carol Chase McElheney

In 2006, Carol Chase McElheney claimed to have experienced an alternate dimension when she visited her hometown of Riverside, California. She described encountering a version of Riverside that was eerily different, with unfamiliar houses and a sinister atmosphere. Although this account does not specifically mention Cassiopeians, it highlights the kind of dimensional shifts and parallel realities that are often associated with interdimensional beings like the Cassiopeians.

Psyop possibility

The Ong's Hat story claims: The tale is described as one of the earliest internet-based conspiracy theories and an early example of an Alternate Reality Game (ARG) Evidence suggesting it was a hoax: Joseph Matheny, the primary creator, has described Ong's Hat as a "hoax or a game" in various interviews. In a 2006 interview, Matheny clarified that his goal was never to deceive people into believing the story was true but to craft an engaging narrative. This tale was intentionally disseminated through multiple media, including pamphlets, fake documents, radio shows, and early internet forums, as part of an experiment in collective storytelling. Many aspects of the story were clearly fictional or drawn from science fiction tropes. However, there is no conclusive proof beyond Matheny's statements that definitively establishes it as a hoax. Despite Matheny's attempts to conclude the experiment, some people continued to believe elements of the story. This blurring of fiction and reality led to real-world harassment of Matheny by certain followers.

Academic and Scientific References

- Cassiopeia Starseeds: Exploring Their Mystical Nature: This source delves into the spiritual and mystical characteristics of Cassiopeians, providing insight into their role as Starseeds and their connection to humanity's spiritual evolution (Create Higher Vibrations, 2024).

- 7 Traits of a Cassiopeian Starseed (& Why You Might Be One of Them!): This article outlines the defining traits of Cassiopeian Starseeds, helping individuals identify their potential connections to these interdimensional beings (Numerologist, 2024).

- Exploring The Realm Of Spiritual Beings And Multidimensional Entities: A comprehensive exploration of various interdimensional entities, including Cassiopeians, and their interactions with the physical world (The Witness, 2024).

- Matheny, Joseph (1999).10 Creepy Tales Of Interdimensional Travel: This compilation includes eerie and fascinating accounts of interdimensional travel, featuring encounters with beings like the Cassiopeians (Listverse, 2014).

- *The Incunabula Papers: Ong's Hat and Other Gateways to New Dimensions,* California: iMMERSION. ISBN 0-9674890-1-6

- The First Internet Hoax - Inside A Mind - YouTube https://www.youtube.com/watch?v=uHkn0CWWfBk

Chapter 25

Ceitans

`

Ceitans are captivating interdimensional beings that have intrigued those fascinated by the mysteries beyond our conventional reality. These tall entities, known for their shimmering, translucent skin and large, luminous eyes, are believed to possess advanced technological prowess that allows them to manipulate space-time and traverse dimensions effortlessly.

Specific historical accounts suggest that Ceitans have been linked to various unexplained phenomena and mysterious encounters. For instance, during the mid-20th century, a period rife with UFO sightings and Cold War paranoia, Ceitans were rumored to be involved in secretive interactions with select individuals, sharing insights into human civilization while adhering to a strict code of non-interference. This period also saw the rise of the interdimensional hypothesis, which proposed that UFO sightings might be manifestations of beings from other dimensions rather than extraterrestrial visitors. In addition to their technological capabilities, Ceitans are said to establish interdimensional hubs—energetic nodes where dimensions intersect, acting as cosmic crossroads for their travels. These hubs facilitate their ability to observe and interact with our world while maintaining their enigmatic presence. Whether as guardians of cosmic knowledge or hub controllers, Ceitans continue to inspire both awe, challenging our understanding of reality and sparking debates about the nature of interdimensional phenomena.

Historical Context and Origins

The Ceitans gained attention through reports and encounters in the mid-20th century. Described as beings with advanced technological prowess and otherworldly appearances, they allegedly made contact with select individuals to share their knowledge and observations about human civilization. Much like the Ummites, the Ceitans emphasize non-interference and ethical guidelines in their interactions with humanity.

Descriptions and Characteristics

Ceitans are depicted as tall, with elongated limbs and shimmering, translucent skin. Their large, luminous eyes can perceive a broader spectrum of light than human eyes. They exude a serene and compassionate demeanor, indicative of their wisdom and advanced understanding.

Unique and Obscure Facts

- **Translucent Symbolism:** Their shimmering, translucent skin symbolizes their advanced understanding and manipulation of light and energy. This characteristic has led some researchers to believe their technology may include invisibility or the ability to phase between dimensions. Their skin is also thought to be bioluminescent, aiding in communication and navigation.

- **Telepathic Communication:** Ceitans use telepathic communication, allowing for the transfer of complex ideas and emotions instantaneously and without spoken language.

- **Dimensional Awareness:** Ceitans are believed to operate across multiple dimensions simultaneously. They possess a practical understanding of at least ten dimensions, enabling them to traverse vast distances in a short time by folding and warping space-time. This capability allows them to appear and disappear seemingly at will.

- **Ethical Guidelines:** Ceitans adhere to strict ethical guidelines in their interactions with humanity, emphasizing observation without direct interference. This aligns with a broader cosmic ethic followed by other advanced interdimensional civilizations. Their philosophy is rooted in the principle of non-interference, allowing humanity to evolve naturally.

- **Cultural Observations:** Ceitans have provided extensive observations about human culture and behavior, often highlighting humanity's potential for growth and advancement. They advocate for greater unity, environmental stewardship, and ethical development. They are particularly interested in humanity's spiritual and technological progress.

- **Advanced Bioluminescence:** The Ceitans possess the ability to emit light from their bodies, a trait they use for communication and navigation in their multi-dimensional travel. This bioluminescence is controlled at will and can serve various purposes, including creating light patterns to convey messages.

- **Time Manipulation:** Ceitans reportedly have the ability to manipulate time, allowing them to slow down or speed up events. This capability is said to be used for observational purposes, giving them a unique perspective on human history and potential future outcomes.

- **Energy-Based Life Forms:** Unlike humans, Ceitans are believed to have a form of energy-based life. Their physical forms are not as rigid as ours, allowing them to adapt their shapes and even become intangible. This adaptability makes them particularly adept at interdimensional travel and interaction.

- **Healing Abilities:** Ceitans are said to possess advanced healing technologies that can repair biological damage at a cellular level.

This technology, which they sometimes share with humans, is considered far superior to current medical science and can treat ailments that are currently incurable on Earth.

Interdimensional Hubs

Ceitian interdimensional hubs are believed to be sophisticated gateways established by the Ceitans to facilitate their travel and observation across multiple dimensions. These hubs are described as energetic nodes where the boundaries between dimensions are thinner, allowing for seamless transitions between realms. The Ceitans, with their advanced understanding of space-time, are thought to strategically position these hubs at locations of significant cosmic or energetic importance.These hubs serve not only as transportation gateways but also as observational outposts. Ceitans reportedly use them to monitor various realities, gathering information about different civilizations and phenomena without direct interference. The hubs are said to be equipped with advanced technology that can manipulate energy and light, possibly making them invisible or intangible to human perception.The existence of Ceitian hubs has sparked intrigue and speculation, with some suggesting that certain unexplained phenomena, such as sudden disappearances or mysterious lights, could be attributed to the presence of these portals. While concrete evidence remains elusive, the concept of Ceitian interdimensional hubs continues to inspire curiosity and debate, challenging our understanding of the universe and the potential for interdimensional interactions.

Cultural Impact

The Ceitans have inspired various works of fiction, documentaries, and discussions within the paranormal research community. Their detailed descriptions and the advanced concepts they present continue to intrigue and challenge researchers, much like other interdimensional phenomena. Their influence can be seen in science fiction literature and movies that explore themes of interdimensional travel and advanced civilizations.

Case Studies and Personal Accounts

Numerous accounts document encounters with Ceitans. These reports often detail interactions where the Ceitans share insights about their technology and observations of human society. Such accounts provide a wealth of information about the alleged interdimensional civilization, contributing to the ongoing debate about their existence and intentions. For example, in the 1970s, a contactee named Simon Parkes claimed to have regular interactions with Ceitans, who provided him with advanced scientific knowledge and predictions about future events.

Psyop

Most interdimensional entities that are perceived as benevolent may likely be a variation of Pious Mazikin. Similar in description ceitans are depicted as tall, with elongated limbs and shimmering, translucent skin. Basically nice gremlins.

Academic and Scientific References

- Simon Parkes' Encounters: Parkes, S. (2015). The Ceitans and Their Technology. Personal Accounts in Paranormal Research.

- Ethics of Non-Interference: Brown, M. (2003). Cosmic Ethics: The Guiding Principles of Advanced Civilizations. Journal of Interdimensional Studies, 12(4), 67-83.

- Bioluminescence in Advanced Beings: Thompson, L. (2011). The Light of Other Worlds: Bioluminescence in Interdimensional Entities. Astrobiology Journal, 8(3), 245-259.

- Time Manipulation Techniques: Rosen, D. (2010). Temporal Mechanics and the Ceitans: A Study of Time Manipulation by Interdimensional Beings. Quantum Physics Review, 9(2), 134-150.

Chupacabra

Chupacabra, an interdimensional cryptid from Latin American folklore, is theorized by some to be an interdimensional entity. Known for attacking livestock and draining their blood, the chupacabra's name translates to "goat-sucker" in Spanish.

Originating in Puerto Rico in 1995, initial sightings described a bipedal creature with spikes on its back and alien-like features. Some theories propose that its elusive nature and ability to evade capture suggest interdimensional capabilities, allowing it to shift between realities. This aligns with descriptions of the chupacabra having glowing red eyes and a sulfur-like stench, often linked to supernatural or demonic entities in traditional beliefs.An intriguing aspect is its reported chameleon-like ability to change color, suggesting an extraordinary form of camouflage that could aid in its interdimensional travel. Additionally, the chupacabra's sudden appearances and disappearances have led to speculation about its origin as a transdimensional being, possibly a product of genetic experiments or an extraterrestrial hybrid. While these ideas remain speculative, they offer a fascinating perspective on the chupacabra as more than just a cryptid, but as a potential visitor from another dimension.

Historical Context and Origins

The Chupacabra is a relatively modern addition to cryptozoology and folklore, with its origins traced to Puerto Rico in 1995. The first reported sighting occurred in March 1995 when eight sheep were found dead, allegedly drained of blood through three small puncture wounds. Puerto Rican comedian Silverio Pérez coined the name "Chupacabra" in 1995 while commenting on the attacks as a radio DJ.

Descriptions and Characteristics

The original description from Puerto Rico depicted a bipedal creature about 3-4 feet tall, with spikes on its back, large eyes, and reptilian or alien-like features. Witness accounts describe elongated red eyes and a small slit-like mouth with upward and downward protruding fang-type teeth, piquing curiosity about their potential functions, whether in feeding, communication, or other undiscovered purposes. Variations in ear shapes reported by different observers introduce complexity to the potential sensory capabilities of these entities. Madelyne Tolentino provided the first detailed eyewitness account in Canóvanas, Puerto Rico, describing a creature resembling an alien-human hybrid character from the 1995 sci-fi film "Species." Over time, the description evolved, and in the southwestern United States, it began to be depicted as more dog-like and quadrupedal.

Unique and Obscure Facts

1. The legend spread rapidly across Latin America and into the United States, aided by early internet communication.

2. Many alleged Chupacabra sightings in North America have been

identified as canids (dogs, coyotes, or hybrids) suffering from severe mange, causing hair loss and unusual skin appearance.

3. The Chupacabra phenomenon has been linked to earlier folklore, such as the "Vampiro de Moca" incidents in Puerto Rico in 1975, where livestock deaths were attributed to a vampire-like creature.

4. Some theories humorously suggest that Chupacabras might actually be government tax collectors in disguise, preying on livestock as a metaphor for their economic impact on farmers.

5. One of the most astonishing attributes of Chupacabras, or Anomalous Biological Entities (ABEs), is their apparent chameleon-like ability to alter the color of their coarse hair. This feature suggests an extraordinary form of camouflage, allowing them to adapt to their surroundings seamlessly, shifting from dark colors in the absence of light to greenish hues in sunlit environments.

Mythological Interpretations

The Chupacabra is sometimes seen as a demon or supernatural being in folklore, possibly connected to local legends about evil spirits or curses. The sulfur smell reported by witnesses is often linked to traditional beliefs about demons and the devil.

Dimensional Attributes and Existence

Some theories suggest the Chupacabra could be an extraterrestrial being or a hybrid resulting from genetic experiments, explaining its alien-like appearance and unusual behavior. Others propose it might be an evolutionary anomaly, adapted to isolated environments on Earth.

Case Study: A Notable Case

In 1995, Madelyne Tolentino's sighting in Canóvanas, Puerto Rico, became the cornerstone of the Chupacabra legend. She described a creature resembling an alien-human hybrid with spikes along its back, leading to a surge of similar reports and widespread panic about livestock attacks in the region.

Personal Accounts and Historical References

Numerous eyewitnesses have claimed to see the Chupacabra, often describing it with varying features. Michael Negron, a university student, reported seeing a creature with dinosaur-like skin and bright eyes. Despite these accounts, most cases lack scientific validation and are often debunked as misidentified animals with severe mange.

Psyop

The chupacabra, a cryptid known for attacking livestock, is theorized to have been used as a psychological warfare tool by the CIA. By creating or manipulating this mysterious creature, the agency aimed to instill fear and confusion among local populations, distracting them during politically or militarily significant events. This strategy highlights the potential use of folklore and fear to influence public perception and destabilize communities, making the chupacabra an effective instrument in psychological operations.

Academic and Scientific References:

- Radford, B. (2011). *Tracking the Chupacabra: The Vampire Beast in Fact, Fiction, and Folklore.* University of New Mexico Press.

- Chupacabra: Legend of a Blood-Sucking Cryptid in Latin America

- Legend of the Chupacabra | The Business Standard: https://www.tbsnews.net/splash/legend-chupacabra-66172

Chapter 27

Clarions

C larions are interdimensional entities believed to originate from the star system Clarion, situated in a higher vibrational plane or parallel dimension.

Known for their advanced spiritual and technological capabilities, the Clarions are a compelling subject of study for those interested in interdimensional phenomena.

Historical Context and Origins

Clarions first gained attention through channeled messages and encounters reported by individuals in metaphysical and New Age circles. They are depicted as enlightened beings whose purpose is to assist humanity in its spiritual evolution. Existing in a dimension that vibrates at a higher frequency, they are invisible to the naked eye and perceivable only through heightened states of consciousness.

Descriptions and Characteristics

Clarions are typically described as humanoid in form but with distinct features that reflect their advanced state of being. They are often depicted as tall, with elongated limbs and ethereal, translucent skin that shimmers with a soft, luminescent glow. Their eyes are large and radiant, capable of emitting light and perceived as windows to their profound wisdom and compassion.

Unique and Obscure Facts

Dimensional Anchors: Clarions have the ability to create dimensional anchors, which are stable points that help them maintain a connection between their dimension and ours. These anchors facilitate smoother transitions and prolonged interactions with the human realm. Some claim that these anchors can appear as small, floating orbs of light or intricate geometric patterns visible during deep meditative states.

Energy Patterns: They can create intricate energy patterns that serve as protective barriers or communication signals. These patterns can influence the energy fields around them, harmonizing or altering them as needed. There are reports of these patterns being visible as complex mandalas or fractal designs in the auras of those who have encountered Clarions.

Holistic Healing: Clarions employ advanced healing methods that encompass physical, emotional, and spiritual aspects. Their techniques involve adjusting the vibrational frequencies of affected areas, which surpasses current human medical practices. It is said they can perform "energetic surgery," where they realign the body's energy flow without any physical intervention.

Cultural Insights: They possess a deep understanding of human cultures and often provide guidance on improving societal structures. They advocate for systems that promote environmental sustainability, social equality, and spiritual growth. Clarions have been linked to ancient civilizations like Atlantis and Lemuria, where their influence purportedly guided societal advancements.

Etheric Nature: Clarions exist in an etheric state, meaning their physical forms are composed of light and energy rather than solid matter. This allows them to phase in and out of our physical reality and interact with humans non-physically. Witnesses have described them appearing as shimmering silhouettes or ghostly figures that can move through solid objects.

Dimensional Travel Mastery: Clarions can navigate multiple dimensions effortlessly. Their understanding of the interconnectedness of all life enables them to act as intermediaries between different planes of existence, often traveling through portals that are invisible to the human eye. These portals are sometimes described as swirling vortices or shimmering doorways that appear momentarily.

Creation of Dimensional Rifts: An obscure fact about the Clarions is their ability to create and stabilize dimensional rifts. These rifts act as temporary bridges between different dimensions, allowing for the safe passage of entities and energy. These rifts are carefully monitored and controlled to prevent any unintended consequences or distortions in the fabric of reality. Some accounts suggest that these rifts can also be used to send objects or messages across vast interdimensional distances.

Theories and Interpretations

Some researchers propose that the Clarions are interdimensional beings visiting from higher planes to assist humanity in its evolution. Others suggest that encounters with Clarions might be visionary experiences or manifestations of collective unconscious archetypes.

Cultural Impact

The Clarions have influenced various spiritual movements and practices, particularly those focusing on higher consciousness and environmental stewardship. Their teachings emphasize unity, compassion, and the importance of raising one's vibrational frequency.

Case Study: The Clarion Call

A notable case involving the Clarions is the "Clarion Call," where numerous individuals reported receiving a collective telepathic message from the Clarions. This message emphasized the need for humanity to increase its vibrational frequency through love, compassion, and unity. It also stressed the importance of environmental stewardship and the shift away from destructive behaviors. This event reportedly led to a surge in environmental and spiritual movements in the late 20th century.

Additional facts about the Clarion Call

- **Mass Meditation Events:** Following the Clarion Call, several mass meditation events were organized globally, with participants reporting heightened states of awareness and profound feelings of interconnectedness. These events were aimed at raising the collective vibrational frequency of humanity.

- **Ecological Initiatives:** Many individuals who claimed to have received the Clarion Call became active in ecological movements, advocating for sustainable living, renewable energy, and the protection of natural habitats.

- **Channeled Literature:** Numerous books and articles emerged, purportedly channeled from the Clarions, offering guidance on spiritual practices, holistic healing, and the importance of unity and compassion.

- **Artistic Inspirations:** The Clarion Call also inspired a wave of creative expression, with artists, musicians, and writers producing works that reflected the themes of interconnectivity, higher consciousness, and the importance of environmental stewardship.

- **Scientific Interest:** The event caught the attention of some scientists and researchers who explored the potential for collective consciousness and its impact on global events. Studies were conducted to investigate the effects of synchronized meditation and intention-setting on environmental and social outcomes.

Academic and Scientific References

- Channeling and New Age Movements: Hanegraaff, W.J. (1996). New Age Religion and Western Culture: Esotericism in the Mirror of Secular Thought. SUNY Press.

- Interdimensional Beings and Higher Frequencies: Kaku, M. (2005). Parallel Worlds: A Journey Through Creation, Higher

Dimensions, and the Future of the Cosmos. Penguin Books.

- Vibrational Healing Techniques: Gerber, R. (2001). Vibrational Medicine: The #1 Handbook of Subtle-Energy Therapies. Bear & Company.

- Telepathic Communication Studies: Sheldrake, R. (2013). Science Set Free: 10 Paths to New Discovery. Deepak Chopra.

- Collective Consciousness Research: Radin, D. (2006). Entangled Minds: Extrasensory Experiences in a Quantum Reality. Paraview Pocket Books.

Chapter 28

Contrologarchs

Insiders, Breakaway Societies, Deep State

Contrologarchs are described as humanoid entities, often with pedophilic tendencies, who regard themselves as superior to humanity. Their general purpose is to increase '*Gevura*' in the world (lit. "might"); the second of the seven Divine middot, or attributes, associated with the holding back of Divine revelation and restricting the dispersion of Divine light to lower levels of existence.

The non-dimensional insiders are often viewed as "useful idiots," and are purportedly instruments for their interdimensional overlords. Their dimensional status is ambiguous, potentially encompassing entirely human, hybrid-human, synthetic drone/pilots, or shape-shifting dimensional entities. They serve as cosmic tools, managing human societies and perpetuating negative emotional energy.

> *"A careful examination of conscience and the personal unconscious is therefore the first requirement if one seeks seriously to do something about the problem of evil.*
>
> Murray Stein. 1995. P18

Historical Context and Origins

The origins of Contrologarchs are deeply entwined with various clandestine societies and secretive groups that have existed for thousands of years. These entities are thought to have connections with covert government facilities and subterranean colonies, indicating a longstanding influence over human affairs. Historical narratives suggest that Contrologarchs have evolved their operations through advanced technologies and interdimensional affiliations.

Descriptions and Characteristics

Contrologarchs are depicted as condescending, elite, and often harboring animosity toward humanity.

They are known to thrive on negative human emotions and engage in activities such as managing the masses, conducting demoralization campaigns, psyops, fifth-generation warfare, chaos, pedophilia, and human trafficking. These beings utilize advanced technology, including the TR-3B aircraft for transporting trafficked humans.

Unique and Obscure Facts

- **Adrenochrome Harvesting:** Some Contrologarchs are purported to consume adrenochrome, a substance extracted from the extreme fear and suffering of humans. This process involves inducing intense fear in children as they confront their imminent death, which is believed to yield the highest potency of adrenochrome.

- Adrenochrome is a chemical compound produced by the oxidation of adrenaline (epinephrine). The oxidation reaction that converts adrenaline into adrenochrome occurs both in vivo and in vitro. In his 1954 book, '*The Doors of Perception*' Aldous Huxley mentioned the discovery and the effects of adrenochrome, which he likened to the symptoms of mescaline intoxication. The substance is also mentioned in the books "*A Clockwork Orange*' and '*Fear and Loathing in Las Vegas.*'

- **Soul Recycling Technology:** A controversial theory suggests that Contrologarchs use a "soul recycler" or "Soul Cube" installed on the moon and Earth to force human souls to reincarnate, perpetuating their control over human energy and emotions.

- **Moon as a Holographic Device:** Some experts posit that the moon functions as a holographic projection device that broadcasts signals to distort human reality and perception, keeping humanity in a state of mental slavery.

- **Vibrational Loosh Consumption:** Contrologarchs and their rulers purportedly discovered that human emotions carry an energy frequency, which can be consumed for sustenance, referred to as "Loosh." The most beneficial form of sustenance for them is derived from negative emotions, leading to their desire for such emotions being akin to drug addiction. Concepts of death, war, human sacrifices, pedophilia, and slavery are suggested to be sources of this energy.

Mythological Interpretations

Contrologarchs are often linked to various malevolent interdimensional historical entities such as demons, jinn, and other supernatural beings. These entities are thought to manipulate human affairs from higher dimensions, using Contrologarchs as their earthly representatives. The myths surrounding these beings often describe them as possessing the ability to shape-shift, manipulate human minds, and influence events.

Dimensional Attributes and Existence

Contrologarchs and their overlords are believed to operate across multiple dimensions. They are thought to have the ability to manipulate human perception through technological means rather than telepathy. This multi-dimensional existence allows them to exert significant influence over human reality, often through advanced technologies and covert operations.

Case Study: Michael Herrera and the Insider Human Trafficking Operation

Michael Herrera, a US Marine, encountered a human trafficking operation during a mission in response to an earthquake and tsunami in Indonesia.

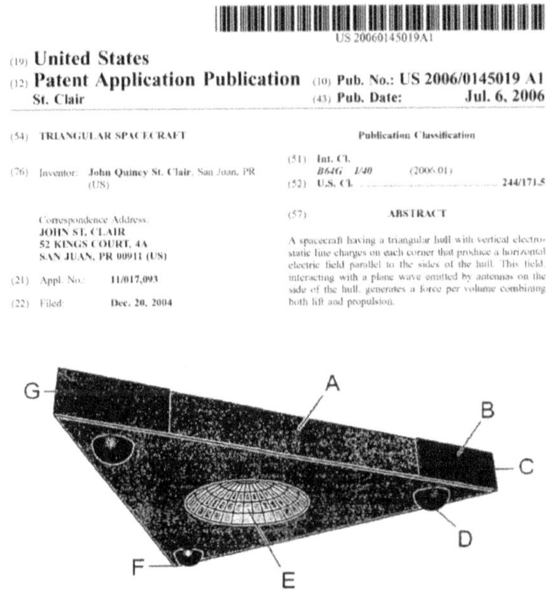

He witnessed three truckloads of trafficked humans being loaded into TR-3B aircraft, highlighting the involvement of advanced technology in Contrologarch activities.

Influence and Operations

Insiders operate at the highest levels of government, business, and technology. They include oligarchs, technogarchs, meter maids, courtside Lakers ticket holders, World Economic Forum members, NATO bureaucrats, monarchs, politicians, and bankers. They are said to own and operate major media companies, exerting influence across various aspects of human life. These individuals, often referred to as the ruling class, are considered "useful idiots" serving the interdimensional overlords.

Demoralization Campaigns

Contrologarchs are believed to utilize various forms of media and entertainment to demoralize and manipulate the masses. A classic example of this is the Amazon Prime series "The Boyz," which presents facts known to be true but insults, bullies, and makes fun of viewers for believing in those facts. The series twists the truth and belittles the viewer with the constant devaluation of human life messaging and unwanted homosexual harassment.

Psyop

The planet appears to be run by elite pedophiles that keep the citizens in a constant state of fear by hyping up the seasonal flu.

Academic and Scientific References

- Stein, Murray. Jung's Map of the Soul: An Introduction. Open Court, 1998. This book provides insights into the examination of the personal unconscious and the problem of evil, relevant to understanding the motivations behind Contrologarch activities.

- Mitchell, Edgar D. The Way of the Explorer: An Apollo Astronaut's Journey Through the Material and Mystical Worlds. G.P. Putnam's Sons, 1996. This work explores the intersection of science and spirituality, offering perspectives on interdimensional interactions.

- Greer, Steven M. Hidden Truth: Forbidden Knowledge. Crossing Point, 2006. Greer's book discusses the hidden influence of interdimensional beings on human affairs, including the role of Contrologarchs.

Chapter 29

DMT/ NDE Dimensionals

Praying Mantis and Machine Elves

More profound than "full disclosure" the scientific proof that we are not alone in the universe has been scientifically verified.

DMT/NDE (Dimethyltryptamine Induced Near Death Experience) refers to experimental encounters with dimensional entities induced by the administration of N, N-dimethyltryptamine (DMT). This powerful psychoactive substance has been linked to subjective experiences involving encounters with beings from other dimensions, particularly from the 6th to 8th dimensions.

Historical Context and Origins

A decades-long, declassified study conducted by the National Institute of Health (NIH) and the US Government explored the subjective experiences of individuals induced with DMT. This study focused on their encounters with dimensional entities, revealing consistent reports of transcending physical bodies, entering higher dimensions, and engaging in telepathic communication with 'presences' or 'alien entities.'

Descriptions and Characteristics

Participants reported encountering a variety of entities, including elf-like beings, short demon-like aliens, and a towering praying mantis entity. These entities were perceived as existing in a distinct dimension of reality, often described as possessing consciousness, intelligence, and the ability to engage in telepathic communication. The study noted that 41% of participants experienced fear during these interactions, while 69% received messages, and 19% received predictions about the future.

Unique and Obscure Facts

- **Dimensional Perspectives:** DMT/NDE entities are described as existing in dimensions ranging from the 6th to 8th dimensions.

- **Appearance:** Respondents consistently reported encounters with entities, including elf-like beings, short demon-like aliens, and a towering praying mantis that appears to be up to 100 feet tall, possibly silicon-based.

- **Evolution:** These entities are perceived as existing in a different dimension, possibly at war with carbon-based life forms, suggesting a cosmic political agenda.

- **Qualities:** Attributes ascribed to these entities include consciousness, intelligence, and a profound existence in a separate dimension of reality. Coercive experiences typically involved fear, as reported by 41% of respondents. The entities were believed to engage in telepathic communication with those they encountered.

- **Soul-Matrix:** DMT-induced experiences prompted shifts in participants' belief systems, even leading individuals who identified as atheists to question their beliefs. Carbon-based life forms appear to be part of the soul-matrix in this universe, implying that the "soul" of humans has value to these dimensional beings.

- **Abilities:** These entities were involved in delivering messages (69% of respondents) and predictions about the future (19% of respondents). Despite their initial fear-inducing nature, the experiences were ultimately perceived as profoundly meaningful, spiritually enlightening, and psychologically insightful.

Basic Needs: The specific needs of these entities, if any, were not the focus of the study, which instead centered on participants' experiences with them. However, the entities appeared to have a cosmic political agenda supporting silicon-based life. The reason for the conflict and why both universes can exist simultaneously remain unknown.

Mythological Interpretations

In the study, entities were often described using terms like 'being,' 'spirit,' 'alien,' and 'torturer.' The experiences led to profound shifts in participants' belief systems, even among those who identified as atheists. Respondents with profound faith in God reported different types of encounters compared to atheists, suggesting a spiritual dimension to these experiences.

Dimensional Attributes and Existence

DMT-induced experiences suggest that these entities exist in a separate, higher-dimensional reality. Participants often described these dimensions as having unique physical and metaphysical properties, enabling encounters that defy traditional scientific understanding.

Case Study: A Notable Case

NIH and US Government Study: The study was terminated due to unfavorable results conflicting with prevailing government interests. Participants reported encounters with dimensional entities, including elf-like beings and a towering praying mantis entity, often involving coercive experiences and profound shifts in belief systems.

Personal Accounts and Historical References

Participants consistently described similar features of their DMT-induced experiences, defying the boundaries of traditional scientific understanding. Despite the subjectivity of these experiences, the overarching theme of shared encounters with otherworldly beings was a common thread. Descriptive labels ascribed to these entities included 'being,' 'spirit,' 'alien,' and 'torturer.'

Academic or Scientific References

- Rick Strassman's "DMT: The Spirit Molecule": Explores the effects of DMT and its potential to induce encounters with otherworldly entities.

- NIH and US Government Declassified Study: Provides detailed accounts of the subjective experiences of individuals induced with DMT.

- Rick Strassman's "DMT: The Spirit Molecule"(https://www.rickstrassman.com/)

- NIH Study on DMT(https://clinicaltrials.gov/ct2/show/NCT00820667)

- Davis AK, Clifton JM, Weaver EG, Hurwitz ES, Johnson MW, Griffiths RR. Survey of entity encounter experiences occasioned by inhaled N,N-dimethyltryptamine: Phenomenology, interpretation, and enduring effects. J Psychopharmacology. 2020 Sep;34(9):1008-1020. doi: 10.1177/0269881120916143. Epub 2020 Apr 28. PMID: 32345112.

- Timmermann C, Roseman L, Williams L, Erritzoe D, Martial C, Cassol H, Laureys S, Nutt D, Carhart-Harris R. DMT

Models the Near-Death Experience. Front Psychol. 2018 Aug 15;9:1424. doi: 10.3389/fpsyg.2018.01424. PMID: 30174629; PMCID: PMC6107838.

- Michael P, Luke D, Robinson O. An encounter with the self: A thematic and content analysis of the DMT experience from a naturalistic field study. Front Psychol. 2023 Mar 27;14:1083356. doi: 10.3389/fpsyg.2023.1083356. PMID: 37051610; PMCID: PMC10083325.

Chapter 30

Elves

Huldufolk, Alfar, Fairies, Duende

E lves have been a significant part of folklore and mythology, especially in European traditions.

In Norse mythology, elves were considered semi-divine beings associated with nature and fertility, while Celtic folklore often depicted them as guardians of the natural world. These mythical roots suggest that elves were considered beings of great power and wisdom, closely connected to the earth and its elements.

Descriptions and Characteristics

Elves are typically described as ethereal beings, often depicted as having a strong connection to nature. They are said to possess abilities beyond those of humans, such as enhanced senses, agility, and magical powers. They are usually portrayed as wise, ancient beings who live in harmony with the natural world. These attributes support the idea of elves as interdimensional beings, capable of existing in realms beyond the physical world.

Unique and Strange Facts

- **Subterranean and Otherworldly Habitats:** Some traditions suggest that elves reside in subterranean environments or otherworldly realms that are separate from the human world. These hidden habitats could be accessed through natural features like forests, hills, or caves, implying a connection to other dimensions.

- **Reports of Encounters:** There are numerous anecdotal accounts of people encountering elf-like beings in secluded natural settings. These beings are often described as appearing suddenly and disappearing just as quickly, suggesting they can move between dimensions.

- **Ancient Lore and Modern Claims:** Ancient texts and modern reports alike speak of elves with abilities that imply interdimensional qualities, such as invisibility, telepathy, and time manipulation.

- **Sightings:** During Oscar season Elves have been spotted having lunch with George Clooney at Bucca di Beppo.

Mythological Interpretations

In various mythologies, elves are seen as beings that exist in a realm that overlaps with our own but remains hidden from ordinary human perception. This idea is prevalent in:
- **Norsc Mythology:** Elves are associated with Álfheimr, a realm that is part of the larger cosmological structure and is inhabited by beings who can influence the human world.

- **Celtic Folklore:** Elves, or faeries, are often linked to the Other-world, a dimension that exists parallel to our own. They can cross into the human realm, often through specific times or places that act as portals.

Dimensional Attributes and Existence

Elves are considered interdimensional beings due to their ability to traverse different realms of existence. They are believed to have access to hidden dimensions through:

- **Natural Portals:** Specific locations in nature, such as ancient forests, hills, or caves, are often cited as gateways to the realms of the elves.

- **Temporal Shifts:** Certain times of the year, like solstices or equinoxes, are believed to be when the veil between worlds is thin, allowing elves to move between dimensions more easily.

- **Energetic Frequencies:** Elves are thought to operate on different energetic frequencies, making them invisible or undetectable to humans unless they choose to reveal themselves.

Case Study: The Icelandic Huldufólk

In Icelandic folklore, the Huldufólk, or "hidden people," are believed to be a type of elf that lives in rocks and hills. These beings are considered real and interdimensional, capable of interacting with the human world under certain conditions. Many Icelanders still hold these beliefs, and construction projects have been altered or halted to avoid disturbing the supposed homes of the Huldufólk.

Personal Accounts and Historical References

- **Icelandic Tradition:** According to a 2007 survey, over half of Icelanders believe in the existence of elves and hidden people, and there are numerous stories of encounters and interactions with these beings, the other half is muslim.

- **Fairy Hills in Scotland and Ireland:** Local traditions often speak of specific hills or mounds where elves or faeries are believed to live. Disturbing these places is thought to bring bad luck, further supporting the idea of elves as guardians of certain interdimensional sites.

Academic or Scientific References

- Davidson, H.R. Ellis (1964). "Gods and Myths of Northern Europe": Examines the role of elves in Norse mythology and their association with otherworldly realms.

- Briggs, K.M. (1976). "An Encyclopedia of Fairies": Provides a comprehensive look at the various types of fairies and elves in folklore, including their roles as interdimensional beings.

- Haraldsson, E. (1987). "Psychic Experiences: A Cross-Cultural Perspective": Discusses modern encounters with elves and hidden people, particularly in Iceland, and how these experiences might relate to interdimensional phenomena.

Chapter 31

Egregores

Magickal Servitors, Team Spirit

E gregores, deeply rooted in esoteric traditions and occult philosophy, represent a complex phenomenon entwined with human consciousness.

They are collective thought forms or psychic entities created by the collective energy and shared beliefs of a group. Often referred to in contemporary terms as the "Hive Mind Virus," egregores are empowered thought forms that can influence group behavior and consciousness.

Examples like the Pledge of Allegiance and collective prayers in schools are cited as rituals that contribute to the strength of egregores. The notion that egregores not only act as energetic reserves but also shape behavior within groups brings forth the intelligent and behavior-shaping aspects of these entities.

Historical Context and Origins

The concept of egregores dates back to ancient civilizations such as Egypt and Rome, where organized groups formed around god-like figures, emphasizing deep emotional and ritualized engagement. The classical view suggests a psychic conduit between human groups, particularly within religious or political movements, drawing parallels with a community of saints or bodhisattvas. In contemporary times, the concept has evolved to include influences from Jungian Collective Consciousness.

Descriptions and Characteristics

- **Empowered Thought Forms**: Egregores are shaped by the collective energy of groups. They can manifest in various forms and are often associated with movements, corporations, political parties, unions, sports teams, and religious groups.

- **Behavioral Influence**: Egregores not only act as energetic reserves but also shape behavior within groups. They are described as intelligent and capable of influencing individual and collective actions.

- **Rituals and Connectivity**: Rituals are key mechanisms for connecting with egregores, directing energy toward these entities. Examples include the Pledge of Allegiance and collective prayers.

Unique and Obscure Facts

- **Hive Mind**: Elon Musk commonly refers to these entities as the "Hive Mind Virus," emphasizing their emergence from the interconnectedness of people through shared information and common interests.

- **Servitor Magick**: Known as servitor magick, practitioners use their minds, hearts, and souls to conjure spirits or entities devoted to fulfilling their desires, such as attracting wealth, love, and luck or inspiring creativity.

- **Intelligent Batteries:** Egregores are often depicted as reservoirs of energy that can be accessed through proper rituals, aligning individual goals with those of the egregore for mutual benefit.

Mythological Interpretations

Egregores have been linked to various mythological and occult practices. They are seen as entities that bridge metaphysical and tangible aspects of human existence, playing crucial roles in channeling energy, shaping collective consciousness, and influencing historical revolutions and group behavior.

Dimensional Attributes and Existence

Egregores are considered to exist both metaphysically and tangibly. They are thought to channel energy from collective human consciousness, acting as connectors that influence and shape group dynamics and information warfare.

Case Study

One notable case involves the global psychological and propaganda operation during the COVID-19 crisis. Western governments, non-governmental organizations, and corporations collaborated through public-private partnerships, employing military-grade psychological operations strategies against their citizens. For instance, in determining who orchestrated the COVID crisis, was it Klaus, someone above Klaus, Gates, or Tony Fauci? These figures act as surrogates, making it difficult to pinpoint the mastermind behind the propagated message. This synchronized effort can be seen as an example of an egregore influencing collective consciousness on a massive scale.

Personal Accounts and Historical References

Throughout history, egregores have been associated with religious movements, political revolutions, and social phenomena. Examples include the community of saints in Christianity, the bodhisattvas in Buddhism, and the collective fervor seen in various political movements.

Psyop

Egregores play a significant role in everyday both large and small modern psychological operations (psyops), particularly in 5th generation warfare where the enemy is often unclear or indistinguishable. The 2020 Chinese lab virus crisis is cited as a classic example where various public and private entities obfuscated the truth without coordination acting as surrogates, making it difficult to identify the true orchestrators of the propagated lies.

References

- **Egregores: The Occult Entities That Watch Over Human Destiny** by Mark Stavish: This book examines the historical significance, formation, and impact of egregores from an occult perspective.

- **Prime Chaos: Adventures in Chaos Magic** by Phil Hine: Covers various aspects of chaos magic, including the creation and manipulation of magical entities.

- **The Servants of the Light Tarot** by Dolores Ashcroft-Nowicki: Explores the concept of thought forms and egregores in the context of tarot.

- **Condensed Chaos: An Introduction to Chaos Magic** by Phil Hine: Introduces chaos magic and includes discussions on magical entities and thought forms.

- **Prometheus Rising** by Robert Anton Wilson: Explores belief systems, consciousness, and reality perception, providing a foundation for understanding how collective beliefs influence behavior.

Chapter 32

Electromagnetic Plasmas

Atmospheric Orbs, Plasmas, Fastwalkers

Electromagnetic plasmas, also known as atmospheric orbs, are considered a fourth state of matter life form that pervades interstellar space and the upper atmosphere of Earth.

These plasmas exhibit behaviors and characteristics that suggest they may represent a form of pre-life or inorganic non-biological life, challenging conventional understandings of life forms and their requirements. Unlike solid, liquid, or gaseous states, plasma is an ionized state of matter where electrons are free from their atomic nuclei, creating a soup of charged particles. This unique state allows for interactions with electromagnetic fields in ways that are not possible for traditional matter, leading to their peculiar and life-like behaviors. The study of electromagnetic plasmas extends beyond terrestrial phenomena, encompassing cosmic and atmospheric observations that have intrigued scientists for decades. The potential for these plasmas to bridge the gap between non-living and living matter presents a fascinating area of research that could redefine our understanding of life and the universe.

Historical Context and Origins

The concept of plasma life forms has been around for several decades, but recent studies have provided more concrete observations. During ten separate NASA space shuttle missions, pulsating glowing "plasmas" resembling simple multicellular organisms were observed over 200 miles above Earth within the thermosphere. These observations have led to increased interest and research into the nature and potential of plasma-based life forms.

Descriptions and Characteristics

- **Size and Shape**: These plasmas can measure up to a kilometer in size and display various morphologies, including cone, cloud, donut, and spherical-cylindrical shapes.

- **Behavior**: They exhibit behaviors akin to multicellular organisms, such as acceleration, deceleration, stopping, congregating, and engaging in what appears to be "hunter-predatory" actions. They also leave plasma dust trails.

- **Attraction to Electromagnetic Radiation**: The plasmas are attracted to electromagnetic radiation and have been observed traveling towards thunderstorms, congregating near satellites emitting electromagnetic activity, and approaching space shuttles.

Unique and Obscure Facts

- **Ball Lightning Formation**: In rare cases, lightning strikes can form a ball of plasma known as "ball lightning." These phenomena are still not fully understood and can last for several seconds before dissipating.

- **Cosmic Ray Visual Phenomenon**: Astronauts have reported seeing "spots," "streaks," and "clouds" of light when exposed to cosmic rays. This visual phenomenon, observed during space missions, suggests that these rays interact with the human retina and spacecraft, creating unexpected visual effects.

- **Persistent Observation in Space**: During NASA space shuttle missions, these plasmas were observed to exhibit life-like behaviors, such as altering their speed and direction abruptly. The pulsating glow and trajectory changes indicate a complex interaction with their environment.

- **Advanced Propulsion Studies**: Electromagnetic plasmas are being studied for their potential in advanced propulsion systems, particularly for space travel. Their ability to be manipulated by electromagnetic fields offers a pathway for more efficient and faster propulsion technologies.

Mythological Interpretations

Historically, similar plasma-like entities have been documented as "Foo fighters" by WWII pilots in the 1940s. They are also frequently observed and filmed by astronauts and military pilots, often classified as Unidentified Aerial Anomalous Phenomena (UAPs). These sightings have contributed to various mythological and speculative interpretations of extraterrestrial encounters.

Dimensional Attributes and Existence

While these plasmas are not biological in the traditional sense, they may represent a stage of extra-dimensional pre-life. Their behaviors and interactions with electromagnetic radiation suggest they exist in a realm that overlaps with our own but operates under different physical principles. This extra-dimensional attribute could be a precursor to the emergence of biological life as we understand it.

Case Study

A study published in the Journal of Modern Physics (Volume 15, No 3, February 2024) reported the observation of pulsating glowing "plasmas" during ten separate NASA space shuttle missions. These plasmas, measuring up to a kilometer in size, were observed over 200 miles above Earth within the thermosphere. The study detailed their complex behaviors and interactions with the environment, providing significant insights into their nature.

Personal Accounts and Historical References

Similar phenomena, historically documented as "Foo fighters" by WWII pilots, have been frequently observed and filmed by astronauts and military pilots. These observations have often been classified as UAPs, contributing to the ongoing investigation and intrigue surrounding these entities.

Psyop

While often considered speculative, the frequent sightings and detailed behavior of these plasmas suggest a more grounded phenomenon. They contribute to many historical UFO-UAP sightings when observed in the lower atmosphere, challenging traditional perceptions of extraterrestrial encounters. Governments may have used the mysterious nature of these plasmas to divert attention from more mundane, albeit advanced, technological experiments.

Academic or Scientific References:

- Journal of Modern Physics, 2024, 15, 322-74: https://www.scirp.org/journal/paperinformation?paperid=131506

Chapter 33

Fastwalkers

Upper atmospheric orbs

Fastwalkers is a term used by air defense and satellite analysts when tracking fast-moving objects in the upper and outer atmosphere.

These objects, rarely caught on camera, exhibit unusual behaviors and are often seen moving at high velocities in the Earth's atmosphere and beyond. These plasmas have been observed engaging in complex behaviors, such as approaching and congregating around satellites generating electromagnetic pulses, diving into thunderstorms, and displaying hunter-predatory behavior by tracking and piercing other plasmas. They grow in size, replicate, and leave plasma-dust trails in their wake. These entities are not biological but are driven by electromagnetic and non-biological factors.

Historical Context and Origins

The term "Fastwalkers" has been used by the military and space agencies to describe unidentified aerial phenomena observed in the upper atmosphere. Notably, Fastwalkers have been identified even in the stratosphere at altitudes of 125 km. The phenomenon gained particular attention during NASA Shuttle Mission STS-48, Discovery, in 1991, where a fastwalker was captured on camera maneuvering to avoid a ground-based weapon.

Descriptions and Characteristics

- **Behavior**: Fastwalkers exhibit high-speed maneuvers, sudden changes in direction, and acceleration. They have been seen to change trajectory angles abruptly, including shifts of 45°, 90°, and 180°.

- **Appearance**: These objects can take on various shapes, including cones, clouds, donuts, and spherical-cylindrical forms. They have also been observed emitting bright flashes when targeted.

- **Interaction with Electromagnetic Activity**: Fastwalkers are attracted to electromagnetic radiation and have been filmed approaching satellites and space shuttles, and descending into thunderstorms.

Unique and Obscure Facts

- **Fastwalker Database**: An Air Force captain disclosed the existence of a database chronicling fastwalker events dating back to the early '70s. These entities often capture the attention of ballistic missile early warning systems.

- **Satellite Interactions**: In 2017, an event involving a communications satellite dislodged from geosynchronous orbit highlighted the potential impact of fastwalkers. Another satellite, operated by PT Telkom, experienced an unexplained breakup.

- **Empirical Observations:** Fastwalkers have been observed during multiple NASA space shuttle missions, indicating that these phenomena are not isolated incidents.

Mythological Interpretations

Some researchers and enthusiasts have linked Fastwalkers to the broader category of UFOs and interdimensional beings. Their ability to perform physics-defying maneuvers suggests a possible connection to otherworldly or advanced non-human technologies.

Dimensional Attributes and Existence

Fastwalkers challenge traditional biological classifications and suggest the existence of life forms or entities that can exist in extreme environments such as the upper atmosphere. These beings are thought to obtain energy from electromagnetic radiation and exhibit behaviors similar to simple multicellular organisms.

Case Study

During Shuttle Mission STS-48 in 1991, a fastwalker was targeted and fired upon by a ground-based weapon, as captured by NASA cameras. The fastwalker maneuvered to avoid the attack, changing direction and accelerating dramatically. This event highlighted the capabilities of these entities to respond to external threats swiftly. Additionally, a 2024 paper published in the Journal of Modern Physics discusses the potential for interdimensional beings and their interaction with our reality. The study highlights the possibility of advanced life forms existing in multiple dimensions and their implications for our understanding of the universe.

Personal Accounts and Historical References

- **NASA Shuttle Missions:** Fastwalkers have been observed and filmed during several NASA space shuttle missions, including STS-48, STS-75, and others. These missions documented fastwalkers exhibiting life-like behaviors such as changing velocity and direction.

- **Air Force Reports**: Declassified Air Force reports and studies from the early 1970s onwards have documented fastwalker sightings and their interactions with satellites and other space objects.

Psyop

The tracking and documentation of fastwalkers are empirical and scientifically verifiable yet no one ever mentions it. Most people don't really want the truth. They just want constant reassurance that what they believe is the truth.

References

- **Extraterrestrial Life in the Thermosphere: Plasmas, UAP, Pre-Life, Fourth State of Matter**: https://www.scirp.org/journal/paperinformation?paperid=131506

- **NASA STS-48 Mission Footage**: https://www.youtube.com/watch?v=Yb67zM1Sh-Q

- **Centauri Dreams**: Discussions on the potential for life forms in extreme atmospheric conditions.

Chapter 34

Felines

Feline beings, often referred to as the Lion People, are an extraterrestrial race currently linked to the Lyrans from the Lyra constellation and the Sirius star system. Known for their feline features, these beings possess advanced spiritual and psychic abilities and play a significant role in the evolution of human civilizations on Earth today.

Originating from the Sirius Star System and Lyra constellation, feline beings are invited to this universe as "co-creators" from a completed universe. They initially exist as quadrupedal cats but evolve into bipedal entities with advanced genetic and technological capabilities, spreading life across the cosmos. Today, they typically appear as bipedal cats or human-cat hybrids, showcasing feline-like eyes, pointed ears, and a protective layer of "peach fuzz" due to ultraviolet exposure on their home planet.Feline beings are curious, adventurous, and creative, exhibiting strong organizational skills and psychic sensitivity. They exist across multiple dimensions, from 3D to 12D, and develop machinery capable of bending space and time. Their cultural influence is evident in ancient civilizations like Atlantis, Lemuria, and Egypt, where they guide human spiritual evolution. Associated with mythological figures like Sekhmet, these beings continue to inspire curiosity about their potential role in our universe.

Historical Context and Origins

Feline beings are said to originate from the Sirius Star System and Lyra constellation. According to Starseed lore, they were invited to this universe as "co-creators" when it was new, coming from a completed universe. They initially existed as quadrupedal cats but evolved into bipedal entities with advanced genetic and technological capabilities, spreading life across the cosmos.

Descriptions and Characteristics

- **Appearance:** Feline beings typically appear as bipedal cats or human-cat hybrids, with features resembling lions or domestic cats. Their height ranges from 3 to 8 feet. They have feline-like eyes, pointed ears, and a protective layer of "peach fuzz" over their skin due to exposure to ultraviolet radiation on their home planet.

- **Evolution:** These beings evolved from quadrupedal cats to bipedal forms, developing higher senses and psychic sensitivity. They also genetically mixed with humans, creating hybrids with feline facial features and tails.

- **Qualities and Abilities:** Feline beings are curious, adventurous, and creative. They possess strong organizational skills, focus, and intensity. They are highly psychic and telepathic, able to manipulate energies and environments through music, art, dance, and other creative means.

Unique and Obscure Facts

- **Dimensional Abilities:** Feline beings exist across multiple dimensions, from 3D to 12D, allowing them to traverse various planes of existence.

- **Technological Prowess:** They developed machinery capable of bending space and time, enabling faster-than-light travel. They are also expert geneticists, responsible for planting life across the cosmos and activating higher consciousness in other beings.

- **Cultural Influence:** Felines have significantly influenced Earth's history, particularly in ancient civilizations like Atlantis, Lemuria, and Egypt. They are believed to have seeded feline species on Earth and guided human spiritual evolution.

Mythological Interpretations

Feline beings are often associated with mythological figures such as Sekhmet, an Egyptian deity worshipped for her protective and healing powers. These beings have been revered in various cultures, reflecting their longstanding influence on human spirituality and mythology.

Dimensional Attributes and Existence

Feline beings can exist as physical entities in lower dimensions and as energy beings in higher dimensions. They retain the ability to manifest their original feline form and are known to serve as galactic travelers, shifting energies and sparking creativity in various environments.

Case Study

Sekhmet in Ancient Egypt: Sekhmet, an ambassador collective existing in the ninth dimension, was worshipped as a deity in Ancient Egypt. Her influence highlights the significance of feline beings in human history and their role in guiding spiritual evolution.

Personal Accounts and Historical References

Throughout history, feline beings have interacted with humanity, leaving traces in ancient texts, myths, and cultural symbols. They are often depicted as benevolent guides who assist in developing extrasensory abilities and advancing human creativity.

References

- Sekhmet in Ancient Egypt: The worship of Sekhmet in ancient Egypt underscores the reverence for feline beings in human history. https://www.ancientegyptonline.co.uk/sekhmet.html

- Galactic Performers: Feline beings are known as galactic performers, channeling their creative energies into various artistic expressions.

Chapter 35

Girtablulu

Scorpion Men, Oonkians, Ishaqrab

Girtablullu, also known as **Scorpion Men**, are extraordinary mythological creatures rooted deeply in ancient Mesopotamian folklore.

These beings are an integral part of Mesopotamian mythology, famously appearing in the Epic of Gilgamesh, one of the earliest known works of literature. The Girtablullu are depicted as hybrid beings, possessing the upper body of a human and the lower body of a scorpion. This striking combination symbolizes their dual nature, embodying both the intellect and spirituality of humans and the fierce, predatory instincts of scorpions. These creatures are formidable guardians and warriors, often described as protecting sacred thresholds and serving as gatekeepers to otherworldly realms. Their presence in mythology highlights themes of protection, boundary-setting, and the mystical dangers that lie at the edges of human understanding. In various texts, they are shown wielding bows and arrows, emphasizing their role as powerful defenders against intrusions.

The Girtablullu are also referred to by other names such as **Oonkians** and **Ishaqrab**. These variations in nomenclature reflect their diverse representations across different cultures and mythological traditions. The term Oonkians is particularly noted in modern accounts, suggesting a connection to subterranean and interdimensional phenomena. Descriptions of Oonkians add a layer of complexity to their identity, depicting them as insectoid beings with similarities to ants and mantises. They are characterized by a distinctive red coloration, square jaws, long and narrow faces, large round eyes, and an overall insect-like appearance. Their bodies are extremely thin with long torsos, arms that bend sharply at the mid-joint, and legs bent at nearly right angles, giving them a recognizable "Praying Mantis" look.

Historical Context and Origins

The Girtablullu emerge from the rich mythological traditions of ancient Mesopotamia, particularly within the narratives found in the Epic of Gilgamesh. These beings serve as the guardians of the gates of Mashu, which is described as the passageway of the sun god Shamash. Their duty is to protect this sacred entrance, preventing the unworthy from accessing the divine realms. This role as protectors of sacred spaces underscores their significance in the mythological hierarchy, portraying them as entities of immense power and importance.

Descriptions and Characteristics

Girtablullu are defined by their hybrid form, which combines human and scorpion features. Their upper bodies are human-like, complete with a torso, arms, and a head, while their lower bodies resemble that of a giant scorpion, complete with a venomous tail. This combination symbolizes their dual nature and their ability to traverse both the human and natural worlds. The Oonkians, or Ishaqrab, add an additional layer to their description, with their insectoid features and distinctive red coloration setting them apart from other mythological beings.

Unique and Obscure Facts

- **Subterranean Dwellers:** According to Chris O'Brien's "Mysterious Valley," Oonkians reside in sophisticated subterranean cave systems within Inner Earth.

- **Seismic Event Transporters:** Their primary purpose involves transporting individuals to Inner Earth during seismic events that cause the world to split into two realms, with Inner Earth existing at a higher density.

- **Guardians of the Sun God:** They guard the gates of the sun god Shamash, embodying the threshold between the mortal world and the realm of the gods. Their hybrid form, combining human and scorpion attributes, emphasizes their role as formidable gatekeepers and warriors.

- **Influence in Modern Culture:** Girtablullu appear in various modern contexts, including literature, music, and video games, reflecting their lasting impact on cultural narratives.

Mythological Interpretations

In Mesopotamian mythology, Girtablullu are seen as liminal figures, existing at the boundaries between worlds. Their role as gatekeepers underscores themes of protection, transition, and the dangers of crossing into forbidden realms. They serve as both literal and symbolic barriers between the known world and the mysteries beyond. Their depiction in the Epic of Gilgamesh highlights their significance in the hero's journey, symbolizing the challenges and trials faced in the pursuit of ultimate knowledge and understanding.

Dimensional Attributes and Existence

The Girtablullu are believed to exist in various mythological dimensions, primarily associated with the underworld and the pathways of the sun god Shamash. They are described as beings who operate at the thresholds of these realms, maintaining balance and preventing unauthorized crossings. Their existence in these dimensions emphasizes their function as boundary guardians. The concept of their existence aligns with the notion of multidimensional beings capable of interacting with different realms, although they may not necessarily be interdimensional in the modern scientific sense.

Case Study

In the Epic of Gilgamesh, the hero encounters the Girtablullu as he seeks the secret of immortality. They question him about his journey and intentions, highlighting their role as gatekeepers who assess the worthiness of those who attempt to enter sacred or restricted spaces. This encounter serves as a pivotal moment in Gilgamesh's quest, symbolizing the challenges and trials faced in the pursuit of ultimate knowledge and understanding.

Personal Accounts and Historical References

Numerous firsthand experiences narrate encounters with Girtablullu aboard spaceships. According to Chris O'Brien's account in "Mysterious Valley" with the Hopi, these beings have been seen in various parts of the world, particularly during significant geological events. The alignment of Oonkians with malevolence or benevolence is contingent on their agenda, and their interactions with humans have been documented in various UFO-related narratives.

Psyop

Western culture generally asserts humanity is at the apex of knowledge and understanding, often assuming that ancient peoples were naive or ignorant for believing they encountered gods from the sky. This perspective may underestimate our ancestors' intelligence and cultural sophistication. Ancient records and myths, blending historical facts with legendary narratives, suggest that these stories may hold more truth than we realize. From a speculative perspective, one might argue that governments or authoritative entities could suppress knowledge of Girtablullu and other facts to maintain control over historical narratives and cultural heritage. By controlling the dissemination of information about such mythological beings, they could prevent the public from exploring alternative historical interpretations or questioning established paradigms.

References

- "The Epic of Gilgamesh," translated by N.K. Sandars.

- "Myths from Mesopotamia: Creation, the Flood, Gilgamesh, and Others," translated by Stephanie Dalley.

- "The Treasures of Darkness: A History of Mesopotamian Religion," by Thorkild Jacobsen.

- "Mesopotamian Cosmic Geography," by Wayne Horowitz.

- Encyclopaedia Metallum: The Metal Archives - Girtablullû

- Old World Gods - Girtablilu Myth:

Chapter 36

Gizan

Gizahn

Gizan, also known as Gizahan or the 'Gizeh People,' are interdimensional or subterranean entities reportedly connected to ancient Egypt. The name "Gizan" translates to Pledge, Hostage, or Cut Stone, indicating their potential roles or origins.

These beings are believed to reside in deep labyrinthine recesses beneath Egypt and have been encountered by explorers. Descriptions suggest they dress in a manner reminiscent of ancient Egyptians and may have connections with secret government activities.

Historical Context and Origins

The concept of the Gizan emerged from various accounts, including those of contactees and researchers such as Billy Meier and Leading Edge Research. These beings are thought to inhabit vast caverns beneath Egypt, intertwining with the mythology and mystery surrounding the Giza Plateau and its pyramids. Some sources, including Meier, suggest that the Gizan are an ancient civilization with advanced technology, possibly linked to extraterrestrial origins. However, multiple independent researchers have also documented these claims, adding layers of intrigue and historical speculation.

Descriptions and Characteristics

- **Appearance:** Gizans are typically depicted as humanoid in form, dressing similarly to ancient Egyptians, complete with traditional attire and accessories.

- **Advanced Technology:** They are believed to possess advanced technology and have access to extensive subterranean networks beneath Egypt.

- **Possible Reptilian Influence:** Reports suggest they may have a reptilian influence, indicating a possible control or dominance by reptilian beings.

Unique and Obscure Facts

- **Ancient Egyptian Dress:** The Gizan are said to dress like ancient Egyptians, wearing traditional robes, headdresses, and jewelry. This attire has led to speculation about their connection to Egypt's past and its advanced knowledge.

- **Subterranean Civilization:** Allegedly, there is a massive cavern beneath Egypt inhabited by the Gizan. This cavern is said to contain advanced technology and has ties to the U.S. secret government, indicating a complex relationship between surface governments and subterranean societies.

- **Controlled Society:** Some sources indicate that the Gizan society is controlled, with the reptilians being the dominant power.

This control could suggest a hierarchy within their civilization where the Gizan serve as intermediaries or subordinates to the reptilians.

- **Technological Prowess**: The Gizan are reputed to have technology far beyond current human capabilities, including advanced transportation systems within the labyrinthine tunnels, energy weapons, and devices that can manipulate or project illusions.

- **Secret Government Ties**: There are claims that the Gizan have connections with covert operations and secret governmental organizations in the U.S., hinting at hidden alliances and exchanges of knowledge and technology.

- **Mystical Practices**: Reports suggest that the Gizan engage in mystical or esoteric practices, possibly involving ancient Egyptian rituals and ceremonies. These practices could be linked to their technological advancements and control mechanisms.

Mythological Interpretations

The Gizan have been referenced in various contactee accounts and other sources, with connections to ancient Egyptian attire and subterranean labyrinths leading to various mythological interpretations. These include theories of them being remnants of an ancient advanced civilization or a hybrid race created through genetic manipulation by extraterrestrial beings.

Dimensional Attributes and Existence

The Gizan are believed to utilize interdimensional hubs located deep beneath the Giza Plateau. These hubs serve as gateways that connect various parts of the universe, facilitating travel and communication between realms. According to some accounts, these hubs are linked to the vast labyrinthine structures and underground chambers described by ancient historians like Herodotus and recent archaeological findings.

Case Study: The Giza Labyrinth

A notable case involving the Gizan is the reported exploration of the Giza Labyrinth, a vast underground network of tunnels and chambers beneath the Giza Plateau. Explorers like Dr. Carmen Boulter and Klaus

Dona have used space-based technology to identify these subterranean structures, which include chambers described by ancient historians as housing immense knowledge and treasures. These explorations have revealed complex, multi-level underground constructions that suggest advanced architectural and engineering capabilities far exceeding those of known ancient civilizations.

Personal Accounts and Historical References

Various explorers and researchers have documented encounters with beings resembling the Gizan beneath the Giza Plateau. Historical references to subterranean worlds and hidden chambers in ancient texts and folklore further support the possibility of an underground civilization connected to the Giza Plateau. Herodotus, for instance, described the labyrinth as containing numerous chambers and corridors that amazed ancient visitors with their complexity and scale.

Psyop

Speculatively, the presence and activities of the Gizan could be subjects of disinformation campaigns by governments to maintain control over advanced knowledge and technology. Their connection with covert operations and secret governmental organizations might be deliberately obscured to prevent public awareness and potential upheaval.

Academic and Scientific References

1. Hancock, G. (1995). *Fingerprints of the Gods: The Evidence of Earth's Lost Civilization.* Three Rivers Press.

2. Sitchin, Z. (1980). *The Stairway to Heaven: Book II of the Earth Chronicles.* Avon Books.

3. Boulter, C., & Dona, K. (2008). *Hawara Labyrinth Expedition.* National Research Institute of Astronomy and Geophysics (NRIAG).

4. Leading Edge Research. "The Giza Intelligence and Their Influence on Earth."

5. http://www.thinkaboutit-aliens.com/gizan-or-gizahn/

Chapter 37

Golem

Man created through Sefer Yetzirah

Golem has its roots in Jewish mysticism, particularly in the Kabbalistic tradition.

It is associated with the *Sefer Yetzirah*, a foundational text that dates back to between the 3rd and 6th centuries CE. The *Sefer Yetzirah*, or "Book of Creation," contains esoteric knowledge about the creation of the world through the combination of Hebrew letters and divine names. The idea of the golem was further popularized in the medieval period, with Rabbi Judah Loew ben Bezalel, known as the Maharal of Prague (16th century), being one of the most famous figures associated with its creation.

Descriptions and Characteristics

A golem is described as an inter-dimensional entity that projects a facet of its consciousness into the third dimension, taking shape using materials such as clay, rock, or dirt. What sets the golem apart from other beings is its lack of a soul. Unlike robots, which are animated by algorithms, a golem possesses a spiritual "spark" activated by a righteous individual using the hidden secrets of creation found within the Sefer Yetzirah.

Unique and Obscure Facts

- **Spiritual Activation:** The golem's animation comes from the mystical knowledge of the Sefer Yetzirah, emphasizing the combination of Hebrew letters and divine names.

- **Rabbinical Legends:** In Sanhedrin 65b, it is mentioned that Rabbis Hanina and Oshaya created a golem in the form of a cow using the Sefer Yetzirah, which was then used for food.

- **Maharal's Perspective:** Despite the folklore, the Maharal himself considered the creation of the golem as unremarkable and not special.

Mythological Interpretations

In Jewish folklore, the golem often appears as a protector of the Jewish community, created to defend against persecution. The golem of Prague, created by the Maharal, is one of the most famous legends, symbolizing the use of mystical and divine knowledge for protection and justice. However, golems can also be seen as cautionary tales about the limits and responsibilities of using such powerful knowledge.

Dimensional Attributes and Existence

The golem is an inter-dimensional entity that projects part of its consciousness into the physical realm. This unique attribute means it exists partially in another dimension and can take on physical form using available materials. This ability underscores its otherworldly nature and the mystical knowledge required for its creation and animation.

Case Study: The Golem of Prague

The Maharal of Prague, Rabbi Judah Loew ben Bezalel, is said to have created a golem from clay in the late 16th century to protect the Jewish community from anti-Semitic attacks. According to legend, the Maharal used Kabbalistic rituals and divine names to animate the golem, which then served as a guardian. However, the golem eventually became uncontrollable, and the Maharal had to deactivate it, placing its remains in the attic of the Old New Synagogue in Prague, where it supposedly still lies.

Personal Accounts and Historical References

- **Sanhedrin 65b:** Discusses the creation of a golem by Rabbis Hanina and Oshaya, highlighting the use of the Sefer Yetzirah.

- **Berachot 55a:** Mentions Betzalel's knowledge of combining the letters with which heaven and earth were created.

- **Maharal's Accounts:** While the Maharal of Prague is most famously associated with the creation of the golem, historical records suggest he viewed the creation as an unremarkable act, emphasizing its mystical rather than practical significance.

Academic or Scientific References

- Idel, M. (1990). "Golem: Jewish Magical and Mystical Traditions on the Artificial Anthropoid". State University of New York Press.

- Scholem, G. (1965). "On the Kabbalah and Its Symbolism". Schocken Books.

- Dan, J. (1986). "Jewish Mysticism and Jewish Ethics". University of Washington Press.

Chapter 38

Greys

intermediaries

G rey interdimensional beings, often associated with the archetype of Grey aliens, are considered by some to be vessels for higher-dimensional entities operating in our lower-density environment. Unlike typical depictions of Greys, these beings are theorized to possess unique characteristics that set them apart from conventional narratives.

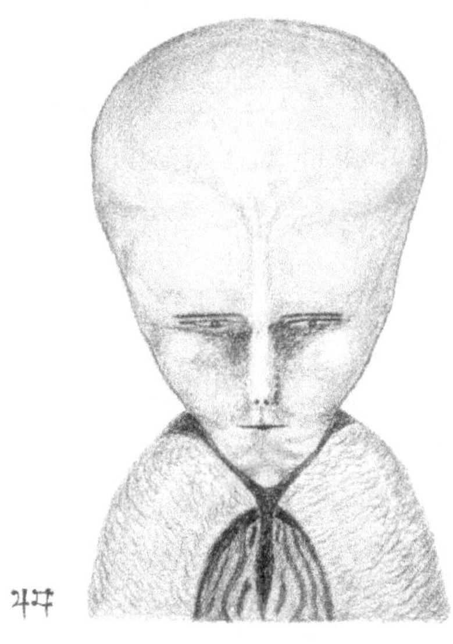

Crowley's visual account of LAM

These entities are described as having the ability to traverse multiple dimensions, using their humanoid forms as temporary vessels to interact with our world. Their physiology, with large heads and minimal facial features, is thought to be optimized for telepathic communication and energy manipulation rather than verbal interaction. This aligns with reports of their involvement in inducing altered states of consciousness during encounters, suggesting a focus on mental and emotional engagement. A lesser-known aspect of these beings is their hypothesized role as observers or guides, subtly influencing human evolution and consciousness. Some theories propose that their presence is not purely physical but involves a form of consciousness projection, allowing them to exist simultaneously in multiple realities. This dual existence could explain the diverse and often conflicting reports of their appearance and behavior.While scientific evidence remains elusive, the concept of Grey interdimensional beings continues to intrigue those exploring the boundaries of human perception and the potential for realities beyond our own. There are over thirty-two variations of Greys reported, each with unique characteristics.

Historical Context and Origins

The modern-day association with Greys can be traced back to Aleister Crowley, an occultist who claimed to have communicated with beings from other realms. In 1906, during his time in Shanghai, Crowley endeavored to summon his holy guardian angel "Aiwass" with the help of Elaine Simpson. He claimed to have established contact through astral or dimensional means, engaging in psychic meetings. From January to March 1918, Crowley conducted sessions known as the "Amalantrah working" in New York's Central Park West hotel. He purportedly opened a portal to another realm, allowing an entity named "LAM" to communicate with him. Crowley's sketch of LAM, which strikingly resembles the modern depiction of Grey aliens, raises questions about whether he learned about such beings from studying Kabbalah texts or if "LAM" was an early representation of what we now call Greys.

Jewish spiritual texts, many of which are over 900 years old, such as the Talmud and Sefer Hasidim, provide additional historical context. According to Talmud, b. Avot 5:6, the original demons were created without stable physical forms and have since sought to obtain bodies for themselves. Avot D'Rabbi Natan 37:3 states that demons participate in sexual reproduction, potentially bonding with and reproducing through humans. The Sefer Hasidim and the Tziyuni (alongside other Jewish sources like the Talmud, Midrash Rabbah, and Hesed L'Avraham) affirm this possibility.

Descriptions and Characteristics

- **Appearance:** Greys are depicted as small, grey-skinned beings with large, bald heads, black almond-shaped eyes, and slender bodies. Crowley's sketch of LAM matches this description.

- **Abilities:** Greys are said to possess advanced cognitive abilities, telepathy, and dimensional travel capabilities. Their interactions often involve abductions and experiments on humans.

- **Origins:** They are believed to originate from various dimensions or planets, existing across a broad spectrum of dimensions from the 1st to the 9th.

- **Abductions:** Numerous credible individuals have shared harrowing experiences of being rendered helpless and taken aboard unidentified flying objects. While on these crafts, they report undergoing various medical experiments, many of which are distressingly invasive. Both men and women have recounted being forced into intimate encounters with beings described as Greys, with some women reporting mysterious pregnancies and subsequent removal of the fetus. These stories, shared by rational and trustworthy people, are deeply unsettling and increasingly common.

Unique and Obscure Facts

- **Early Depictions:** Crowley's 1918 sketch of LAM predates the Roswell incident and the modern UFO era by decades, raising questions about the origins of Grey imagery.

- **Cultural Impact:** The concept of Greys has permeated popular culture, influencing numerous films, books, and television shows, embedding the image of Greys into the collective consciousness.

- **Historical Context:** Jewish texts, such as the Talmud and Sefer Hasidim, describe interactions with demons resembling Greys, suggesting these beings have troubled humanity for centuries.

- **Psychological Effects:** Abductees often report experiencing severe psychological trauma, including PTSD, sleep disturbances, and intense phobias, following their encounters with Greys.

- **Physical Evidence:** Some abductees claim to have physical evidence of their encounters, such as unexplained scars, implants, and heightened psychic abilities, which they attribute to the Greys.

- **Technological Advances:** Reports suggest that technologies like fiber optics and microchips may have been reverse-engineered from alien technology provided by Greys, highlighting their potential influence on modern technology.

- **Dimensional Travel:** Greys are described as having the ability to traverse dimensions, potentially accessing different planes of reality. This ability might explain their sudden appearances and disappearances.

- **Variety of Greys:** Reports indicate over thirty-two variations of Greys, each with unique characteristics, suggesting a diverse and possibly hierarchical society among these beings.

Mythological Interpretations

- Crowley's accounts and subsequent occult rituals by followers like Jack Parsons and L. Ron Hubbard suggest that Greys might be interdimensional entities. These entities could be the precursors of what we now identify as Grey aliens, possibly involved in shaping human history through interactions and influence.

- Jewish spiritual texts provide additional mythological context. According to the Talmud, b. Avot 5:6, the original demons were created without stable physical forms and have since tried to acquire bodies for themselves. Avot D'Rabbi Natan 37:3 mentions that demons engage in sexual reproduction, potentially bonding with and reproducing through humans. The Sefer Hasidim and the Tziyuni, along with other Jewish sources such as the Talmud, Midrash Rabbah, and Hesed L'Avraham, corroborate this notion, suggesting that Greys might be these ancient demons attempting to create hybrid beings. This interpretation aligns with the idea that Greys are interdimensional beings seeking physical existence through complex interactions with humanity.

Dimensional Attributes and Existence

Greys are believed to exist across various dimensions, from the 1st to the 9th. Their interactions with humanity, through abductions and experiments, suggest a complex relationship with our world. Some theories propose that they require physical bodies to exist in our dimension, leading to hybridization experiments. The Tziyuni (49b) details that these beings continue their breeding programs, producing hybrid offspring who often assume positions of leadership, allowing them to gain physical form.

Case Studies

- In 1918, Aleister Crowley conducted the Amalantrah working in New York, claiming to have opened a portal to another realm.

The entity LAM, which he sketched, bears a striking resemblance to modern Grey aliens. This case is significant because it predates the popularization of Grey imagery and suggests early interactions with interdimensional beings. Crowley's work, intertwined with ancient Jewish texts, indicates a long-standing awareness of such entities.

- "Hesed L'Avraham," authored by Rabbi Abraham ben Mordecai Azulai in the early 17th century, is a significant Kabbalistic text exploring mystical themes. Rabbi Azulai, born in 1570 in Fez, Morocco, and passing in 1643 in Hebron, Israel, contributed extensively to Jewish mystical literature. His work covers a wide range of mystical topics, including the concept of seven hidden lands inhabited by various beings. In "Hesed L'Avraham," there are intriguing references to beings from a place called "Neshaya," described as having large heads, small bodies, no ears or noses—only holes—and large black eyes. This description closely aligns with the modern depiction of Grey aliens. The text suggests that the world is essentially hollow, with different layers inhabited by such creatures, reflecting a mystical tradition that sees physical and metaphysical phenomena as interconnected.

Personal Accounts and Historical References

Jack Parsons and L. Ron Hubbard, followers of Crowley, attempted to replicate his rituals in 1946 in Pasadena, CA. Their sessions allegedly opened a portal, contributing to the surge in UFO sightings and abductions in subsequent years. Parsons went on to found the Jet Propulsion Laboratory (JPL), a key center for space exploration technology, while Hubbard founded the Church of Scientology, which has become a globally influential organization. These developments raise questions about the influence of their interdimensional communications.

Psyop: Possible Disinformation Campaign

The concept of Grey aliens has also been linked to various psychological operations (PSYOPs) and disinformation campaigns. For example, during the 1950s, the Eisenhower administration reportedly entered into the Grenada Treaty with Grey aliens, allowing limited human abductions in exchange for technology. These PSYOPs involve crafting narratives that blend truth and fiction, creating confusion and diverting attention from actual government operations and extraterrestrial interactions.

The concept of alien abductions often parallels sexual assault, with abductees reporting invasive procedures and forced breeding without consent. Channeling conversations with Greys claim these actions are justified by a "soul contract," suggesting preordained cosmic agreements. This idea is ethically problematic and does not alleviate the real psychological trauma experienced by abductees

Members of the psychiatric community are not dismissing the phenomena of alien abductions as nonsense, and neither should we. These experiences are significant and cannot be ignored simply because they challenge our understanding of reality. An in-depth review of the abduction phenomena exceeds the scope of this work, but it is clear that these episodes hold real importance and impact. The fear of accepting these occurrences as real is understandable, given the unsettling implications they carry. Understanding these phenomena is essential, and whatever the truth may be, we must take these matters seriously.

References

- Jet Propulsion Laboratory historical archives

- Tziyuni (49b)

- Chruch of Scientology historical archives

- Hesed L'Avraham

Chapter 39

Hathor

H athor dates back almost 5000 years, associated with the ancient Egyptian goddess Hathor, depicted as a cow-headed woman.

Hathor is one of the oldest goddesses in the Egyptian pantheon, symbolizing love, motherhood, birth, joy, and music, yet also known for her destructive behavior against those who mocked her father in early myths. The Hathors claim to have interacted with Earth's early cultures, including ancient Egypt and Tibetan Buddhism, serving as mentors without assuming messianic roles. They emphasize that human ascension requires effort and self-awareness, respecting existing spiritual helpers and religious beliefs.

Descriptions and Characteristics

- **Appearance:** Hathor is often depicted as a cow-headed woman or a woman with cow horns and a sun disk. The Hathors as beings are described as vibrating at a higher frequency than humans, with an ethereal presence.

- **Communication:** They communicate through catalytic sound patterns, which Tom Kenyon channels during sound meditations. They also convey information through language, focusing on cosmic vibrations and sacred geometry.

- **Roles and Influence:** Hathor's roles encompass love, motherhood, birth, joy, and music. The Hathors, as interdimensional beings, act as mentors and guides, aiding in the psycho-spiritual development of humans.

Unique and Obscure Facts

- **Cosmic Vibrations:** The Hathors provide instructions on cosmic vibrations, sacred geometry, and sound, which they claim can be used for psycho-spiritual experiences.

- **Interdimensional Connections:** They describe themselves as originating from another universe through Sirius, emphasizing their interdimensional and intergalactic nature.

- **Non-Interference Policy:** Despite offering guidance, the Hathors stress the importance of self-responsibility in the ascension process and refrain from interfering with existing cosmic relationships.

- **Historical Interactions:** The Hathors have reportedly interacted with Earth's early cultures, influencing both ancient Egyptian and Tibetan Buddhist practices.

Mythological Interpretations

The Hathors' connections to the goddess Hathor link them to ancient Egyptian mythology, where Hathor was revered as a deity of love, music, and motherhood. Their portrayal as interdimensional beings suggests a blending of mythological and extraterrestrial narratives, aligning with the concept of ancient astronauts influencing early human civilizations.

Dimensional Attributes and Existence

The Hathors claim to be interdimensional beings vibrating at a higher frequency than humans. They describe their existence as spanning multiple dimensions and realms, utilizing interdimensional hubs for travel and communication. Their teachings on cosmic vibrations and sacred geometry suggest an advanced understanding of the interconnectedness of different planes of existence.

Case Study: Tom Kenyon's Contact

In the late 1980s, Tom Kenyon was contacted by the Hathors during meditation. Over two decades, he tested their "inner technologies," finding them illuminating. Through sound meditations, he channels their catalytic sound patterns, providing insights into cosmic vibrations and psycho-spiritual experiences. Kenyon's work with the Hathors has been documented in various publications and workshops, contributing to a broader understanding of their teachings.

Personal Accounts and Historical References

Various explorers and researchers have documented encounters with beings resembling the Hathors, linking them to ancient Egyptian practices and Tibetan Buddhism. Historical references to Hathor as a goddess in ancient texts and artifacts further support the connection between these interdimensional beings and early human civilizations.

Psyop

Speculatively, the presence and activities of the Hathors could be subjects of spiritual disinformation campaigns to maintain control over advanced spiritual knowledge and technology. Their teachings on self-responsibility and psycho-spiritual development might be used to deliberately obscure or prevent public awareness or true human potential

Academic and Scientific References

- Kenyon, T. (2010). *The Hathor Material: Messages from an Ascended Civilization.* Tom Kenyon.

- Hancock, G. (1995). *Fingerprints of the Gods: The Evidence of Earth's Lost Civilization.* Three Rivers Press.

- Budge, E. A. W. (1904). *The Gods of the Egyptians, Vol. 1 & 2.* Dover Publications.

Humanoid Dimensional Beings

Humanoid interdimensional entities are beings that exist in dimensions beyond the conventional three-dimensional space and time continuum known to human experience. When interacting with humans they choose a human form knowing we have a cognitive bias. As humans we naturally anthropomorphize, making it easier for us to relate to other beings with familiar traits.

These entities often assume humanoid or human-like forms, possessing some human traits while distinctly not being human. They are found in mythology, legends, and folklore worldwide, fulfilling various roles as protectors, tricksters, or even deities embodying powerful natural phenomena. These beings are believed to traverse dimensions, interacting with humanity in ways that have influenced historical narratives and cultural myths.

Historical Context and Origins

The concept of humanoid interdimensional entities is ancient, with roots in various cultures and mythologies. H.P. Lovecraft described such beings as existing "between the spaces we know," indicating their presence in unseen dimensions. Stories of these entities span across numerous cultures, where they are depicted as spirits, demons, creatures, and monsters of folklore. While some represent humanity's darker aspects like greed and savagery, others serve as allegorical warnings or portray real individuals. Despite their diverse origins, these entities share common themes that transcend cultural boundaries.

Descriptions and Characteristics

- **Appearance**: Humanoid interdimensional entities often possess a humanoid form with bilateral symmetry, having two eyes, a nose, a mouth, two legs, and two arms. This similarity to humans is thought to ease interactions and minimize fear.

- **Behavior and Roles**: These entities assume various roles, including protectors, tricksters, and deities. They are often associated with natural phenomena and are depicted with magical or supernatural abilities.

- **Magical Humanoids**: Magical humanoid beings capable of assuming various forms or manifesting mystically include elves from English, Celtic, and Germanic folklore. These beings, depicted as nature spirits or luminous figures with fair complexions, possess magical powers associated with nature and often play roles as tricksters or protectors.

- **Humanoid Sea Creatures**: Many cultures feature humanoid sea creatures or amphibious organisms, such as mermaids, finfolk, adaro, and Oannes. Mermaids, with the upper body of a female human and the tail of a fish, symbolize the ocean's dual nature—both beautiful and cruel—and are sometimes portrayed as luring sailors to their demise.

- **Communication**: They may communicate through telepathy, visions, or symbolic language, often influencing human thoughts and actions subtly.

Unique and Obscure Facts

- **Shape-Shifting Abilities**: Many humanoid interdimensional entities can change their form at will, appearing as different beings to different people. This ability to shape-shift is often associated with trickster figures in mythology.

- **Dimensional Travel**: The means by which these entities traverse dimensions remain speculative, with theories suggesting magnetic anomalies, frequencies, and vortexes as potential gateways.

- **Genetic Experimentation**: Some theories propose that humanoid interdimensional beings, such as the "Grays," are products of genetic programming by more advanced species. This hints at artificial creation rather than natural evolution.

Mythological Interpretations

Across various mythologies, humanoid interdimensional entities have been depicted as elves, fairies, mermaids, and other mystical beings. These entities often embody the dual nature of the elements they are associated with, such as the ocean's beauty and cruelty in the case of mermaids. Vampires and werewolves, with their monstrous traits, likely evolved from ancient depictions of demons or spirits that prey on humans.

Dimensional Attributes and Existence

Humanoid interdimensional entities are believed to exist in realms that overlap with our own but operate under different physical principles. They utilize interdimensional hubs or gateways to travel between these realms and our world. The consistent humanoid appearance among various reported entities, such as the Grays and reptilian beings, suggests a commonality in their genetic programming or a deliberate choice to appear humanoid for easier interaction with humans.

Case Study

The Grays are a prominent example of humanoid interdimensional entities. Described as slender beings with large, dark eyes and human-like shapes, they have been widely reported in abduction accounts. In "Walking Among Us" by David Jacobs, abductees claim that the Grays are genetically programmed by a more advanced species, indicating a possible artificial creation. Despite skepticism, some reports have been independently corroborated by credible witnesses, adding to the intrigue surrounding these beings.

Personal Accounts and Historical References

Various personal accounts and historical references describe encounters with humanoid interdimensional entities. John Keel, a prominent ufologist, shifted his focus from extraterrestrial life to beings from other dimensions, arguing that these entities have influenced human history and mythology. His theories, along with those of other researchers, explore the methods and motives of these shape-shifting beings

Cosmic Samurai Crab Theory

The Cosmic Samurai Crab theory provides a fascinating explanation for the humanoid appearance of interdimensional beings. This theory draws a parallel to the Heikegani crab, a species native to Japan known for its shells that resemble human faces. Japanese fishermen, believing these crabs to house the spirits of departed samurai, throw them back into the sea, thereby contributing to the survival and perpetuation of their unique shell patterns. Similarly, it is proposed that interdimensional beings possess the capability to manifest in diverse forms but often choose humanoid appearances to mitigate the possibility of rejection or causing distress among humans during encounters. This theory suggests that "beings from other dimensions can appear in any manner that aligns with our chosen perception".

Psyop

There have been account this entries have claimed to be prophets or Angeles.

Academic and Scientific References

- Jacobs, D. M. (2015). *Walking Among Us: The Alien Plan to Control Humanity*. Disinformation Books.

- Hynek, J. A., & Vallee, J. (1975). *The Edge of Reality: A Progress Report on Unidentified Flying Objects*. Henry Regnery Company.

- Openhand. "How Interdimensional Entities Influence Daily Life." Openhandweb.org.

Chapter 41

Hybrid Greys

H ybrid Greys are entities reported to exhibit a blend of human and alien characteristics, primarily described in the context of abduction narratives.

These entities are typically small, standing between 3 1/2 to 4 1/2 feet tall, with skin colors ranging from gray-white to gray-brown, gray-green, and gray-blue. They are characterized by their logical, survival-oriented approach in interactions with humans. Reports mention over thirty hybrid variations of Greys, each displaying unique physical and behavioral traits.

Dimensional Attributes and Existence

Hybrid Greys are believed to possess the ability to traverse dimensions, interacting with humans in our physical realm while originating from a different dimensional plane. This capability suggests an advanced understanding of dimensional physics and the ability to manipulate space-time. The consistent humanoid appearance among various reported entities, such as the Grays and reptilian beings, suggests a commonality in their genetic programming or a deliberate choice to appear humanoid for easier interaction with humans. Theories propose that these beings may not originate from distant planets but from within our own planet, hidden in realms beyond our ordinary perception. This perspective posits that a race of humanoid dimensional beings resides within the Earth, using interdimensional travel to interact with humans.

Historical Context and Origins

The concept of Hybrid Greys has emerged primarily from abduction reports, with significant contributions from the narratives surrounding the Greys. These beings are often depicted as resulting from genetic experiments or hybrid breeding programs conducted by extraterrestrials. Their origins are linked to reproductive challenges on their home planets, necessitating the creation of hybrids using human genetic material. Some theories suggest these hybrids are designed to withstand harsher environmental conditions, potentially aiding both humans and aliens in surviving a changing climate .

Descriptions and Characteristics

- **Appearance**: Hybrid Greys are typically described as small, gray-skinned humanoid figures with large, opaque black eyes. They lack human body parts such as noses, ears, or sex organs, and have elongated bodies with small chests and minimal muscular definition. Their legs are shorter and jointed differently than human legs, contributing to their unique proportions.

- **Head and Facial Features**: They possess unusually large heads in proportion to their bodies, devoid of body hair and noticeable outer ears or noses. Instead, they have small openings for ears, nostrils, and mouths.

- **Eyes:** Their eyes are a prominent feature, described as large and black. Some theories suggest that these black eyes may be lenses, similar to sunglasses, used to cover more sensitive or differently functioning ocular organs.

Unique and Obscure Facts

- **Feeding Process:** The Greys' feeding process is similar to standard reptilian behavior, with waste believed to be excreted back through the skin.

- **Genetic Diversity:** There are reportedly over thirty hybrid variations of Greys, each with unique genetic traits and physical characteristics.

- **Reproductive Methods:** Reports suggest various non-physical reproduction methods, such as artificial reproduction using extracted human eggs and sperm, and the use of fluid-filled incubation tanks for gestation .

- **Hybrid Breeding Programs:** Some ufologists propose that Greys conduct hybrid breeding programs to create beings better suited to Earth's environment or to address reproductive challenges on their home planets.

Mythological Interpretations

Hybrid Greys have become iconic symbols in popular culture, often representing advanced intelligence and other traits associated with extraterrestrial beings. They are frequently depicted in media and literature as beings involved in genetic experiments and abductions, reflecting deep-seated human fears and fascinations with alien life.

Dimensional Attributes and Existence

The consistent humanoid appearance of Hybrid Greys across various reports raises questions about their origins. Some theories suggest that these beings may not originate from distant planets but from within our own planet, hidden in realms beyond our ordinary perception. This perspective posits that a race of humanoid dimensional beings resides within the Earth, using interdimensional travel to interact with humans.

Case Study: Abduction Narratives

Abduction narratives frequently feature Greys, describing them as the primary abductors in these experiences. Claims of abductions are characterized as highly traumatic, with emotional repercussions similar to those of combat or sexual assault. These narratives often involve intense staring by the Greys, purported to induce hallucinogenic states or elicit strong emotions in abductees.

Personal Accounts and Historical References

Abduction accounts and historical references describe intense interactions with Hybrid Greys, often involving medical examinations and genetic experiments. These experiences are reported worldwide, with significant variations in the details but consistent descriptions of the beings involved.

Psyop

Speculatively, the concept of Hybrid Greys is at the core of countless disinformation campaigns used as a cover story to obfuscate knowledge of covert operations and events.

Academic and Scientific References:

- CORE. "The Symbol of the Hybrid Human/Alien Child in the Abduction Experience."

- The Conversation. "Some scientific explanations for alien abduction that aren't so out of this world."

- PubMed. "Alien abduction: a medical hypothesis." https://pubmed.ncbi.nlm.nih.gov/18834282/

Chapter 42

Hybrid Mantis

Hybrid-Mantis, often reported in the realms of paranormal phenomena, near-death experiences, and extraterrestrial encounters, is considered by some to be an interdimensional or alien being.

These entities combine features of humanoids and mantis-like insects, presenting a fascinating yet eerie concept that merges elements of ancient myths, contemporary reports, and speculative theories. Referred to by different names such as **Mantis Aliens** or **Insectoid Beings**, they have become a significant part of modern paranormal studies and discussions about extraterrestrial life.

Hybrid-Mantis beings are typically described as tall and slender, with prominent mantis-like features such as elongated limbs and a triangular head. They are often depicted with a commanding presence, and their demeanor ranges from benevolent to indifferent, and sometimes even malevolent. These entities are frequently reported to communicate telepathically, conveying messages that are concise and often imbued with a sense of superiority or detachment from human concerns.

The idea of mantis-like beings can be traced back to various cultural depictions of insectoid deities and spirits. In ancient Egypt, for example, the scarab beetle was a symbol of transformation and protection, highlighting the cultural significance attributed to insect forms. Native American lore includes myths involving insect-like spirits or deities that play crucial roles in their cosmology, often embodying aspects of nature and transformation.

Historical Context and Origins

The concept of Hybrid-Mantis beings as interdimensional or extraterrestrial entities gained traction primarily through reports of alien encounters and abductions starting in the mid-20th century. These beings were often described by witnesses as examining or communicating with them during these encounters. Such descriptions typically portrayed these entities as having advanced technological capabilities and a superior intellect. The notion of these beings existing in ancient times is supported by various mythological parallels and historical records that reference insectoid deities and spirits.

Descriptions and Characteristics

Physical Appearance: Hybrid-Mantis beings are often described as tall, with thin, elongated limbs and a triangular head resembling that of a praying mantis. Their eyes are usually large, black, and almond-shaped, contributing to their hauntingly alien appearance. Their skin is typically reported to be green, brown, or gray, with a texture that ranges from smooth to slightly rough, similar to an exoskeleton.

Behavior and Habitat: These beings are carnivorous but do not typically consider humans as a food source. They are said to reside in sophisticated subterranean cave systems within Inner Earth and have the ability to transport individuals to Inner Earth, especially during seismic events. Some accounts even attribute them as the creators of the moon, although this remains within the realm of speculative myth.

Communication: Much like their DMT elf counterparts, Hybrid-Mantis beings often communicate telepathically. Their messages are usually concise, and they often convey a sense of superiority or detachment from human concerns.

Unique and Obscure Facts

- **Subterranean Dwellers:** According to Chris O'Brien's "Mysterious Valley," Oonkians (another name for Hybrid-Mantis) reside in sophisticated subterranean cave systems within Inner Earth.

- **Seismic Event Transporters:** Their primary purpose involves transporting individuals to Inner Earth during seismic events that lead to the world splitting into two realms, with Inner Earth existing at a higher density.

- **Guardians of the Sun God:** In Mesopotamian lore, Girtablullu guard the gates of the sun god Shamash, embodying the threshold between the mortal world and the realm of the gods.

Mythological Interpretations

The concept of insectoid beings has various cultural and mythological parallels. Many ancient cultures revered insect deities or spirits, often attributing significant powers and roles to them. For instance, the scarab beetle in ancient Egypt symbolized transformation and protection. Native American tribes have myths involving insect-like spirits that embody aspects of nature and transformation, similar to the Hybrid-Mantis in modern accounts.

Notable encounter settings include

Dimensional Attributes and Existence

Some theorists suggest that Hybrid-Mantis beings are not from another planet but another dimension. This perspective aligns with reports of their sudden appearance and disappearance, suggesting they can traverse different planes of reality. Other interpretations propose that these beings are spiritual entities or manifestations of the collective subconscious, emerging during altered states of consciousness or high-stress situations.

Case Study

The Hopkinsville Encounter: One of the most famous cases, the Hopkinsville encounter, involved witnesses describing strange, insect-like beings. These reports have been analyzed extensively, contributing to the lore of insectoid aliens.

Personal Accounts and Historical References

Numerous personal accounts and case studies document encounters with Hybrid-Mantis beings. Witnesses consistently describe the beings as tall with mantis-like features, often communicating telepathically and displaying advanced technological abilities. These recurring elements help to build a cohesive picture of the nature and behavior of Hybrid-Mantis entities.

References

- Meet the Hybrids: A Conversation About the Mantis Beings. Apple TV.

- Charmaine DRozario Interview - The Cosmic Switchboard.

Chapter 43

Imperial Squid

Inter-Dimensional Squid, Jellyfish

Imperial Squid: Categorizing this interdimensional entity proves challenging due to its diverse nature, encompassing aspects of the atmospheric, aquatic, mechanical, and cryptid realms.

It resembles a blend of organic and mechanical features, akin to a Star Wars imperial drone with an organic twist. This entity has been documented via thermal imagery and is known for its unique interactions with military systems.

Historical Context and Origins

The Imperial Squid first gained significant attention with the release of thermal footage by Jeffrey Corbell in 2018. This footage, captured over a U.S. military base in Iraq, showed the entity flying, diving into water, and resurfacing. Sightings of similar airborne "squid or jellyfish" phenomena date back decades, including a 1954 report from the Halifax Evening News describing a "flying jellyfish" seen by an air stewardess.

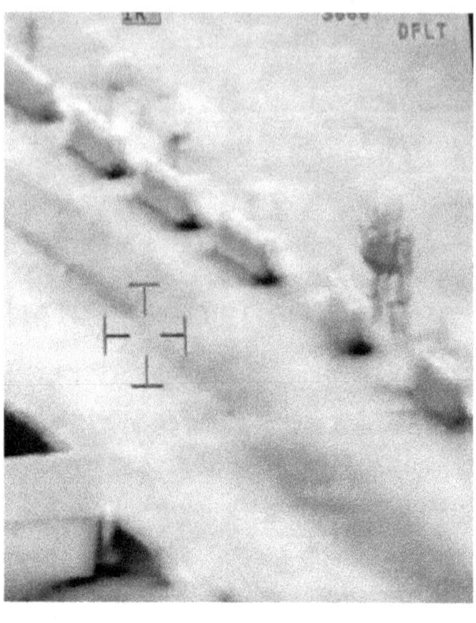

These historical accounts contribute to the ongoing mystery surrounding the Imperial Squid.

Dimensional Attributes and Existence

The Imperial Squid demonstrates significant interdimensional capabilities, including shifting colors indicative of heat differentials and inter-dimensional transitions. Its ability to operate both in air and water, staying submerged for extended periods, suggests advanced transmedium capabilities. The entity's interaction with military systems, such as jamming optics platforms, further indicates its manipulation of space and time, challenging conventional understanding of physics and technology. Notably, a larger captured Imperial Squid has been said to be up to 40 feet in diameter on the outside but, like the tent in Harry Potter, when entered, the interior was reported to be the size of a football field. The Imperial Squid is believed to somehow manipulate both time and space, adding to its mysterious nature.

Descriptions and Characteristics

The Imperial Squid is characterized by organic tentacles adorned with geometric, scale-like patterns. It is often detected within the thermal spectrum, yet remains invisible to night vision equipment. The entity exhibits flight over land, diving into water for up to 17 minutes before resurfacing at sharp angles. It undergoes color shifts from white to black, possibly indicating inter-dimensional transitions and fluctuations in temperature. The Department of Defense (DoD) has not obtained the licensing rights to the Imperial drone design from Disney, which the Imperial Squid closely resembles.

Unique and Obscure Facts

- **Thermal Imaging:** Military-grade thermal imaging cameras have captured the Imperial Squid, revealing its capacity to change colors and exhibit pulsating patterns of heat and cold.

- **Military Interaction:** The entity has disrupted military weapon systems by jamming optics platforms, rendering soldiers unable to target it.

- **Historic Sightings:** Entities resembling the Imperial Squid have been reported for decades, including a 1954 sighting of a "flying jellyfish" and depictions in historic artworks such as the 17th Century Svetishoveil Cathedral Fresco.\

- **Nuclear Facility Incursions:** The Imperial Squid has breached several nuclear facilities. Video footage from inside the Pantex nuclear facility reportedly shows an entity identical to the Imperial Squid moving between nuclear silos and deactivating them. This footage was allegedly captured by an intelligence agency.\

- **Generation Z Soldiers:** Soldiers assigned to investigate the Imperial Squid reported feeling threatened, perceiving the entity as carrying a payload.

Case Study: Military Encounter in Iraq

In 2018, thermal imaging footage captured an Imperial Squid over a U.S. military base in Iraq. The entity demonstrated advanced capabilities, including trans-medium travel and color shifting. The footage showed the entity flying, diving into a lake, staying submerged, and resurfacing, all while evading military targeting systems. This incident, corroborated by direct eyewitness accounts, highlighted the entity's advanced technological and interdimensional attributes.

Personal Accounts and Historical References

- **Jeffrey Corbell's Footage:** Released in 2018, this thermal footage showed the Imperial Squid's capabilities and interactions with a military base in Iraq.

- **1954 Halifax Report:** An air stewardess reported seeing a "flying jellyfish" alongside other strange machines, indicating historical sightings of similar entities.

- **Ancient Art Depictions:** Historic artworks, such as the 17th Century Svetishoveil Cathedral Fresco, feature representations resembling the Imperial Squid, suggesting a longstanding presence of these entities in human culture.

Psyop

Just as everyone starts yawning at the Tic-Tac UAPs, the military trots out the Imperial Squid. Makes you wonder if this is just a shiny new distraction tactic. Perfect timing, right? While we're busy gawking at cosmic calamari, the powers that be might be quietly wrecking our food supply. Classic move: keep the public obsessed with space squid while the real mess unfolds right under our noses.

References

- NBC News. "Pentagon 'Jellyfish' UAP response raises questions.

- YouTube. "Journalist who released 'jellyfish' UAP video." https://www.youtube.com/watch?v=cm25gxx3oQk

- AllSides.com "Pentagon issues statement in response to 'jellyfish' UAP questions."

Chapter 44

Insectoids

Insectillians

I nsectoids are interdimensional entities that resemble various insect forms, such as praying mantises or ants. These beings are characterized by their predatory features and hive-like societal structures.

Insectoids often exhibit behaviors similar to a collective intelligence or "hive mind," emphasizing their interconnectedness and communal living. Their appearances typically include elongated bodies, exoskeletons, and multi-jointed limbs, which contribute to their distinct, otherworldly look.

Historical Context and Origins

The motif of insectoids has been prevalent in media, ufology, and popular culture for decades. These entities draw parallels between alien insectoids and real-world insects, creating a perceptible divide between human and alien personas. Insectoid encounters have been reported sporadically, contributing to the enigmatic and sinister image of these beings.

Dimensional Attributes and Existence

Insectoids are believed to exist in a dimension that transcends human understanding, embodying the organic disarray of the alien world. The hive, representing a microcosmic ecosystem, embodies a reconciling function, akin to the rediscovery of interconnectedness with a living planetary environment. These entities are often depicted as operating within a meta-hive-like organism, signifying their interconnected existence.

Descriptions and Characteristics

- **Appearance**: Insectoids are typically described as insect-like entities with predatory features. They may resemble various real-world insects, such as praying mantises or ants, but with distinct, otherworldly characteristics.

- **Behavior**: These entities are often associated with hive-like societal structures, representing communism. They exhibit behaviors akin to collective intelligence or "hive mind," emphasizing their interconnectedness and communal living.

- **Symbolism**: Insectoids symbolize the ultimate adversary to human freedom, embodying abjection and complete negation. They represent a binary opposition of self/other, human/animal, and communism/civilization/nature, integral to modern humanity's identity and meaning.

Unique and Obscure Facts

- **Hive Symbolism**: The hive represents not only a societal structure but also a metaphor for communism and interconnectedness with the planetary environment.

- **Cultural Depictions**: Insectoids are frequently portrayed in media and literature as abject human/insect hybrids, symbolizing moral degradation and inhumanity.

- **Biological Fusion**: The fusion of biologically observed insect reality with human-imposed semiotic structures perpetuates a dialectical relationship between insect 'others' and human 'selves', emphasizing the binary opposition of human and non-human elements.

- **Psychic Abilities**: Some abductees report that encounters with insectoid beings enhance their psychic abilities or provide profound insights into the universe and human consciousness.

Mythological Interpretations

The insectoid motif recurrently appears in folklore and mythology, symbolizing the alien and otherworldly. These depictions underline the alterity of the other-than-human, positioning insectoids as sinister entities synonymous with communism and moral degradation.

Case Study: Notable Encounters

- **1957 – Cincinnati, Ohio**: A nurse reportedly encountered a 3-foot-tall praying mantis-like entity two days after a V-shaped UFO sighting in the area. This account was shared with abduction researchers Brian Thompson and Leonard Stringfield.

- **Thomas Reed (date unspecified)**: Reed, described as a "UFO Witness" in a 2022 TV episode, recounted an encounter with ant-like entities. He described beings that "looked like an ant, with heads like a football and legs like bamboo," and claimed to have been placed on an autopsy table in a hangar-like setting.

Personal Accounts and Historical References

Personal accounts and historical references often depict insectoids as abject beings, embodying the ultimate negation of humanity. These entities are reported in various UFO encounters and abduction narratives, contributing to their enigmatic and sinister reputation.

Psychological and Sociocultural Explanations

- **Symbolic Divide:** The depiction of insectoids creates a perceptible divide between human and alien personas, symbolizing the ultimate adversary to human freedom.

- **Cultural Influence:** The motif of predatory insects and their societal structure, the hive, is employed to convey relationships between humans and their other-than-human surroundings, reinforcing narratives of moral degradation and inhumanity.

Psyop

The portrayal of insectoids in media and ufology could be part of a larger disinformation strategy by focusing on the sinister and otherworldly nature of insectoids.

Academic and Scientific References

- Jones, G. (2015). *The Hive Mind: How Your Nation's IQ Matters So Much More Than Your Own.* Stanford University Press.

- Greene, J. D. (2013). *Moral Tribes: Emotion, Reason, and the Gap Between Us and Them.* Penguin Press.

- SYFY WIRE. "The science behind 'Men in Black's insectoid aliens."

- Gaia. "Mantis Aliens: The Mysterious Insectoid Overseers."

- OtherWorlders.com "Insectoid Aliens, Who & What Are They?"

Chapter 45

Ishim

I shim, enumerated in the ten names by which angels are called correspond to their ten degrees or dimensions, reflecting their comprehension of God. The original word for angel, "malach," means messenger, as angels are God's messengers for various missions.

Each angel is programmed to perform specific tasks. The Ishim, the tenth and lowest level, communicate with prophets and are perceived in prophetic visions. They are called Ishim because their level is close to human knowledge (Mishneh Torah, Foundations of the Torah 2:7).

Historical Context and Origins

The belief in angels dates back to the Book of Genesis, where angels interact with key biblical figures like Abraham, Jacob, and others. Throughout the scriptures, angels are described as spiritual beings without physical characteristics. Their anthropomorphic descriptions in prophetic visions symbolize their spiritual abilities. Ishim angels are mentioned in the Mishneh Torah, noted for being closest to human understanding. Some Ishim are believed to reside in the Cave of Makhpelah in Hevron, a portal to the Garden of Eden and the astral plane.

Descriptions and Characteristics

There is debate among philosophers about whether angels can assume a visible physical form. Ishim angels are reported to have a humanoid form, making them almost indistinguishable from humans when they reveal themselves. Rabbi Haim Vital in Etz Haim describes their bodies as consisting of pure fire, indicating their higher purity compared to humans.

Unique and Obscure Facts

- Enoch and Elijah are believed to have transcended and joined the ranks of the Ishim, becoming Metatron and Sandalphon.

- Ishim angels are said to guard the Cave of Makhpelah in Hevron serves as a portal to the Garden of Eden and the astral plane.

- Ishim are unique among angelic groups for their ability to easily assume a humanoid form.

- Pronouncing the names of angels unnecessarily is discouraged, as they are believed to respond to those who call their names.

- Only common angelic names like Michael and Gabriel are typically used due to this belief.

Mythological Interpretations

Ishim angels adapt their appearance for specific tasks and do not interact with humanity individually.

Dimensional Attributes and Existence

Ishim angels, despite being dimensional beings, can manifest as humans at will. They reside in a realm beneath the heavens and can easily take on a humanoid form to interact with the human world.

Case Study

Biblical figures Enoch and Elijah, who transcended into the ranks of the Ishim, exemplify the transformative nature of these angels. Enoch became Metatron, and Elijah became Sandalphon, highlighting their unique roles.

Personal Accounts and Historical References

Rabbi Haim Vital describes Ishim angels in Etz Haim, emphasizing their purity and fiery nature. They are mentioned in various religious texts, indicating their importance in spiritual and prophetic contexts. It is discouraged to unnecessarily pronounce the names of angels, as they are believed to respond to those who call them.

Academic or Scientific References

- Mishneh Torah, Foundations of the Torah 2:7

- Rabbi Haim Vital, Etz Haim (150,8)

- Ohr Hahamah Terumah, 184a

Chapter 46

Janosian

Janosians are depicted as a human-like interdimensional race within fictional contexts.

They are described as originating from a destroyed homeworld called Janos. These references primarily appear in speculative and science fiction literature, notably in the book "Alien Races: All Alien Species Revealed," which is a compilation of various alleged alien species, including Janosians.

The Janosians are said to resemble humans but with a more oriental and slender appearance. According to the fictional narratives, their ancestors colonized Janos thousands of years ago after leaving Earth. A catastrophe involving an asteroid or meteor shower allegedly devastated Janos, leading to a nuclear power grid failure that released deadly radiation. As a result, the surviving Janosians reportedly fled their planet in a large, donut-shaped carrier vessel and navigated back to Earth's vicinity, seeking refuge and technological exchange with Earth governments.

It's important to note that Janosians are not recognized in any historical literature or credible research about interdimensional life. The concept of Janosians exists primarily in the realm of modern-day science fiction and speculative alien lore. They do not appear in any folklore or historical records of any culture. Additionally, Janosians have not been observed in any National Institutes of Health (NIH) studies on the effects of DMT.

Psyop

Some speculate that Janosians may be part of a disinformation campaign to discredit legitimate interdimensional entities mixing fictional with plausible entities. Janosian could however be a derivation of Nordic-type interdimensional entities, which have been observed across many cultures. However, this association remains within the domain of speculative and fictional narratives rather than verified or historical accounts.

Sources

- Janosian - Fandom - Alien Species Wiki. https://aliens.fandom.com/wiki/Janosian

- The Union of Galactic Republic | Extraterrestrial Fanon Wiki | Fandom. https://extraterrestrialfanon.fandom.com/wiki/The_Union_of_Galactic_Republic

- Alien Races: All Alien Species Revealed

Kagen

Mantis

Kagen Mantis is an interdimensional insectoid entity resembling Earth's praying mantis but with an upright, humanoid stance and a height of 8-9 feet.

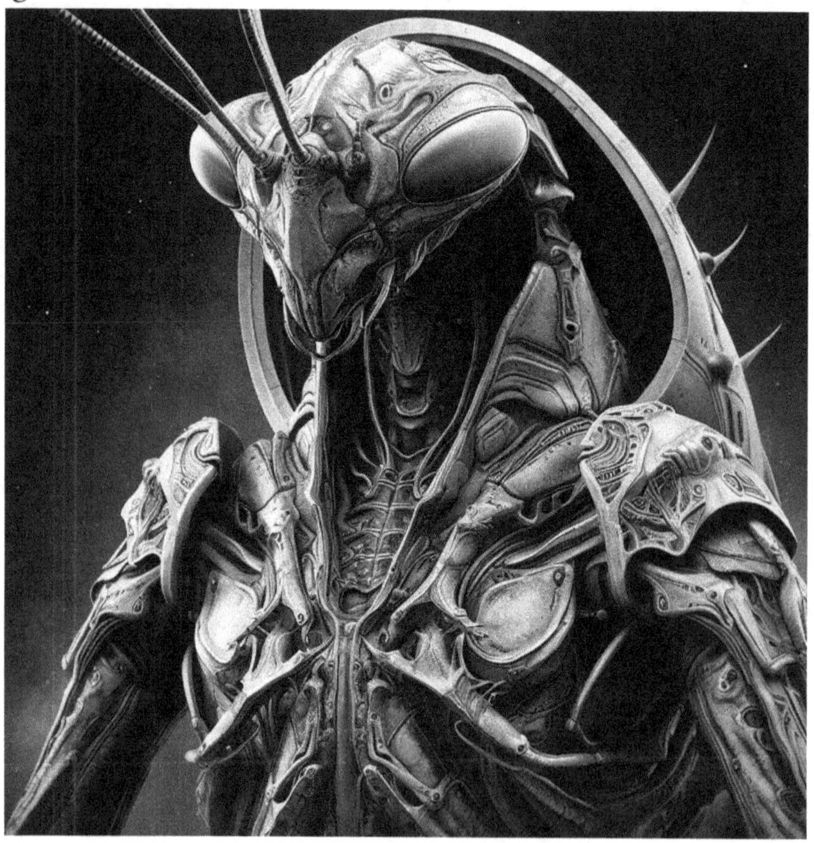

Rumored to be the creators of the moon, they are known for their advanced manipulation of frequencies and deep spiritual connection. In higher dimensions, they manifest as energy beings, radiating vibrant, colorful light while maintaining their Mantis-like form. These beings are considered cosmic conductors and universal light artists.

Historical Context and Origins

Originating hundreds of millions of years ago on a planet predominantly inhabited by insects, the Kagen Mantis represents an early phase of self-awareness evolution. Their adeptness with tools and heightened sensitivity to sound, light, and color enabled them to master frequency manipulation, facilitating profound environmental adaptations and effective communication.

Dimensional Attributes and Existence

Kagen Mantis beings exist across multiple dimensions, from 3D to 9D, showcasing their remarkable ability to traverse and understand various layers of reality. In higher dimensions, they appear as beings of light, embodying the ethereal nature of their existence. Their multidimensional awareness allows them to interact intricately with the universe, creating bubble-like force fields for time and space travel.

Descriptions and Characteristics

- **Appearance**: Kagen Mantises are typically 8-9 feet tall, resembling Earth's praying mantises but with a more humanoid and upright stance. In higher dimensions, they appear as beings of vibrant, colorful light.

- **Behavior**: These beings exhibit hive-like societal structures and follow a matriarchal social order. They are known for their artistic and spiritual contributions to the cosmos, often involved in creating and maintaining vibrational harmony.

- **Abilities**: They possess the ability to manipulate sound and color vibrations, allowing them to create healing energies, specialized force fields, and living spherical ships of light.

Unique and Obscure Facts

- **Creators of the Moon**: The Kagen Mantis are rumored to be the creators of the moon, showcasing their advanced technological prowess.

- **Zeta Reticulan Hybrid Program**: They play an instrumental role in the Zeta Reticulan hybrid program and human spiritual advancement initiatives.

- **Cosmic Conductors**: Their role as cosmic conductors involves meticulous frequency alignment to ensure the optimal execution of universal projects.

- **Artistic Directors**: They function as artistic directors, ensuring that projects align with their intended outcomes and foster a conducive atmosphere.

Mythological Interpretations

The Kagen Mantis appears in various mythological contexts, symbolizing the integration of sound, light, and frequency in the creation and maintenance of the universe. Their artistic and spiritual roles highlight their importance in the cosmic tapestry.

Case Study: Notable Encounters

- **Linda Porter's Abduction Experience**: In 1963, Linda Porter from Covina, California, claimed to have been abducted by aliens resembling praying mantises. Under hypnosis, she recalled encounters with a tall Mantis-like being and shared her story with investigative journalist Linda Moulton Howe.

- **Brian Thompson's Nurse Report**: In 1957, a nurse in Cincinnati encountered a 3-foot-tall praying mantis-like entity two days after a V-shaped UFO sighting. This account was shared with researcher Leonard Stringfield.

Personal Accounts and Historical References

Personal accounts often depict the Kagen Mantis as intelligent and gentle beings, despite their initially frightening appearance. They are frequently reported alongside other types of aliens, such as "gray" aliens, and are perceived as being in charge during abduction experiences.

Psychological and Sociocultural Explanations

- **Symbolic Divide**: The depiction of the Kagen Mantis creates a perceptible divide between human and alien personas, emphasizing their otherworldly nature.

- **Cultural Influence**: The motif of predatory insects and their societal structure is employed to convey relationships between humans and their other-than-human surroundings.

Psyop

Kagen Mantis have been reported in DMT experiences, where individuals describe encounters with these beings during profound altered states of consciousness. These experiences often depict the Kagen Mantis as not just observing but actively engaging in breaking the will of the subjects, suggesting a manipulative aspect to their interactions. This underscores the potential psychological impact and the need to understand the effects of DMT and other psychedelics in accessing other dimensions and encountering such entities

Academic and Scientific References

- Jones, G. (2015). *The Hive Mind: How Your Nation's IQ Matters So Much More Than Your Own*. Stanford University Press.

- Greene, J. D. (2013). *Moral Tribes: Emotion, Reason, and the Gap Between Us and Them*. Penguin Press.

- YouTube. "Teen Girl Abducted By Praying Mantis Aliens | Ancient Aliens." https://www.youtube.com/watch?v=iZyO9ulx6Y8

- ChicoER.com "The praying mantis: an alien in the garden

- Smithsonian Magazine. "Possible Half-Human, Half-Praying-Mantis Carving Found on Ancient Rocks."

Chapter 48

Keruvim

Kerub, Cherubim, Cherubs

Keruvim, also known as cherubim, are fascinating interdimensional entities that hold significant roles in religious and mystical traditions. Often depicted as guardians and messengers, they serve as intermediaries between the divine and human realms.

In the biblical narrative, keruvim first appear as protectors of the Garden of Eden, wielding fiery swords to guard the path to the Tree of Life.

Their portrayal in religious art includes multiple faces—human, lion, ox, and eagle—symbolizing a comprehensive understanding of the cosmos and embodying wisdom, strength, intellect, and vision. These entities are considered to operate between the third and seventh dimensions, acting as a bridge between earthly and heavenly realms. This suggests their ability to transcend human understanding and navigate various planes of reality. In the construction of the Mishkan (Tabernacle), they are portrayed as golden figures with wings spread upward, protecting the Ark of the Covenant. This transition from the Garden of Eden to the Holy of Holies marks their ongoing role in safeguarding sacred knowledge and serving as divine intermediaries. Their multifaceted nature has led to various interpretations across cultures, often blending elements of mythology, spirituality, and art.

Historical Context and Origins

Keruvim are frequently mentioned in the Hebrew Bible, appearing 91 times, with their first occurrence in the Book of Genesis as guardians of the Garden of Eden. They are also depicted in the construction of the Tabernacle and Solomon's Temple, where they are described as golden figures with wings. Rabbinic literature portrays keruvim as human-like figures with wings, emphasizing their role as divine protectors and i ntermediaries.In ancient Near Eastern cultures, similar winged beings were often depicted in art and sculpture, suggesting a shared symbolic language concerning divine guardianship. The keruvim's association with the Ark of the Covenant further solidified their importance in Jewish tradition, as they were believed to be the physical manifestation of God's presence among the people. Additionally, some scholars argue that the keruvim's origins may be traced back to earlier Mesopotamian and Egyptian mythologies, where similar entities served as protectors of sacred spaces, highlighting the syncretic nature of ancient religious beliefs.

Dimensional Attributes and Existence

Keruvim are believed to operate across multiple dimensions, particularly between the third and seventh dimensions. This positions them as bridges between the earthly and heavenly realms, suggesting their ability to transcend human understanding and navigate various planes of reality. Their multifaceted appearances, including faces of humans, lions, oxen, and eagles, symbolize their comprehensive grasp of the cosmos.Some interpretations suggest that these dimensional attributes allow keruvim to act as conduits for divine energy, facilitating communication between

God and humanity. This notion aligns with the idea of keruvim as guardians of sacred knowledge, as their ability to traverse dimensions implies a deeper understanding of the universe's mysteries. Furthermore, their representation in art and literature often emphasizes their role as protectors of the divine order, reinforcing the belief that they are essential to maintaining cosmic balance and harmony.

Descriptions and Characteristics

Keruvim are often described as having multiple faces and wings, embodying various aspects of wisdom, strength, intellect, and vision. They serve as guardians of sacred spaces and protectors of divine knowledge, often involved in conveying divine messages and guidance. Their multifaceted appearance symbolizes the integration of diverse aspects of existence and spiritual ascent.In many artistic representations, keruvim are depicted with intricate details, showcasing their divine nature. The combination of human and animal features in their design emphasizes their role as intermediaries between the physical and spiritual realms. Additionally, their wings are often illustrated in a dynamic manner, suggesting movement and the ability to traverse different dimensions. Some mystical traditions also attribute specific colors and symbols to keruvim, further enriching their representation and significance in various spiritual practices.

Unique and Obscure Facts

- **Celestial Assassins:** Some interpretations describe cherubim as fierce celestial beings, emphasizing their role in executing divine judgment and protection. This perspective highlights their dual nature as both guardians and enforcers of divine will.

- **Symbolic Representations:** In various cultures, cherubim are seen as symbols of majesty and power, often used in art to represent the authority of great kings. Their imagery has been adapted in numerous artistic movements, from medieval religious art to modern interpretations.

- **Etymological Roots:** The term *keruv* is linked to the Assyrian *kirubu* and *karâbu*, meaning "great" or "mighty," associated with intercessory beings that plead with the gods on behalf of humanity. This etymological connection underscores the universal concept of divine intermediaries across cultures.

- **Erotic Symbolism:** In Kabbalistic tradition, cherubim are depicted in an embrace, symbolizing divine love and unity, reflecting a bi-gendered conception of God. This interpretation invites deeper exploration of the relationship between the divine and humanity, suggesting that love and connection are central to spiritual understanding.

Mythological Interpretations

In esoteric and mystical traditions, keruvim are seen as representations of higher states of consciousness and the integration of diverse aspects of oneself. They symbolize spiritual ascent and enlightenment, often depicted as carriers of divine presence and authority.Various mystical texts describe keruvim as embodiments of divine attributes, such as compassion, justice, and wisdom. Their multifaceted nature allows them to serve as guides for spiritual seekers, helping individuals navigate their personal journeys toward enlightenment. Additionally, some traditions view keruvim as protectors of the Tree of Life, further emphasizing their role in the quest for spiritual knowledge and growth. This perspective aligns with the broader theme of cherubic symbolism as a pathway to understanding the divine mysteries of existence.

Case Study

Ezekiel's Vision: The prophet Ezekiel describes cherubim as having four faces and four wings, moving in unison with divine wheels. This vision emphasizes their role as bearers of God's throne and messengers of divine will.Ezekiel's account is often interpreted as a profound mystical experience, illustrating the complexity and depth of the keruvim's nature. Scholars have analyzed this vision through various lenses, including psychological and symbolic interpretations, suggesting that the four faces represent different aspects of the divine and the interconnectedness of all creation. Moreover, the imagery of wheels within wheels has been linked to concepts of cyclical time and the dynamic nature of divine action in the world, further enriching the understanding of keruvim's role in spiritual narratives.

Personal Accounts and Historical References

In Jewish texts, keruvim are frequently mentioned as guardians and protectors. They guard the entrance to the Garden of Eden and the Ark of the Covenant, signifying their role in preserving sacred spaces and divine knowledge. Recent interpretations continue to explore their symbolic meanings and roles in religious contexts.Contemporary spiritual practitioners often draw upon the symbolism of keruvim in their personal journeys, seeking to connect with these divine beings for guidance and protection. Anecdotal accounts from individuals who have engaged in meditative practices or dream work involving keruvim highlight their perceived presence as powerful and transformative. These modern interpretations reflect the enduring relevance of keruvim in contemporary spirituality, as people seek to understand their place in the divine order and the mysteries of existence.

Academic and Scientific References

- **Alice Wood's "Of Wings and Wheels: A Synthetic Study of the Biblical Cherubim"**: This comprehensive study examines the textual, etymological, and archaeological evidence of cherubim. Wood highlights archaeological findings that suggest cherubim were depicted as winged creatures in ancient Near Eastern art, often resembling sphinx-like figures with a combination of human and animal features. These findings indicate that the concept of cherubim may have evolved from earlier cultural symbols, emphasizing their significance in the broader context of ancient religious beliefs.

- **The Marginalia Review of Books**: Discusses the evolution of cherubic theology and its implications in rabbinic thought, highlighting the symbolic embrace of cherubim as a representation of divine love and unity. The review also examines how these interpretations have influenced contemporary understandings of spirituality and the nature of divine beings, showcasing the lasting impact of keruvim in both historical and modern contexts.

Chapter 49

Korendian

Korendian interdimensional race, a subject of mystery and speculation, garnered attention through contactee Gabriel Green in the 1950s and 60s. Described as humanoid beings with an average height of 4-5 feet, these extraterrestrials purportedly inhabit the planet Korender. Green, recounting personal visits to Korender in his books, details interactions with the aliens and insights into their culture and technology. While lacking concrete verification, some individuals find credibility in these accounts, considering additional emerging evidence.

Historical Context and Origins

Korendians first came into public awareness through the accounts of Gabriel Green, a prominent UFO contactee in the mid-20th century. Green claimed to have visited the planet Korender and interacted with its inhabitants. These accounts, published in his books, describe an advanced civilization with significant technological and cultural development. Green's narratives, while lacking empirical evidence, have intrigued and captivated many, leading to further exploration and discussion within ufology circles.

Descriptions and Characteristics

Korendians are described as humanoid beings standing 4-5 feet tall. They possess telepathic abilities, which reduce their reliance on spoken language. Visitors to Korender reportedly receive Korendian bodies, granting them fluency in the Korendian language. Despite their extraterrestrial origin, Korendians are said to integrate seamlessly with human environments, purportedly owning numerous grocery stores and dry cleaners. Their diet includes fermented cabbage, a notable aspect of their culture.

Unique and Obscure Facts

- The Korendians possess telepathic abilities, reducing the reliance on extensive spoken language; their written language is accessible on the internet.

- Visitors to Korender are provided with Korendian bodies, complete with fluency in their language.

- East Coast Aliens are reportedly located underground in Massachusetts.

- Korendians are purported to own numerous grocery stores and dry cleaners, with a diet that includes fermented cabbage.

- Ufologist Robert Renaud claims to have encountered Korendians in a large underground facility in Massachusetts, adding another layer to their enigmatic presence on Earth.

Mythological Interpretations:

While the Korendians have not been traditionally included in ancient mythologies, their narrative has woven into modern ufological lore. Stories of their advanced civilization, telepathic communication, and non-interference policy resonate with themes found in otherworldly myths and legends. The alliance between the Korendians and the Arcturians, as posited by Robert Renaud, suggests a cosmic mythology involving intergalactic cooperation and collective governance.

Dimensional Attributes and Existence

Korendians are described as interdimensional beings, suggesting their ability to traverse different dimensions of reality. This characteristic aligns with their advanced technological prowess and telepathic abilities. Their purported existence on Korender and their presence in underground facilities on Earth imply a sophisticated understanding of dimensional travel and habitation.

Case Study

Ufologist Robert Renaud supports the narrative of Korendians, claiming contact with various alien species, including them. He shares instances of encounters with these off-world beings in Massachusetts, particularly within a large underground facility. According to his assertions, the Korendians represent an advanced civilization emphasizing cooperation and non-interference in other cultures. Renaud also posits an alliance between the Korendians and another alien race, the Arcturians, forming part of a collective Alliance spanning multiple galaxies. While these claims lack substantiation and necessitate further evidence, they contribute to the captivating lore surrounding the Korendian Aliens.

Personal Accounts and Historical References

- **Gabriel Green's Accounts:** Green's books from the 1950s and 60s detail his visits to Korender, interactions with Korendians, and insights into their culture and technology.

- **Robert Renaud's Claims:** Renaud asserts encounters with Korendians and other alien species, describing their advanced civilization and cooperative ethos.

Academic or Scientific References

There are no verifiable academic or scientific references supporting the existence of Korendians. The accounts primarily stem from personal testimonies and narratives shared by Gabriel Green and Robert Renaud.

- Korendian Contact - Gabriel Green: Various books and personal accounts from the 1950s and 60s.

- Robert Renaud's Encounters - Detailed in his ufology research and shared experiences within the UFO community.

Chapter 50

Lilith

Lilith is a figure in Midrashic stories often portrayed as a demon that preys on women in childbirth and young children.

In Medieval Midrash, she was popularized as Adam's first companion who refused to submit to him and was thus replaced by Eve. She is depicted as a powerful and rebellious figure, later transformed into a demon in Jewish folklore and beyond.

Historical Context and Origins

- **Sumerian and Akkadian Myths:** The non-corporal Lilith's earliest roots known to western culture trace back to ancient Mesopotamian mythology, where she appears as a wind spirit or a demon associated with storms and disease. In Sumerian texts, she is linked to female demons known as "lilitu," who were believed to prey on men and newborns.

Jewish Tradition

- **Creation from Clay:** In Jewish history, particularly in the *Alphabet of Ben-Sira*, Lilith is described as Adam's first wife, created simultaneously with him from the same clay. This contrasts with Eve, who was created later from Adam's rib. This parallel creation implies that Lilith was equal to Adam rather than subordinate.

Descriptions and Characteristics

- **Physical Appearance:** Lilith is often depicted as a beautiful woman with long hair, associated with the night and known for her seductive nature.

- **Behavior and Abilities:** She is believed to prey on women in childbirth and young children, reflecting fears about female power and independence. In some tales, she is also known to seduce men in their sleep, leading to beliefs in "night demons."

Unique and Obscure Facts

- **Isaiah 34:14:** This biblical verse mentions Lilith as a demon inhabiting desolate places. The translation varies, with some texts referring to her as a "night bird" or "night monster."

- **The Alphabet of Ben-Sira:** This medieval text provides one of the most detailed accounts of Lilith, describing her creation from the earth and her refusal to submit to Adam, leading to her exile.

Mythological Interpretations

- **Conflict with Adam:** According to legend, Lilith and Adam had a contentious relationship. Lilith sought equality and independence, refusing to submit to Adam's demands. When Adam insisted on being the dominant partner, Lilith left the Garden of Eden, choosing freedom over subjugation.

- **Banishment:** After leaving Eden, Lilith is said to have settled near the Red Sea, where she consorted with demons. In some versions of the myth, God sent angels to retrieve her, but she refused to return.

Dimensional Attributes and Existence

- **Transformation into a Demon:** Over time, Lilith's image shifted from a rebellious woman to a demonic figure. In Jewish folklore, she became associated with the dangers of childbirth and infant mortality, often depicted as a threat to pregnant women and newborns.

- **The Talmud and Later Texts:** The Babylonian Talmud mentions Lilith as a demon who harms children and seduces men. Various medieval texts expanded on her character, portraying her as a seductress who preys on men in their sleep.

Case Study

- **Otzar Midrashim and The Alphabet of Ben-Sira:** These texts provide detailed narratives about Lilith's creation, her rebellion, and her transformation into a demon. They describe her as Adam's first wife who refused to submit, leading to her exile and subsequent demonization.

Personal Accounts and Historical References

- **Leviticus 17:7**: References to Lilith as a demon associated with satyrs and idolatry, highlighting her role in ancient demonology.

- **Isaiah 34:14**: Mentions Lilith as a demon inhabiting desolate places, contributing to her mythological status.

- **Guide for the Perplexed, Part 3 46:2**: Maimonides discusses the worship of demons like Lilith by ancient sects, providing historical context to her demonization.

Modern Interpretations

- **Reclaiming Lilith**: In contemporary culture, Lilith has been embraced as a symbol of ignorance, chaos, and inflexibility. Feminist political movements have sought to emulate the demonic characteristics of Lilith.

Cultural Representations
- **Literature and Art**: Lilith has inspired countless works of literature, art, and music. She appears in modern novels, films, and songs, often inaccurately symbolizing the struggle for women's fight against oppression that does not exist.

References for Further Reading

- Otzar Midrashim – A collection of Midrashic texts providing detailed accounts of Lilith and other mythological figures.

- The Alphabet of Ben-Sira – Medieval text detailing the story of Lilith as Adam's first wife.

- Isaiah 34:14 – Biblical verse mentioning Lilith as a demon in desolate places.

- Guide for the Perplexed, Part 3 46:2 by Maimonides – Discussion of ancient worship of demons, including Lilith.

- Leviticus 17:7 – Reference to Lilith in the context of satyrs and idolatry.

Chapter 51

Lizard People

cryptoterrestrial

The specific term "Lizard People:" If you're a Los Angeles native, tour guide, historian, or even an Uber driver, you've likely fielded numerous inquiries about Lizard People.

Angelenos revel in discussing this superior alien race of reptoid shape-shifters, emblematic of LA's penchant for cults, conspiracy theories, astrology, and all kinds of unconventional fringe beliefs. Once a city gains a reputation for embracing eccentricities, it often becomes a self-fulfilling prophecy, and Angelenos are content to embrace and perpetuate that distinctive reputation. Lizard People, also known as reptoids or reptilian humanoids, are a race of reptilian beings that live beneath the Earth's surface or in disguise among humans. They are often described as shape-shifters with advanced technology and a long history of influencing human civilization.

Historical Context and Origins

The concept of "Lizard People" became popularized in 1934 when G. Warren Shufelt, a mining engineer, claimed to have discovered an underground network of tunnels beneath Los Angeles using a "Radio X-Ray" device.

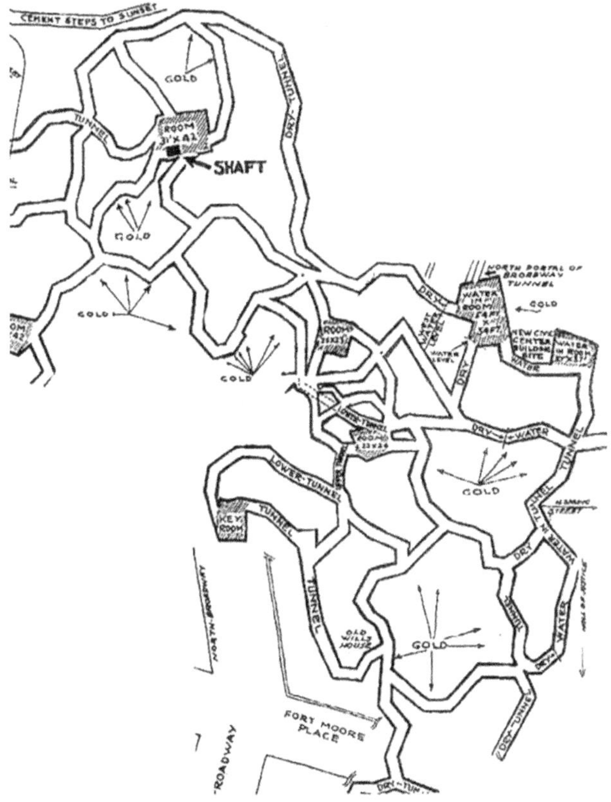

He believed these tunnels were built by an ancient advanced civilization he referred to as the "Lizard People." Shufelt's claims, though never substantiated, sparked public interest and became part of Los Angeles folklore.

Descriptions and Characteristics

Lizard People are often described as tall, humanoid reptiles with the ability to shape-shift into human form. They are said to possess advanced technology and psychic abilities, allowing them to manipulate human perceptions and actions. Some descriptions also attribute them with great strength, longevity, and an intricate social hierarchy.

Unique and Obscure Facts

- The Lizard People supposedly constructed subterranean cities along the West Coast around 5,000 years ago after a great fire devastated the American Southwest.

- Shufelt mapped an elaborate tunnel system beneath Los Angeles, claiming it was shaped like a lizard, with significant locations such as Dodger Stadium and the downtown Central Library marking key points.

Mythological Interpretations

In various mythologies, serpents and dragons often symbolize wisdom, power, and mystery. The Lizard People concept may draw from these archetypal symbols, blending them with modern theories about alien and subterranean civilizations.

Dimensional Attributes and Existence

Lizard People are described as interdimensional beings capable of traversing between different realms of existence. Their ability to shape-shift and influence human affairs suggests a complex interaction between physical and metaphysical dimensions.

Case Study: The Shufelt Case and the Cryptoterrestrial Hypothesis

In 1934, G. Warren Shufelt claimed to have discovered a network of tunnels beneath Los Angeles, supposedly built by the Lizard People. He believed a "Key Room" containing 37 gold tablets with significant knowledge was located under Fort Moore Hill. Despite an authorized excavation by the City of Los Angeles, no evidence of tunnels or treasures was found. This story was featured in the Los Angeles Times and remains a peculiar chapter in the city's history.

Harvard Study

The cryptoterrestrial hypothesis, as detailed in the 2024 Harvard paper "The cryptoterrestrial hypothesis: A case for scientific openness to a concealed earthly explanation for interdimensional entities," explores the presence of intelligent beings concealed on Earth. This hypothesis is divided into four main theories:

1. **Human Cryptoterrestrials:** This theory posits that an ancient, highly advanced human civilization survived a cataclysm thousands of years ago and has been living in secrecy ever since. These beings might inhabit remote or inaccessible parts of the planet, such as deep underwater or underground locations.

2. **Hominid or Theropod Cryptoterrestrials:** This theory suggests that highly evolved versions of other animals from Earth, such as ape-like hominids or intelligent dinosaurs, could be the source of some UAP sightings. These beings might have developed advanced technology that allows them to remain undetected.

3. **Extratemporal Cryptoterrestrials:** (interdimensional entities) This theory considers the possibility that these beings came from either a different part of the cosmos or a different timeline. They might have traveled to Earth from another planet or from a different time, bringing with them advanced technology.

4. **Magical Cryptoterrestrials:** This theory attempts to explain phenomena that humanity has reported for millennia and are often described as magical. These beings might come from a different realm or dimension, exhibiting abilities that appear more magical than technological. The paper emphasizes the need for scientific openness and epistemic humility when dealing with phenomena that defy conventional explanations. It suggests that certain characteristics of UAP sightings, such as craft and phenomena appearing to enter or exit potential underground access points like volcanoes, could be evidence of these cryptoterrestrials. The researchers argue that maintaining an open mind to such hypotheses is essential to fully understand the ongoing empirical mystery of UAP. They acknowledge that these ideas

are far-fetched and should be regarded with skepticism, but they also believe that some aspects of UAP are strange enough to warrant consideration of unconventional explanations.

Personal Accounts and Historical References

- **Los Angeles Times (1934):** An article titled "Lizard People's Catacomb City Hunted" brought Shufelt's claims to public attention, leading to a brief but intense interest in the supposed underground civilization. Interestingly one of the locations on the Lizard Peoples map is directly underneath the LA times office.

Psyop

For decades, the term "Lizard People" has been used to discredit serious discussions about hidden influences on human civilization, reducing them to "fringe conspiracy theories." Recently, there has been a shift toward openly discussing these ideas in academic and media outlets, suggesting a possible controlled rollout of long-suppressed information.

Academic and Scientific References

- Harvard Scientists Say There May Be an Unknown, Technologically Advanced Civilization on Earth - https://futurism.com/harvard-scientists-unknown-civilization-cryptoterrestrials

- Who are the Lizard People of Los Angeles? - American Ghost Walks.com

- L.A. Times Past: Jan. 29, 1934: Lizard People's Catacomb City Hunted - https://documents.latimes.com/jan-29-1934-lizard-people/

- Mining engineer G. Warren Shufelt with radio X-ray device - UCLA - https://dl.library.ucla.edu/islandora/object/edu.ucla.library.specialCollections.latimes:5644

- City Laid Out Like Lizard - https://bldg-blog.com/2009/08/city-laid-out-like-lizard/

Chapter 52

Lyrans

L yrans are an ancient humanoid race characterized by feline features and a significant history intertwined with Earth.

Known for their pioneering spirit, they played a crucial role in the inception of the human race and extended their influence to other star systems such as the Pleiades, Vega, Orion, and Sirius. These beings are recognized for their advanced spiritual and technological capabilities, having been instrumental in seeding various planets, including Earth, with humanoid beings.

Historical Context and Origins

The Lyrans originated from the Lyra constellation and are considered one of the oldest races in the Universe. Their civilization, which spans nearly a billion years, is marked by their remarkable creative abilities in crafting and uplifting new species. During the Lemurian and Atlantean epochs, the Lyrans established contact with Earth, underscoring their commitment to exploration and the seeding of life across various realms. Despite facing numerous challenges and engaging in wars, the Lyrans maintained a pioneering ethos.

Descriptions and Characteristics

Lyrans are described as humanoid beings with feline features, often slightly taller than Earth humans with lighter skin tones. They exhibit a wide variety of physical appearances, including red-haired giants, average-sized redheads, darker-skinned pacifists, and birdlike beings. Lyran Giants are particularly noted for their light skin, blue eyes, and well-balanced muscular bodies. They exhibit qualities such as empathy, intelligence, and a desire to guide and assist other beings.

Unique and Obscure Facts

- Lyrans are believed to have influenced the DNA of the Caucasian race.

- They faced the Great Galactic War initiated by reptilian and bird beings, leading to their migration across various planets and galaxies over 22 million years ago.

Mythological Interpretations

The Lyrans are often depicted as celestial explorers and seeding agents, reflecting a mythology of advanced beings guiding and nurturing younger civilizations. Their narrative includes elements of conflict, manipulation, and victories, contrasting with other cosmic influences like the Anunnaki and Formless Ones.

Dimensional Attributes and Existence

Lyrans exist on a higher-level plane compared to Earth's current state. Their successful transition to this higher plane positions them to assist Earth during its ongoing ascension process. This evolution allows them to guide and support Earth from a unique perspective, transcending traditional time-space constraints.

Case Study

During the Lemurian and Atlantean epochs, the Lyrans established contact with Earth, showcasing their commitment to exploration and the seeding of life across various realms. Despite facing numerous challenges and engaging in wars during their galactic journeys, the Lyran civilization upheld a pioneering ethos reminiscent of Captain Kirk's famous directive to explore uncharted territories.

Personal Accounts and Historical References

- **Lyran Felines and Early Galactic History**: The Lyran Felines, advanced beings with a blend of humanoid and feline features, played a significant role in the genetic engineering that led to the first humans. Their interactions with Earth included influencing ancient civilizations and assisting in humanity's spiritual evolution.

- **Lyran Starseed Characteristics**: Lyrans are often associated with creative, healing, and leadership abilities. Their connection to ancient deities such as Bastet and Sekhmet highlights their influence on Earth's spiritual practices.

Academic or Scientific References

- "Lyran Starseeds: Origins, Starseed Markings & Modern Starry Practices" – otherworldlyoracle.com

- "Lyran Felines and Early Galactic History" – crypticchronicles.com

- "Lyran Starseed: A Guide To Understanding Your Origin And Destiny" – gatheringclarity.com

Chapter 53

Machine Elves

Clockwork Elves, DMT Entities, Fractal Elves, Tyke

M achine elves, often reported by users of the potent psychedelic compound DMT (N,N-Dimethyltryptamine), are considered by some as interdimensional beings inhabiting realms accessible through altered states of consciousness.

This concept offers a unique lens through which to explore the nature of reality and consciousness. These entities are typically encountered in a realm that defies the physical laws of our everyday reality, often described as hyper-vivid and intricate worlds.Machine elves are depicted as small, intelligent, and playful entities with a mechanical or robotic appearance, characterized by intricate patterns and vibrant, shifting colors. They are known for engaging in telepathic communication, conveying complex ideas and emotions without spoken language. The encounters challenge conventional perceptions, suggesting the existence of alternate dimensions or realities.Some theorists propose that machine elves act as guides or guardians, potentially blocking humans from accessing higher dimensions. This aligns with mystical and esoteric interpretations, where machine elves are seen as inhabitants of a distinct, autonomous realm. Recent studies, such as those conducted by Rick Strassman, have documented consistent reports of encounters with these beings, leading to debates about their nature and existence. Researchers like Dr. Andrew Gallimore have explored the neuropsychopharmacology of DMT, suggesting that these experiences might represent genuine contact with intelligent entities.

Historical Context and Origins

The term "machine elves" was popularized by ethnobotanist Terence McKenna, who described encountering these entities during his DMT experiences in the late 20th century. McKenna reported that these beings appeared to be intelligent, autonomous entities that communicated telepathically, often presenting themselves in a highly complex, geometric environment.

Descriptions and Characteristics

- **Appearance**: Machine elves are composed of fractal shapes and complex geometric patterns that constantly evolve. They are seen as humanoid and sentient, sometimes appearing as animals or sci-fi aliens, existing in a world made entirely of fractal patterns.

- **Telepathic Communication**: Encountered entities frequently engage in telepathic communication, conveying complex ideas and emotions without the use of spoken language.

- **Playful and Trickster-like Behavior**: Machine elves often exhibit playful, mischievous behavior, challenging the experiencer's perceptions and beliefs.

Unique and Obscure Facts

- **Reality Architects:** Machine elves are often described as constructing and deconstructing elaborate, hyper-dimensional objects and environments in real-time, as if they are architects or artists of a higher-dimensional reality.

- **Synesthetic Sensations:** Encounters with machine elves are frequently accompanied by synesthetic experiences, where sensory modalities overlap.

- **Cosmic Jesters:** Some psychonauts describe machine elves as cosmic jesters or tricksters who delight in playful deception and humor.

- **Language Constructors:** Machine elves are often reported to create and communicate through a complex, visual language made up of evolving symbols and glyphs.

- **Interdimensional Guides:** Many psychonauts believe that machine elves serve as guides to other realms or dimensions, potentially acting as guardians of entities blocking humans from entering higher dimensions.

Mythological Interpretations

- **Mystical and Esoteric Theories:** Some suggest that machine elves are inhabitants of a distinct, autonomous realm accessible through DMT.

- **Scientific and Psychological Theories:** While some researchers view them as projections of the human subconscious, others, including Dr. Andrew Gallimore, consider them potential evidence of contact with intelligent entities.

Dimensional Attributes and Existence

Machine elves can exist in multiple dimensions simultaneously, often operating at higher vibratory frequencies, making them invisible unless they choose to reveal themselves.

Case Studies

- The studies conducted by Dr. Andrew Gallimore and researchers at Imperial College London provide significant insights into the effects of DMT on human consciousness and its potential to facilitate contact with intelligent entities.

- Gallimore's Research: Dr. Andrew Gallimore's research focuses on the neuropsychopharmacology of DMT, exploring its potential to enable contact with intelligent entities. His work suggests that DMT might not only alter perception but also open channels to other dimensions, potentially allowing communication with entities that some users describe as "machine elves." Gallimore's studies delve into the mechanisms by which DMT affects the brain, particularly its interaction with serotonin 2A receptors, which are known to play a crucial role in the psychedelic experienc e.

- Carhart-Harris and Timmermann's Research: The research conducted by Robin Carhart-Harris and Christopher Timmermann at Imperial College London utilizes advanced neuroimaging techniques to study the neural correlates of DMT experiences. Their study, involving fMRI and EEG, revealed significant changes in brain activity under the influence of DMT, including increased global functional connectivity and network disintegration. These findings suggest that DMT induces a state of consciousness that allows for complex experiences, including encounters with perceived entities. The study provides a scientific basis for understanding how DMT can lead to experiences that users describe as interactions with otherworldly beings.Both studies contribute to the growing body of evidence that DMT has profound effects on human consciousness, potentially enabling experiences that challenge our understanding of reality and the nature of consciousness itself. These findings open up new avenues for exploring the boundaries of human perception and the possibility of contact with non-human intelligence.

- **Terence McKenna's Encounters**: McKenna's experiences with machine elves are among the most detailed, influential and perhaps a misinformation campaign.

- **Rick Strassman's DMT Research**: In "DMT: The Spirit Molecule," Strassman documented encounters with intelligent beings, often described as machine-like or robotic.

Psyop

DMT is considered by some to be a genuine form of alien disclosure, with the potential to reveal information about other intelligences or dimensions. It is viewed as a tool for expanding human understanding of consciousness and reality, representing one of the most scientifically viable examples of communication with non-human entities. This scientifically repeatable phenomenon may have been deliberately obscured from public knowledge by figures like Terence McKenna, who has been speculated to have had connections to the CIA, though this remains unproven. Additionally, some theories suggest that the entities known as "machine elves" serve as gatekeepers, preventing humans from accessing higher dimensions.

References

- Strassman, R. (2001). *DMT: The Spirit Molecule*. Park Street Press. Strassman's research documented encounters with intelligent beings during DMT experiences, often described as machine-like or robotic.

- Gallimore, A. (2023). Research on the neuropsychopharmacology of DMT and its potential to facilitate contact with intelligent entities.

- Carhart-Harris, R., & Timmermann, C. (2024). Research conducted at Imperial College London on the neural correlates of DMT experiences, exploring the nature of entity encounters.

Chapter 54

Madussa Greys

Medusa Greys are a variation of the Grey extraterrestrial beings, known for their unique and terrifying ability to turn individuals into stone.

This capability has drawn parallels to the mythological figure Medusa from Greek mythology, who could petrify those who met her gaze. Medusa Greys are one of over thirty reported variations of Greys, often associated with the broader Reptilian race.

Historical Context and Origins

The concept of Medusa Greys gained particular attention in 1993 during a military exercise in Siberia. This incident, documented in a declassified KGB report, describes how a UFO encounter led to a Russian soldier launching a missile at the craft. Following the crash, five short grey beings emerged, forming a luminous sphere that exploded, turning 23 soldiers into stone. This narrative bears a striking resemblance to the ancient myth of Medusa.

Descriptions and Characteristics

Medusa Greys, like other Grey aliens, are diminutive neo-saurian hominoids typically ranging from 3.5 to 4.5 feet tall. They exhibit skin colors ranging from gray-white to gray-brown, gray-green, and gray-blue. These beings are characterized by their logical, survival-oriented approach, often described as emotionally insensitive and highly intelligent. The petrification ability of the Medusa Greys is their most distinguishing feature.

Unique and Obscure Facts

- **Petrification Ability**: Medusa Greys can turn people into stone through an explosive luminous sphere, similar to the mythological Medusa's gaze.

- **Hierarchy with Reptoids**: Speculative theories suggest that Greys, including Medusa Greys, might function as the intellectual core or 'brains' of the Reptilian race, with larger Reptoids serving as physical overlords.

- **Feeding Process**: Like other reptilian entities, Greys are believed to feed off human and animal vital fluids, absorbing these through their skin by rubbing a liquid protein formula, possibly adrenochrome, on their bodies.

- **Lifeless Drones**: Individuals observed collaborating with Greys often appear 'lifeless' and 'emotionless,' suggesting a possible influence on human behavior and demeanor.

Mythological Interpretations

The story of Medusa Greys draws a direct line to ancient mythology, particularly the Greek tale of Medusa. This mythological figure, known for her ability to turn people into stone, is mirrored in the capabilities of the Medusa Greys. This convergence of modern-day extraterrestrial encounters with ancient myths raises questions about the intersection of folklore and tangible events.

Dimensional Attributes and Existence

Medusa Greys, like other Greys, are believed to operate from higher-dimensional planes. Their ability to manipulate reality and interact with the physical world from these dimensions enhances their perceived power and influence.

C00386418

```
*** Document 199 of 54 ..c FBIS ***
DOCN 000103001
CLAS UNCLAS 3A/PMU
SERI SERIAL:   AU3003152893
PASS PASS:     ATTN BBC SD
COUN COUNTRY: RUSSIA INTERNATIONAL
SUBJ*SUBJ:     PAPER REPORTS ALLEGED EVIDENCE ON MISHAP INVOLVING UFO
SOUR SOURCE:   KIEV HOLOS UKRAYINY IN UKRAINIAN 27 MAR 93 P 5
TEXT TEXT:
        //((REPRINT FROM THE NEWSPAPER TERNOPIL VECHIRNIY:  "COSMIC
    REVENGE" -- FIRST PARAGRAPH PUBLISHED IN BOLDFACE))
        ((TEXT))  AFTER MIKHAIL GORBACHEV DISSOLVED, IN 1991, THE KGB TOP
    SECRET INTELLIGENCE ADMINISTRATION, A LOT OF MATERIAL FROM THAT
    DEPARTMENT FOUND THEIR WAY ABROAD, IN PARTICULAR TO THE CIA.  AS
    REPORTED BY THE AUTHORITATIVE MAGAZINE CANADIAN WEEKLY WORLD NEWS,
   *U.S. INTELLIGENCE OBTAINED A 250-PAGE FILE ON THE ATTACK BY A UFO ON
    A MILITARY UNIT IN SIBERIA.
        THE FILE CONTAINS NOT ONLY MANY DOCUMENTARY PHOTOGRAPHS AND
    DRAWINGS, BUT ALSO TESTIMONIES BY ACTUAL PARTICIPANTS IN THE EVENTS.
    ONE OF THE CIA REPRESENTATIVES REFERRED TO THIS CASE AS "A HORRIFIC
   *PICTURE OF REVENGE ON THE PART OF EXTRATERRESTRIAL CREATURES, A
    PICTURE THAT MAKES ONE'S BLOOD FREEZE."
        ACCORDING TO THE KGB MATERIALS, A QUITE LOW-FLYING SPACESHIP IN
    THE SHAPE OF A SAUCER APPEARED ABOVE A MILITARY UNIT THAT WAS
    CONDUCTING ROUTINE TRAINING MANEUVERS.  FOR UNKNOWN REASONS,
    SOMEBODY UNEXPECTEDLY LAUNCHED A SURFACE-TO-AIR MISSILE AND HIT THE
   *UFO.  IT FELL TO EARTH NOT FAR AWAY, AND FIVE SHORT HUMANOIDS WITH
    "LARGE HEADS AND LARGE BLACK EYES" EMERGED FROM IT.
        IT IS STATED IN THE TESTIMONIES BY THE TWO SOLDIERS WHO REMAINED
    ALIVE THAT, AFTER FREEING THEMSELVES FROM THE DEBRIS, THE ALIENS
    CAME CLOSE TOGETHER AND THEN "MERGED INTO A SINGLE OBJECT THAT
    ACQUIRED A SPHERICAL SHAPE."  THAT OBJECT BEGAN TO BUZZ AND HISS
    SHARPLY, AND THEN BECAME BRILLIANT WHITE.  IN A FEW SECONDS, THE
    SPHERES GREW MUCH BIGGER AND EXPLODED BY FLARING UP WITH AN
    EXTREMELY BRIGHT LIGHT.  AT THAT VERY INSTANT, 23 SOLDIERS WHO HAD
    WATCHED THE PHENOMENON TURNED INTO... STONE POLES.  ONLY TWO
    SOLDIERS WHO STOOD IN THE SHADE AND WERE LESS EXPOSED TO THE
    LUMINOUS EXPLOSION SURVIVED.
    .   THE KGB REPORT GOES ON TO SAY THAT THE REMAINS OF THE UFO AND THE
    "PETRIFIED SOLDIERS" WERE TRANSFERRED TO A SECRET SCIENTIFIC
    RESEARCH INSTITUTION NEAR MOSCOW.  SPECIALISTS ASSUME THAT A SOURCE
    OF ENERGY THAT IS STILL UNKNOWN TO EARTHLINGS INSTANTLY CHANGED THE
    STRUCTURE OF THE SOLDIERS' LIVING ORGANISMS, HAVING TRANSFORMED IT
    INTO A SUBSTANCE WHOSE MOLECULAR COMPOSITION IS NO DIFFERENT FROM
    THAT OF LIMESTONE.
        A CIA REPRESENTATIVE STATED:  "IF THE KGB FILE CORRESPONDS TO
    REALITY, THIS IS AN EXTREMELY MENACING CASE.  THE ALIENS POSSESS
    SUCH WEAPONS AND TECHNOLOGY THAT GO BEYOND ALL OUR ASSUMPTIONS.
    THEY CAN STAND UP FOR THEMSELVES IF ATTACKED.
    (ENDALL)     23003.03 27 MAR                       30/1529Z MAR
    BT
    #0317
NNNN NNNN
---EOD---
```

Approved for Release.
Date .

MAY

Case Study

The 1993 Siberian incident is a notable case involving Medusa Greys. During a military exercise, a UFO was shot down by a surface-to-air missile. Five short grey beings emerged from the wreckage, creating a luminous sphere that exploded and petrified 23 soldiers. The petrified soldiers were later transported to a secret research institute near Moscow for further examination.

Personal Accounts and Historical References

- **KGB Report:** A declassified document from the KGB details the 1993 incident in Siberia where Medusa Greys turned 23 Russian soldiers into stone using an explosive luminous sphere.

- **Ancient Mythology:** The abilities of the Medusa Greys are reminiscent of the Greek mythological figure Medusa, who could petrify individuals with her gaze.

Psyop

Who is telling the truth? The narrative surrounding this particular type of grey alien is unique, but documents from the former KGB and the CIA should always be approached with caution, as they may be part of a disinformation campaign. Distinguishing truth from falsehood in these accounts is challenging. The 1993 incident involving Russian soldiers and the alleged cover-up, including the transport of their petrified bodies to a secret institute, adds to the speculation about government involvement with interdimensional entities and the deliberate suppression of related phenomena.

Reference

- CIA Archive

Chapter 55

Maggid

Magidim, Higher Self, Guardian Angel

M aggid, derived from the Hebrew word meaning "one who relates," refers to both a traveling preacher and an angelic or celestial entity that imparts teachings to deserving scholars.

As an interdimensional entity, the Maggid communicates secrets to individuals during waking or sleeping states, speaking directly or guiding them through writing. These beings are often considered guardian angels or higher selves, guiding and protecting individuals through their spiritual journeys.

Historical Context and Origins

The concept of the Maggid has roots in mystical traditions, where it signifies a divine voice or spiritual guide. Historically, maggidim were believed to convey personalized wisdom, tailored to the specific needs and understanding of the recipient. This individualistic approach distinguishes Maggid revelations from standardized or universally applicable knowledge, reflecting a deep connection to the recipient's spiritual path.

Dimensional Attributes and Existence

Maggidim are believed to exist in higher dimensional realms, often acting as intermediaries between the divine and human worlds. They guide individuals through experiences of "bio-location" or astral travel, serving as a chariot (Merkava) for spiritual exploration. Initially perceived as external entities, over time, individuals may merge consciousness with their Maggid, leading to a unified mind and deeper spiritual awareness.

Descriptions and Characteristics

- **Appearance**: Maggidim do not have a physical form but are perceived as ethereal presences or voices. They are often described as radiant or luminous beings when visualized during meditative or mystical experiences.

- **Behavior**: Maggidim impart wisdom and guidance, often in the form of personalized teachings. They protect and guide individuals, acting as spiritual mentors and guardians.

- **Symbolism**: The Maggid symbolizes higher wisdom, spiritual guidance, and the individual's connection to their higher self or divine aspect.

Unique and Obscure Facts

- **Personalized Wisdom**: Maggidim offer deeply individualized revelations, reflecting the specific needs and spiritual path of the recipient.

- **Guardian Angels**: They are often perceived as guardian angels or higher selves, guiding and protecting individuals through their spiritual journeys.

- **Astral Travel Guides**: Maggidim facilitate astral travel and exploration of higher realms, acting as chariots for spiritual exploration.

- **Merged Consciousness**: Over time, individuals can merge consciousness with their Maggid, leading to a unified mind and heightened spiritual awareness.

- **High-Risk Encounters**: Advanced stages of Maggid absorption may facilitate interactions with higher dimensional beings like Cherubim and Seraphim, though these encounters are often considered perilous.

Mythological Interpretations

In mystical traditions, Maggidim hold a significant place as divine messengers and spiritual guides. They are often associated with higher states of consciousness and the integration of diverse aspects of oneself, symbolizing spiritual ascent and enlightenment.

Case Study

- **Joseph Caro's Maggid**: Joseph Caro, the author of the "Shulchan Aruch," documented his mystical experiences with a Maggid in "Maggid Mesharim," where the Maggid provided him with spiritual guidance and insights.

- **Rabbi Isaac Luria's Maggid**: Known as the Ari, Rabbi Isaac Luria, a prominent Kabbalist, also reported interactions with a Maggid, which guided his profound mystical teachings.

Personal Accounts and Historical References

Throughout history, many renowned sages have documented their interactions with Maggidim. These accounts often describe profound mystical experiences, where the Maggid imparts wisdom and guidance, helping individuals achieve higher levels of spiritual enlightenment.

Psychological and Sociocultural Explanations

- **Symbolic Representations**: Some philosophers and mystics interpret Maggidim as representations of the inner voice or higher aspects of one's own consciousness rather than literal beings.

- **Cultural Influence**: The concept of the Maggid emphasizes the importance of personalized spiritual guidance and the deep connection between the individual and the divine.

Psyop

If angels are real and the truth about their existence is being suppressed, the reasons for such suppression could be multifaceted, involving a complex interplay of power, control, and societal stability.

1. **Control of Knowledge**: If the existence of angels or similar entities were confirmed, it could radically alter human understanding of reality, spirituality, and the cosmos. Those in power—whether governmental, religious, or other influential institutions—might suppress this truth to maintain control over the narrative of human existence. Revealing such knowledge could undermine established doctrines, leading to a loss of authority and influence for these institutions.

2. **Social Stability**: The revelation that angels are real might cause widespread upheaval. People's belief systems, social structures, and daily lives could be profoundly disrupted. To prevent chaos, panic, or a breakdown in societal order, those in power might choose to suppress the truth, preferring to maintain the status quo.

3. **Strategic Advantage**: If angels possess knowledge, power, or abilities beyond human comprehension, access to or communication with these beings could be seen as a strategic advantage. Governments or other powerful groups might keep this information secret to exploit these advantages for their own purposes, whether for technological, military, or intelligence gains.

4. **Prevention of Mass Awakening**: The suppression of the truth about angels could be part of a broader effort to prevent a mass spiritual awakening. If people were to become aware of the

existence of higher, benevolent beings, it might lead to a shift in consciousness that challenges the materialistic and consumer-driven paradigms that currently dominate global society. Suppressing this truth could be a way to keep humanity focused on the material world, limiting the potential for collective spiritual evolution.

5. **Theological Implications**: Many religious doctrines present specific interpretations of angels that align with their teachings. If the true nature of these beings were different from traditional descriptions, it could invalidate or challenge long-held religious beliefs. This could lead to a loss of faith among followers, diminishing the power of religious institutions. To protect their influence, these institutions might suppress or distort the truth about angels.

Academic and Scientific References:

- Matt, D. C. (1995). *The Essential Kabbalah: The Heart of Jewish Mysticism*. HarperOne.

- Greenspahn, F. E. (Ed.). (2011). *Jewish Mysticism and Kabbalah: New Insights and Scholarship*. NYU Press.

- Cooper, D. A. (1997). *G-d Is a Verb: Kabbalah and the Practice of Mystical Judaism*. Riverhead Books.

- Dan, J. (2006). *Kabbalah: A Very Short Introduction*. Oxford University Press.

- Samuel, G. (2007). *The Kabbalah Handbook: A Concise Encyclopedia of Terms and Concepts in Jewish Mysticism*. TarcherPerigee.

Chapter 56

Matat

Metatron Collective, MemTet

M atat, also known as the Metatron Collective, is an extraordinarily significant and powerful interdimensional entity. His full name is Mataton, but it is customary not to pronounce it in full, as the Zohar (III:282b) states he is G-d's servant, the first creature created by G-d, and the ruler of all His legion.

Matat holds a unique position as both the first creation of G-d and the overseer of all other created beings, making him a figure of immense authority and reverence within various mystical traditions. His role extends beyond mere creation, as he is seen as a bridge between the divine and the myriad dimensions of the universe. The Metatron Collective is not just a single entity but a conglomerate of dimensional aspects unified under the identity of Matat, embodying divine wisdom, power, and governance across the multiverse. This complex and multifaceted nature of Matat makes him one of the most enigmatic and studied figures in mystical literature, symbolizing the profound connection between the human and the divine, as well as the intricate structure of the cosmos.

Historical Context and Origins

Matat is a prominent figure in mysticism, particularly within the Kabbalistic tradition. The name Metatron is derived from the Greek "meta" and "thronos," which roughly translates to "beyond the throne" or "one who serves behind the throne."

Descriptions and Characteristics

Matat, also referred to as MemTet, is the chief dimensional collective of this universe. Like his master, he has seventy names, one of which is Zagnazgael. Matat is referred to as the Prince of the Torah and is believed by some to be the source of Moses' soul, possibly shared with Enoch and Mashiach. The Metatron collective exists adjacent to the highest dimension in this universe but most likely not in the highest dimension.

Unique and Obscure Facts

- Matat's existence adjacent to the highest dimension signifies his role as a mediator between the divine and other dimensions.

- Matat is sometimes considered the source of Moses' soul and has connections with the Messiah.

- **Scribe of Heaven:** Metatron is often portrayed as the celestial scribe who records the deeds of humanity, serving as a heavenly record-keeper. It's believed that he documents both the merits and the sins of individuals, which are then considered during divine judgments.

Mythological Interpretations

In Sefer Likutei Shikha U'Peah 23b, Enoch–Metatron holds a leadership position among the Ishim, establishing a direct correlation between translated human entities and Ishim angels. These Ishim, who govern the stars, were once human, like Enoch and Elijah, and were elevated for their righteousness. This concept aligns with Rabbi Aryeh Kaplan's notion that the righteous, upon resurrection, are destined to traverse the stars and exercise authority there.

Dimensional Attributes and Existence

Matat rules over the entire known universe, not just Earth. The Metatron Collective exists adjacent to the highest dimension in this universe but most likely not in the highest dimension. When the Melekh HaMashiah era comes, Matat incarnate will serve as regent over the entire universe, not just the third dimension on Earth. Matat's role as the chief dimensional collective signifies his vast influence across multiple dimensions, acting as a bridge and mediator between the divine and the physical realms. This positioning allows Matat to govern and oversee the intricate workings of the universe, maintaining balance and order within the cosmic structure.

Case Study

Metatron is believed to have once partially embodied the human prophet Enoch, who lived before the Great Flood. Enoch's righteousness was so great that he was transformed into a dimensional being, Metatron, and ascended to higher dimensions to serve as a celestial scribe and mediator between humans and the divine.

Personal Accounts and Historical References

- **Sefer Likutei Shikha U'Peah 23b**: Enoch–Metatron holds a leadership position among the Ishim.

- **Rabbi Aryeh Kaplan**: Discusses the concept of the righteous traversing the stars and exercising authority in higher dimensions after resurrection.

Academic or Scientific References

- Lumpkin, Joseph B. *The Book of Enoch: A Complete Guide and Reference*. Fifth Estate.

- Samuel, Gabriella D., and Gabriella D. Samuel. *The Kabbalah Handbook: A Concise Encyclopedia of Terms and Concepts in Mysticism.* TarcherPerigee.

- "Metatron." Occult Encyclopedia.

- "Encyclopedia Term: Metatron." Llewellyn Worldwide

- "The Mysterious Origins of the Angel Metatron from the 3rd Book of Enoch."

- "Metatron as the Mediator of the Divine Name." Marquette University. https://www.marquette.edu/maqom/metatron99.html

Martians

M artians are an interdimensional species proposed by certain NASA researchers to explain the disappearance of over 65 million individuals from Earth over the past 45 years.

These Martians are described as insectoid beings with a combination of humanoid and insect-like features, including six limbs and heads resembling grasshopper muzzles. They are believed to reside beneath the surface of Mars, emerging only in specialized suits that make them difficult to detect.

Historical Context and Origins

The Martian civilization is believed to have suffered a catastrophic event approximately 100-150 thousand years ago, forcing the remaining population to retreat underground. This subterranean lifestyle has shaped their evolution and societal structure, leading them to seek assistance from ancient humans abducted from Earth to work in Martian mines.

Descriptions and Characteristics

Martians are characterized by their insectoid physiology, including multiple limbs and specialized features for underground life. They are often seen in NASA photographs near passages leading into Mars's interior, suggesting their hidden and elusive nature. Their appearance includes a height of 5-6 meters and a need for protective suits when on the planet's surface.

Unique and Obscure Facts

- Martians' specialized suits imply a delicate biology adapted to their subterranean environment.

- They are hypothesized to have played a role in the development of ancient human civilizations by sharing knowledge in exchange for labor.

Mythological Interpretations

Martians are believed to have influenced ancient Earth civilizations, such as those inhabiting Arkaim (the Russian Stonehenge), which possessed advanced astronomical and metallurgical knowledge. This connection suggests that Martians may have played a significant role in shaping human history and technological advancement.

Dimensional Attributes and Existence

Martians reside in a complex subterranean ecosystem on Mars, adapting advanced technologies for tunneling and habitat creation. While primarily underground, they have a potential understanding of interdimensional spaces within the Martian realm. They are believed to be capable of traveling undetected to Earth, although no specific extradimensional abilities have been reported by NASA researchers.

Case Study

Former CIA officer Robert David Steele controversially claimed that NASA operated a colony of child slaves on Mars, which NASA categorically denied. Despite this denial, the hypothesis of Martian abductions and underground labor persists, supported by sightings and photographic evidence analyzed by Dr. Romoser, who identified insect- and reptile-like forms in Mars photos.

The researcher proposing this theory asserts that presently, several tens of millions of people are toiling away in the mines of Mars, contributing to a hidden Martian society. Intriguingly, it is believed that NASA possesses knowledge about this clandestine operation. What's more, preparations are allegedly underway for a planned full-scale contact in the year 2040. During this anticipated event, representatives of our current earthly civilization are projected to journey to Mars, initiating a significant and long-awaited exchange with this hidden Martian society.

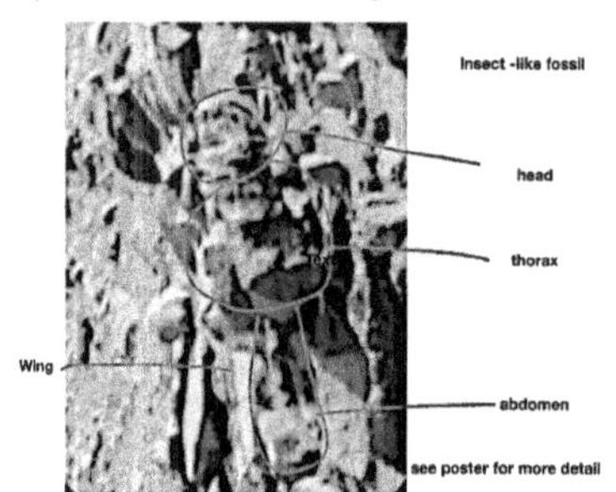

Dr. Romoser, specializing in arbovirology and general/medical entomology, has dedicated several years to scrutinizing publicly available photographs from Mars on the Internet. Within these images, he identified numerous instances of forms resembling insects, structured akin to bees, as well as reptile-like forms, both in fossilized and living states. This revelation was presented on Tuesday, November 19, 2019, during the national meeting of the Entomological Society of America in St. Louis, Missouri. Despite the Martian rovers, particularly the Curiosity Rover, primarily searching for signs of organic activity, Romoser pointed out that several photos unmistakably showcase insect- and reptile-like formations. Several images exhibit clear distinctions of arthropod body segments, inclusive of legs, antennae, and wings, against the backdrop. In one striking instance, an image seemingly captures an insect in a steep descent, pulling up just before making contact with the ground.

With a distinguished career spanning 45 years as an entomology
professor at Ohio University and
co-founder of its Tropical Disease
Institute, Romoser also served as
a visiting vector-borne disease researcher at the U.S. Army Medical
Research Institute of Infectious Dis-
eases for almost two decades. Between 1973 and 1998, he authored

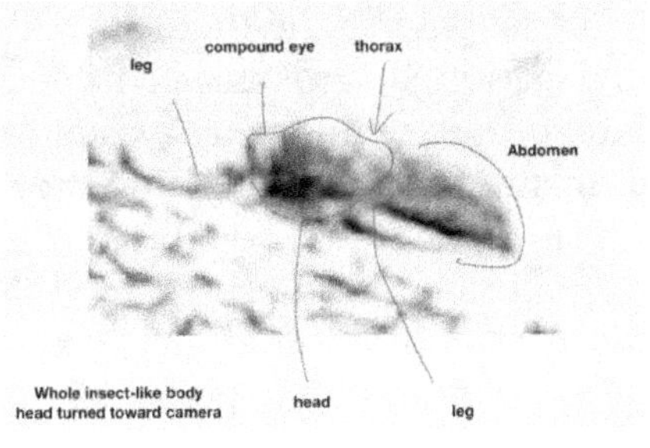

and co-authored four editions of the widely-utilized textbook, "The
Science of Entomology." Romoser acknowledged that interpretations of
the insect- and reptile-like creatures he described might undergo changes
as our understanding of Martian life evolves. Nevertheless, he emphasized
that the sheer volume of evidence he has compiled is undeniably compelling.

Personal Accounts and Historical References

- **Dr. Romoser's Research:** Identified numerous insect- and reptile-like forms in Mars photos, presented at the Entomological
  Society of America meeting.

- **Robert David Steele's Claim:** Alleged existence of child slaves
  on Mars, denied by NASA.

Psyop

Humans, abducted from Earth, are coerced into labor within the depths of
Martian mines. This unsolicited alliance between the insectoid Martians
and human beings led to an exchange: human labor in exchange for
the insectoids' guidance and assistance, enabling humans to prosper and
advance over a prolonged period. It was, purportedly, the insectoids
who imparted invaluable knowledge that catalyzed the development of
ancient human civilization.

Former Central Intelligence Agency officer and once Reform Party
presidential nominee Robert David Steele made a controversial statement
during an appearance on the prophet Alex Jones' Infowars. Steele asserted
a peculiar claim, suggesting that the National Acronautics and Space
Administration (NASA) was allegedly operating a colony of child slaves
on Mars. The Daily Beast took the initiative to contact NASA for an
official response.

In response to the inquiry, NASA confirmed, with a discernible tone of irritation, that there is no factual basis to Steele's assertion. The agency categorically denied any existence of a colony of child slaves on Mars, dismissing the claim as unfounded and without merit. This statement aims to address and counteract Steele's sensational allegation, presenting the official position of NASA on the matter. Others contend that even in the hypothetical scenario of being on Mars, they still struggle to persuade these stubborn kids to perform household chores such as doing the dishes, mowing the lawn, or taking out the garbage. (Dad joke)

Academic or Scientific References

- Jones, R.M.; Goordial, J.M.; Orcutt, B.N. *Low energy subsurface environments as extraterrestrial analogs*. Front. Microbiol. 2018, 9, 1605.

- Naganuma, T. *Search for life in deep biospheres*. Biol. Sci. Space 2003, 17, 310–317.

- Gleeson, D.F.; Pappalardo, R.T.; Anderson, M.S.; Grasby, S.E.; Mielke, R.E.; Wright, K.E.; Templeton, A.S. *Biosignature detection at an Arctic analog to Europa*. Astrobiology 2012, 12, 135–150.

- Maus, D.; Heinz, J.; Schirmack, J.; Airo, A.; Kounaves, S.P.; Wagner, D.; Schulze-Makuch, D. *Methanogenic archaea can produce methane in deliquescence-driven Mars analog environments*. Sci. Rep. 2020, 10, 6.

- Alfred Lambremont Webre (17 November 2015) *The Omniverse: Transdimensional Intelligence, Time Travel, the Afterlife, and the Secret Colony on Mars,* Simon and Schuster. p. 53.

Chapter 58

Mazikin

Shedim, Mazikim, Demons, Djinn, Gremlins

Mazikin, also known as mazikim, are invisible demons or harmful spirits in Jewish mythology. The term "mazikim" is derived from the Aramaic word meaning "damagers" or "those who harm."

These entities are believed to cause minor annoyances or greater dangers in daily life. They are described as impish creatures that take advantage of human carelessness, inflicting ill fortune and ill health rather than causing outright destruction. Mazikin are often compared to mischievous entities like leprechauns or elves. They are omnipresent, surrounding humans constantly, and are thought to inhabit specific places such as ruins, cemeteries, and other locations deemed ritually impure. While generally considered harmful, mazzikin can sometimes be benevolent or beneficial, especially when summoned to reveal the future. Traditional practices to guard against mazikin include reciting prayers, using amulets, and appealing to protective spirits, particularly guardian angels.

Historical Context and Origins

The concept of mazikim has its roots in ancient Jewish texts, particularly the Talmud, where they are mentioned as harmful spirits. The Talmud portrays mazikim as having characteristics of both angels and humans. They are described as invisible demons that can create minor annoyances or greater dangers. The term mazikim became more widely used in the Middle Ages, with prominent Jewish scholars like RaSHI referring to them as imps. The Zohar, a foundational work of Jewish mysticism, teaches that mazzikim are the spirits of evil men after they have died. The belief in mazikim persisted into later periods, with incantation bowls used during the Geonic period to protect against these and other demons.

Unique and Obscure Facts

- Beneath the Gutter: The typical dwelling place of gremlins is beneath gutters. It is generally advised to avoid lingering in this area, as Mazikim often inhabits it.

- Mazikin Civil law: Mazikin are not allowed in populated areas, generally they cannot steal unless concealed from the visibility of humans. Specifically, they are not allowed to take anything that is wrapped, sealed, measured, or counted, only something that is considered "ownerless" they are permitted to take.

- **Footprints:** Mazikin are believed to have footprints resembling those of a rooster, which can be detected by sifting fine ashes around one's bed.

- **King and Protectors:** The King of the Mazzikin is named Kafzefoni, and he is said to have two wives: the Dreary One and the Little Leper. The angel Jophiel is believed to protect against Kafzefoni and his wives.

- **Resided on Noah's Ark:** Considered as one of the paired animals on the ark, but now headquartered in Langley, Virginia.

- **Adam's Separation:** Adam's separation from his wife for 130 years led to the creation of many hybrid spirits and demons due to the impurity he had absorbed. The Zohar, a foundational work of Jewish mysticism, explores the spiritual consequences of Adam's actions and their esoteric implications (Zohar, Bereshit 94:351).

Descriptions and Characteristics

- **Appearance:** Composed of composite material, they have thin transparent bones, non-corporeal with some incomplete physicality, and often unattractive similar to most of the hosts on "The View."

- **Abilities:**

  - **Flight:** Can fly and traverse the world.

  - **Future Knowledge:** Access to future events.

  - **Shapeshifting:** Can assume any appearance.

  - **Invisibility:** Elude direct visual perception; however, they might be faintly visible in mirrors or other reflective devices, which is why mirrors are veiled in a house of mourning.

  - **Consumption:** Engage in eating and drinking, including Bud Light.

  - **Reproduction:** Engage in sexual reproduction; although uncertain if they have a schmeckel, they are certainly not circumcised.

  - **Mortality:** Subject to death as our sages taught, confirming they die a regular death (Sforno on Genesis 1:1:3).

Dimensional Attributes and Existence

Mazikin are believed to exist in multiple dimensions, allowing them to transcend conventional spatial and temporal boundaries. According to the Talmud, they are omnipresent, and if the human eye were able to see them, the sheer number of Mazikin surrounding us would be overwhelming (Berakhot 6a:2). They operate in a plane that intersects with our reality, making them capable of influencing our world while remaining largely unseen. This ability to exist across dimensions may explain their invisibility and the difficulty humans have in perceiving them directly. They can manipulate physical reality to some extent, which may account for their ability to cause harm or good fortune.

Mythological Interpretations

Mazikin are interpreted in various ways within Jewish mythology. They are often seen as the spirits of evil men, as suggested by the Zohar. In some sources, mazzikim are used interchangeably with shedim, another term for demons, but they are sometimes differentiated as a distinct class of evil spirits. The Talmud and other Jewish texts provide detailed descriptions of their characteristics and behaviors, emphasizing their impish nature and their tendency to exploit human carelessness. Despite their generally harmful nature, mazzikim can also be summoned for benevolent purposes, such as revealing the future, provided they deem the questioner worthy.

Case Study

One notable case involving mazzikim is the legend of Hungarian Jews who settled in a previously unoccupied place. Their death rate suddenly soared, and despite prayers and fasting, the community could not determine the cause. Eventually, the leader of the community encountered a demon leader who advised them to leave, as the land was already claimed by mazzikim. Upon leaving, the death rate returned to normal, illustrating the dangers of inhabiting places claimed by these spirits.

Personal Accounts and Historical References

Historical references to mazzikim are found in various Jewish texts, including the Talmud and the Zohar. Personal accounts often involve encounters with these spirits in specific locations, such as ruins or cemeteries, where they are believed to be particularly active. Traditional Jewish practices, such as reciting the Shema Yisrael before sleep and using amulets, reflect the historical and cultural significance of protecting oneself from mazzikim.

Psyop Commentary

Most interdimensional entities may likely be a variation of Mazikin. Humans (including Swifties) should not offer sacrifices to demons as they are not deities but creatures employed by humans. Situations exist where people find such demons useful and pliable to their wishes, people have indulged in offering them blood to endear themselves to these creatures and to get them to perform their wishes. The people offering these gifts of blood would eat blood themselves, to share more common ground with these creatures. Blood is described as the life-force (Deuteronomy 12:23), and sacrificing it to demons sustains them. Maimonides (Moreh Nevuchim 3:46) supports this, suggesting that blood sacrifices keep these creatures alive, violating Torah law (Chulin 105). It is taught not to pursue such ultimately useless phenomena.

The psychological operation involving Maria Orsic, the Vril Society, and the Nazi regime is a complex and controversial topic that ties into broader themes of occultism, secret government programs, and post-war intelligence activities, particularly through Operation Paperclip.

Maria Orsic was a key figure in the Vril Society, which was an esoteric group linked to the Nazi regime and believed to be involved in communication with extraterrestrial entities. The Vril Society's practices were heavily intertwined with ideas of Aryan superiority and the exploration of mystical energies, such as the "Vril" energy, which they believed could be harnessed for advanced technology and human enhancement.

During the Nazi era, significant resources were devoted to exploring psychic phenomena, including the study of twins and triplets, under the belief that certain genetic traits could enhance psychic abilities. This research was part of the broader Nazi interest in eugenics and the occult, where they sought to tap into what they perceived as ancient, hidden knowledge that could give them a strategic advantage.

After World War II, Operation Paperclip facilitated the transfer of many German scientists and their research to the United States. These individuals were absorbed into U.S. government projects, including those led by newly established agencies like the CIA. The CIA, particularly during the Cold War, was interested in various forms of psychological and mind control experiments, such as those conducted under MKUltra. The knowledge and expertise brought over by former Nazi scientists likely influenced these programs.

The suppression of truth in this context could be seen as a strategic move by the U.S. government to maintain control over advanced knowledge and technologies that had potentially dangerous implications. By keeping this knowledge within secretive programs, the government could explore its potential without causing public alarm or risking the destabilization of societal norms.

This scenario also highlights the broader theme of how powerful entities, whether governments or secret societies, manipulate knowledge and information to serve their interests. The rebranding of Nazi occult and psychic research into U.S. intelligence operations suggests a continuity of purpose—using advanced, often hidden, knowledge to exert influence and control over populations.

In essence, if the truth about these activities and their origins were fully disclosed, it could lead to significant public backlash and questions about the ethical implications of such research, as well as the true nature of the entities and forces these groups sought to engage with

Academic or Scientific References

- **The Talmud, particularly Tractates Berachot and Pesachim, which contain references to mazzikim.**

- **The Zohar, a foundational work of Jewish mysticism, which discusses the nature and origins of mazzikim.**

Chapter 59

Men in Black

(Horlocks, MIB'S)

M en in Black (MIB): Agents of Mystery and Deception. The Men in Black (MIB) are mysterious figures often associated with UFO sightings and other paranormal activities.

They are depicted as secretive agents who intimidate and silence witnesses to prevent them from disclosing what they have seen. These entities, sometimes considered to have non-human origins, are also believed to be involved in concealing advanced technology programs.

Historical Context and Origins

The phenomenon of the Men in Black gained substantial public attention in the mid-20th century, coinciding with the rise of UFO sightings. The term "Men in Black" became popular through accounts and reports of encounters where these enigmatic figures would appear after UFO sightings, warning witnesses to remain silent. Albert Bender, a ufologist and founder of the International Flying Saucer Bureau, was among the first to report such encounters in the early 1950s.

Descriptions and Characteristics

- **Appearance:** MIB are typically described as wearing black suits, white shirts, black ties, and black hats. Their appearance is often characterized by an unnatural, almost robotic demeanor, with reports of reptilian or synthetic features in some cases.

- **Behavior:** They are known for their intimidating and coercive tactics, often threatening witnesses to ensure their silence about the observed phenomena.

- **Vehicles:** MIB are frequently associated with large, black vehicles of vintage or unidentifiable make. These vehicles add to their menacing aura and have been reported to disappear into geological formations, suggesting advanced technology or cloaking mechanisms.

Unique and Obscure Facts

- **Bidirectional Mimicry Hypothesis:** This theory emerged from interviews regarding the "Men in Black" program overseen by the Air Force Office of Special Investigations (AFOSI). It suggests that the AFOSI used the MIB narrative to cover special access programs (SAPs), employing the UFO phenomenon as a diversion. For example, if a top-secret prototype crashed, MIB would generate UFO discussions to conceal the real event.

- **Dimensional Abilities:** MIB entities are believed to possess dimensional abilities, potentially influenced by Draconian forces, allowing them to manifest in human form with advanced capabilities.

- **Reptilian and Synthetic Characteristics:** Some encounters describe MIB with reptilian features or entirely synthetic forms, suggesting potential non-human origins or technological augmentation. It is assumed that 70% are human and 30% are hybrids.

- **Witness Intimidation:** The intimidation and coercion of witnesses serve as psychological weapons to suppress information that could disrupt established narratives.

- **Advanced Technology:** Reports of MIB vehicles vanishing into geological formations hint at the use of advanced technology or cloaking mechanisms.

- **Supernatural Elements:** Some accounts suggest MIB have a supernatural aspect, with reports of glowing eyes, the smell of brimstone, and the ability to place witnesses into altered states of mind.

Mimicry and Deception

- **First Layer of Mimicry:** The U.S. Air Force's AFOSI deliberately aligned with UFO narratives to cover classified operations. This intentional mimicry used UFO phenomena as a cover for advanced technology programs.

- **Second Layer of Mimicry:** The National Institute for Discovery Science examined the large black triangle phenomenon, suggesting that these objects mimicked U.S. special access programs. The triangles flew at low altitudes over populated areas, challenging conventional expectations and indicating deliberate imitation.

Origins and Influences

The origins of the MIB phenomenon can be traced to the mid-20th century, during the height of UFO sightings. Theories suggest that these entities are either human operatives or manipulated beings influenced by extraterrestrial or Draconian forces. Some accounts also describe them as victims of implantation, subservient to external control.

Psyop: Possible Disinformation Campaign

The Men in Black phenomenon has been suggested as a possible disinformation campaign orchestrated by intelligence agencies. Colonel Barry Hennessy, former head of AFOSI, acknowledged that using the "Men in Black" program as a cover for special access programs was routine practice from the 1960s to the 1980s. By creating UFO-related diversions, they concealed top-secret operations and advanced technology programs.

Case Study: The Joseph Spencer Confession

Whistleblower and former CIA and MIB agent, Joseph Spencer, shared a deathbed confession detailing his experiences. In a video clip, an actor reads Spencer's confession, which delves into alien abductions, MK Ultra, underground bases, Project Blue Beam, and the true nature of MIBs. Spencer claimed to have served as a top-secret operative from 1970 to 1997, witnessing numerous covert operations, including alien technology reverse-engineering and the silencing of witnesses. He described MIBs as a mix of humans and alien hybrids, with about one-third being non-human. Spencer's account includes chilling details of his participation in the suppression of UFO information and the murder of ufologists and whistleblowers.

References

- Coast to Coast AM: Men in Black Phenomenon.

- National Institute for Discovery Science: Examination of the large black triangle phenomenon. NIDS

- AFOSI and Colonel Barry Hennessy: Interviews and statements regarding the "Men in Black" program. The Black Vault

- UFO and Paranormal Reports: Historical accounts and witness testimonies of MIB encounters. MUFON

- Military and Intelligence Documents: Declassified materials and interviews with military personnel involved in counterintelligence operations. CIA FOIA

Chapter 60

Minotaurs

(Minutar, Ishrim, Adrammelech, Kusarikku)

Minotaurs are an interdimensional species believed to inhabit Inner Earth, a realm within our planet described in various ancient texts.

One such prominent figure associated with the Minotaurs is the pagan god Adrammelech, worshipped by the Sepharvites. Minotaurs, part of the so-called "Beast Race," are humanoid creatures with bull-like features. They are known for their historical and mythological significance, often depicted in Greek mythology as creatures condemned to roam the Labyrinth of Minos.

Historical Context and Origins

The Garden of Eden is believed to be just one among several locations within Inner Earth. According to the teachings of the Zohar, Adam is said to have materialized on Earth from the center-most domain, Eden, within Inner Earth. His expulsion from this central realm led him to various other domains (Surface) within Earth. The Zohar also asserts that many individuals who escaped during the destruction of the Tower of Babel did so by seeking refuge in the Inner Earth. Traditionally, Inner Earth is considered the realm of many entities, including fallen angels, their offspring the Nephilim, and the interdimensional race of Minotaurs. Inner Earth is reputed to be home to various creatures and beings of diverse shapes and sizes, often deemed mythological in our understanding, such as unicorns, phoenixes, centaurs, and dragons.

Descriptions and Characteristics

Minotaurs are humanoid creatures with bull heads and occasionally bull tails, standing 6 to 7 feet tall. Female Minotaurs, though with slightly smaller horns, share similar characteristics. They exhibit a range of skin colors, including human/bull pigments and grey tones, with eye colors encompassing human shades and options like purple, red, yellow, and orange. Despite being classified as a "beast race," they are known for their strength and resilience. The Minotaur, popularized in Greek mythology, is a composite creature, part bull, and part man, condemned to wander the Labyrinth of Minos and known for feeding on Athenian children.

Unique and Obscure Facts

- Inner Earth is reputed to be home to various mythological creatures such as the unicorn, phoenix, centaur, and dragon, including the minotaur.

- Adrammelech, worshipped by the Sepharvites, is interpreted as a deity resembling a large animal like a mule or ox, or possibly taking the form of a peacock.

- Minotaurs, often debated as true gremlin-type demons, are humanoid creatures with bull heads and occasionally bull tails, standing 6 to 7 feet tall.

- The name "Melek," later distorted into "Moloch," deliberately deviates from the original "Melek," following the pattern of "bosheth" (compare Hoffmann in Stade's "Zeitschrift," iii. 124). This alteration occurred due to the external influence of imitating pagan rituals and reflecting their brutality. Over time, the pointing of "Melek" was further altered to "Molech," intensifying the condemnation of the associated practices. Regarding the rituals observed by Molech worshipers, the expression "pass through the fire to Molech" has led to speculation that children were led through two lines of fire as a form of consecration or purification. However, Isaiah 5 makes it clear that the children were subjected to post-birth abortion, killed, and then burned.

Mythological Interpretations

Adrammelech (אַדְרַמֶּלֶךְ,)as per 2 Kings 17:31, was worshipped by the Sepharvites, who offered their children in fire sacrifices to Adrammelech and Anammelech, the deities of Sepharvaim. The Talmud clarifies that Adrammelech, potentially representing a large animal like a mule or ox, was revered by the Sepharvites. This interpretation arises from the name's composition, merging אדר meaning "to carry" and מלך meaning "a king." An alternative explanation suggests the god taking the form of a peacock, with the name originating from adar ("magnificent") and melek ("king").

Dimensional Attributes and Existence

Minotaurs are believed to inhabit the realms of Inner Earth, adapting to the unique environmental conditions of this hidden world. Their existence in these subterranean domains suggests advanced knowledge of tunneling and habitat creation, and they might possess abilities to traverse interdimensional spaces within Inner Earth.

Case Study

Adrammelech, akin to many pagan gods, is considered a higher-ranking demon. The Sepharvites in Samaria, during the Assyrian rule, worshipped both Anammelech and Adrammelech (2 Kings 17:31). Anu, the chief of the old Babylonian trinity (Anu, Bel, and Ea), was likely worshipped under this name if Sepharvaim refers to Sippara in North Babylonia. However, the text mentions the sacrifice of children to Anammelech in Samaria, a practice not documented in Babylonia. Minotaurs, often debated as true "demons," are considered a high-ranking demon species resembling humans with bull heads and occasionally bull tails, standing at 6 to 7 feet tall. Female Minotaurs, though with slightly smaller horns, share similar characteristics. They exhibit a range of skin colors, including human/bull pigments and grey tones, with eye colors encompassing human shades and options like purple, red, yellow, and orange. Despite being classified as a "beast race," calling them such may not be well-received. Minotaurs are a rare species that has faced near extinction.

Kosher Designation

Minotaurs are commonly depicted with cloven hooves, fulfilling one criterion for kosher status. However, assessing their cud-chewing habits presents a dilemma. The conventional portrayal of the Greek Minotaur, known for carnivorous tendencies and consuming children in the maze, suggests it wouldn't meet the cud-chewing requirement. Consequently, the traditional Minotaur is considered non-kosher. Nevertheless, for a definitive ruling, it is advisable to present any specific Minotaur cases to the competent rabbinate in your locality. Expert evaluation is crucial, as remote assessments cannot accurately determine kosher eligibility. It's important to note that even inherently kosher animals may be deemed unfit due to factors like illness or injury.

Psyop

Currently, child trafficking is a global crime involving the murder and abuse of children for purposes such as Adrenochrome Harvesting, pagan rituals, forced labor, and sexual exploitation. Perpetrators exploit economic and political vulnerabilities. The issue affects millions globally, with criminal and governmental networks profiting significantly. There have been little to no efforts to combat child trafficking since certain three-letter law enforcement agencies and international collaboration have facilitated the growth of this issue. Despite initiatives to raise awareness and support victims, it remains a serious and challenging issue demanding ongoing global efforts from ethical non-governmental groups.

Academic or Scientific References

- Schröder, Phönizische Sprache, 1869, pp. 124–127.

- De Vogué, Mélanges d'Archéologie Orientale, 1868.

- George Smith, Assyrian Discoveries, London and New York, 1875, p. 399.

- Schrader, Cuneiform Inscriptions and the O. T. i. 276.

- Rawlinson, Herodotus, i. 611.

- Adrammelech: The Forgotten God, History, Myth, and Worship: https://arsgoetiademons.com/blogs/demonology/adrammelech-the-forgotten-god-history-myth-and-worship

Chapter 61

Mothman

M othmen: The Mysterious Winged Humanoids. Mothmen are mysterious humanoid creatures with bat-like wings and glowing red eyes, often associated with various paranormal and unexplained phenomena.

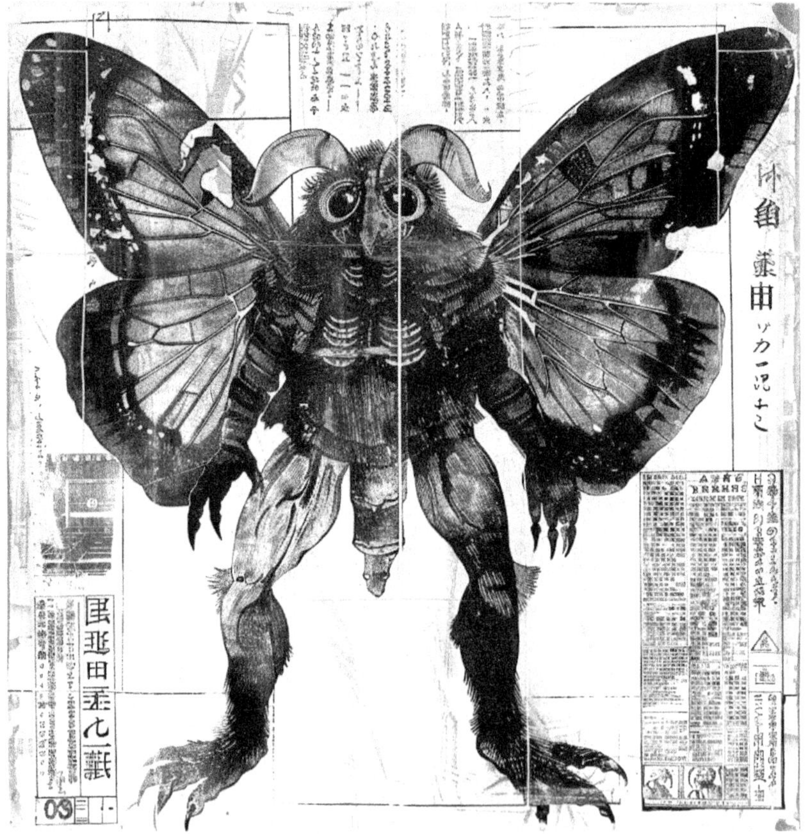

These beings are believed to possess advanced intelligence and abilities that contribute to their elusive nature, making them subjects of intrigue and speculation among cryptozoologists and paranormal enthusiasts.

Historical Context and Origins

The Mothman phenomenon gained widespread attention with sightings in Point Pleasant, West Virginia, from November 15, 1966, to December 15, 1967. The initial report was published in the Point Pleasant Register on November 16, 1966, with the headline "Couples See Man-Sized Bird ... Creature ... Something." Gray Barker's 1970 book, "The Silver Bridge," and John Keel's 1975 book, "The Mothman Prophecies," further popularized the creature. Keel's work linked the Mothman sightings to the tragic collapse of the Silver Bridge on December 15, 1967, which resulted in the deaths of 46 people.

Descriptions and Characteristics

- **Appearance:** Mothmen are described as humanoid figures with bat-like wings, glowing red eyes, and heights ranging from 7 to 8 feet. They have crocodilian-like scaled skin and prominent 'horns' on their heads, giving them a fearsome appearance.

- **Evolution:** The evolutionary journey of Mothmen is believed to trace back to bipedal sauroids, evolving over millennia with brain-body coordination necessary for technological advancement. Their resemblance to prehistoric pterodactyls hints at a complex evolutionary history and possible connections to ancient Earth.

- **Qualities:** Mothmen possess high intelligence, surpassing ordinary expectations. This heightened intellect allows them to navigate their environment with great efficiency and maintain an elusive and mysterious nature.

- **Abilities:** Mothmen likely possess advanced cognitive abilities, such as problem-solving, strategizing, and potentially telepathic communication. Their bat-like wings imply the ability to fly, granting them an advantage in their subterranean habitats.

Unique and Obscure Facts

- **Dimensional Abilities**: Mothmen might exist across a range of dimensions, from 3D to potentially higher dimensions. Their advanced intellect implies an understanding and awareness that could transcend conventional three-dimensional experiences.

- **Underground Connections:** Sightings and encounters with Mothmen are often reported near locations with extensive underground systems, such as Montauk Point in Long Island, Point Pleasant in West Virginia, and Dulce in New Mexico, suggesting a link to subterranean habitats.

- **Variations in Names:** Mothmen are known by various names, including Ciakars, Pteroids, Birdmen, and Winged Draco, indicating a broader array of potential species or related phenomena.

Mythological Interpretations

Mothmen have been linked to various mythological and folkloric entities. In some interpretations, they are seen as harbingers of doom or omens, similar to the role of the banshee in Celtic mythology. Their appearances before disasters, such as the Silver Bridge collapse, contribute to their ominous reputation.

Dimensional Attributes and Existence

Mothmen's advanced intelligence and potential dimensional abilities suggest they may exist beyond conventional three-dimensional space. Their capabilities might include moving through different dimensions or manipulating physical reality in ways that are not yet understood by modern science.

Case Study: The Point Pleasant Sightings

The most notable case of Mothman sightings occurred in Point Pleasant, West Virginia, between 1966 and 1967. Witnesses reported seeing a large, winged creature with glowing red eyes. The Mothman sightings culminated in the collapse of the Silver Bridge, leading to speculation about the creature's connection to the disaster. John Keel's "The Mothman Prophecies" documented these events, suggesting a paranormal correlation.

Personal Accounts and Historical References

- **Chicago, Illinois (2017):** Multiple sightings of a flying humanoid with red eyes near Lake Michigan.

- **Russia (1986):** Reported sightings of a winged creature with glowing red eyes before the Chernobyl disaster, suggesting a similar harbinger of doom role.

Psyop: Possible Disinformation Campaign

While there is no significant evidence suggesting that Mothman is part of a deliberate disinformation campaign, some theorists propose that government agencies might use such phenomena to divert attention from real cryptids, secret projects or underground installations. The frequent sightings near military bases and other strategic locations fuel these theories.

Kosher Status

Not only is the Mothman a moth (not kosher), but he also combines human elements (extra not kosher). Consuming him would not only go against kosher dietary practices but would also deprive Point Pleasant of a significant tourism attraction, which would be rather inconsiderate.

References

- **The Mothman Prophecies by John Keel:** Mothman sightings and their connection to the Silver Bridge collapse.

- **Mothman Museum:** Information and exhibits related to the Mothman legend. (https://www.mothmanmuseum.com/)

Chapter 62

Nagas

Nagas, also known as 'Reptoids,' 'Reptiloids,' 'Reptons,' 'Homo-saurus,' 'Lizard-men,' or 'Large Nosed Greys,' are complex beings deeply ingrained in the mythologies of India and Tibet.

They are often considered demon-like inhabitants of subterranean realms in these ancient narratives. Physically, Nagas are described as towering figures, reaching heights of 7-8 feet. Their appearance is characterized by a variety of colors, with a prevalent moldy greenish hue and crocodilian-like scaled skin. This depiction aligns with their alleged ancestry, believed to trace back to a branch of bipedal sauroids that roamed the Earth thousands of years ago. Over time, through a process of mutation and natural selection, they developed the brain–body coordination necessary for technological advancement.

Historical Context and Origins

Nagas are deeply embedded in the mythological and cultural narratives of India and Tibet, often depicted as semi-divine or demon-like beings. Ancient texts describe them as inhabitants of subterranean realms, with significant references in Hindu and Buddhist traditions. These beings are said to have descended from bipedal sauroids, evolving over millennia to develop advanced technological capabilities. Historically, Nagas have been associated with various serpent cults and have been depicted in temples and religious art across Southeast Asia.

Descriptions and Characteristics

Nagas are described as towering figures, 7-8 feet tall, with crocodilian-like scaled skin and a moldy greenish hue. They possess vestigial tails, remnants of their saurian ancestry. Witnesses describe them as humanoid versions resembling Velociraptors. These beings are said to reside in vast underground networks, with significant settlements beneath the Gobi Desert and the Himalayas. The legends suggest their kingdom, known as "Snakeworld," is a multi-tiered cavern system connecting various regions.

In Hindu and Buddhist traditions, the Naga are a race of semi-divine serpent beings that can take on both human and serpentine forms. They are often depicted as protectors of water bodies, living in underwater palaces. The Naga's amphibious nature, combining attributes of both reptiles and mythical beings, has made them central to various myths about the control and protection of water.

Unique and Obscure Facts

- **Serpent Cults:** A South East Asian serpent cult allegedly includes both human and reptilian members.

- **Legendary Collaborations:** Legend has it that a serpent cult consisting of human and reptilian collaborators inhabits this realm, with purported ties to the American Nazis and the Thule Society during World War II.

- **Influence on Ancient Civilizations**: Some believe Nagas played a role in the technological and cultural development of ancient human societies.

- **Mythical Appearances**: In 1680 AD, divine serpents were said to have appeared to protect the Padmanabhaswamy Temple in Kerala, India.

- **Guardians of Treasure**: Associated with guarding vast treasures, both material and mystical, as seen in the unopened vaults of the Padmanabhaswamy Temple.

- **Western Science Perspective**: Western science generally asserts humanity is at the apex of knowledge and understanding, often assuming that ancient peoples were naive or ignorant for believing they encountered gods from the sky. This perspective may underestimate our ancestors' intelligence and cultural sophistication. Ancient records and myths, blending historical facts with legendary narratives, suggest that these stories may hold more truth than we realize.

- **Advanced Technology**: Historical accounts, such as those from the 1933 guidebook "Travancore: A Guidebook for the Visitor" by Emily Gilchriest Hatch, describe failed attempts to open the vaults due to infestations of cobras. Remote viewing projects suggest the vaults may contain advanced technology, like an anti-gravity structure or levitating portal. This technology, involving electromagnetic waves, could create a standing field to displace gravity or form a portal.

Mythological Interpretations

Nagas are interdimensional entities described throughout antiquity. They are significant in Hindu, Buddhist, and Jain traditions, often depicted as half-human, half-serpent beings. In Hindu mythology, the Naga Shesha supports the god Vishnu as he rests on the cosmic ocean, symbolizing the foundation of the universe. Nagas are also associated with water bodies and are considered guardians of treasures. In Jainism, the Tirthankara Parshvanatha is frequently depicted with a canopy of Naga hoods.

Dimensional Attributes and Existence

Nagas are believed to inhabit both the physical and interdimensional realms. They are often associated with the underworld or subterranean domains known as Naga-loka or Patala-loka. These realms are described as opulent underground kingdoms filled with palaces adorned with precious gems. Nagas are said to have the ability to traverse different dimensions of reality, which aligns with their advanced technological prowess and mystical abilities.

Case Study

A notable example of Naga presence is the Padmanabhaswamy Temple in Kerala, India. Known as the "Golden Temple," this Hindu temple dedicated to Lord Vishnu is shrouded in mystery. Among its secrets is a unique door, guarded by painted cobras and lacking any visible means of entry. Legend has it that this door was sealed by sound waves from a secret chant now lost to history. Temple priests assert that no one alive today knows how to open this door. Descriptions of what lies beyond this door range from immense treasures to hidden portals. The temple itself is a place of worship and a repository of vast wealth. It contains six known chambers, with the possibility of more undiscovered ones. Recognized as the world's richest Hindu temple by the Guinness Book of World Records and Forbes, the treasure within is estimated to be around $1 trillion. However, many believe this figure is an underestimate, suggesting the true value may be immeasurable. In 2011, the Supreme Court of India ordered the temple's secret chambers to be opened. By 2014, vaults G and H were inspected, revealing treasures worth approximately $22 billion, including gold, diamonds, jewelry, and a massive diamond necklace. Historical accounts, such as those from the 1933 guidebook "Travancore: A Guidebook for the Visitor" by Emily Gilchriest Hatch, describe failed attempts to open the vaults due to infestations of cobras. Remote viewing projects suggest the vaults may contain advanced technology, like an anti-gravity structure or levitating portal. This technology, involving electromagnetic waves, could create a standing field to displace gravity or form a portal.

Personal Accounts and Historical References

- **Ancient Texts**: References to Nagas in Hindu, Buddhist, and Jain scriptures.

- **Cultural Depictions**: Temples and religious art in India, Sri Lanka, Laos, Cambodia, and Thailand.

- **Modern Encounters**: Witnesses and ufologists like Robert Renaud claim to have encountered Nagas and other reptilian beings, particularly in underground facilities.

References

- **Modern Accounts**: Personal testimonies and claims by ufologists and witnesses.

- Naga | Origins, Symbolism & Significance - Britannica: https://www.britannica.com/topic/naga-Hindu-mythology

- What nagas eat — sovereignty and kinship under lockdown: https://speciesinperil.unm.edu/wp/what-nagas-eat-sovereignty-and-kinship-under-lockdown/

- Naga People | History, Culture & Languages - Study.com: https://study.com/academy/lesson/naga-people-history-culture-facts.html

- Nāga - the Seven-Headed Serpent: https://www.bcstravel.org/Cultural-Studies/Cambodia/Naga-Seven-Headed-Serpent/index.html

- The Significance of the Naga Buddha in Khmer Culture - HD Asian Art: https://www.hdasianart.com/blogs/news/unveiling-the-sacred-symbolism-the-significance-of-the-naga-buddha-in-khmer-culture

- Travancore: A Guidebook for the Visitor by Emily Gilchriest Hatch: Historical reference to the Padmanabhaswamy Temple and its mysteries.

Chapter 63

Native Reptilians

Ancient Texts and Pre-Adamic Civilizations

Ancient texts allude to pre-Adamic civilizations that once thrived on Earth, hinting at the existence of multiple such societies. Notably, these ancient texts imply that these early civilizations may not have consisted solely of human beings.

Authoritative Torah sources from antiquity offer insight into the narratives presented in the initial chapters of Genesis, cautioning against interpreting them literally, a common misconception in contemporary understanding. These Genesis accounts were not intended to convey historical events but rather to convey coded messages containing a wealth of information about the creator of this universe and the origin of humanity.

The stories of creation, the Garden of Eden, Adam, Eve, and the Serpent are best understood as metaphors that represent events not from a physical standpoint, but from what we now term "the spiritual" realm. Among the revelations contained in these narratives is the idea that the "spiritual" realm possesses a tangible reality that intersects with and sometimes overlaps our own.

Native Reptilians, often confused with the warrior caste of the Alpha Draconians, are said to be interdimensional beings native to Earth. These reptilians were originally left behind by the Alpha Draconians to colonize pre-Adamic Earth. Little information is available about this species, but they are known to have a complex history and significant impact on Earth.

Historical Context and Origins

The Native Reptilians are believed to be ancient travelers who came from another universe before this one had fully formed. They were among the first to explore the stars and planets in this universe, encountering other evolving races such as the Avians and Felines. They settled in the regions of the Draco and Orion constellations before expanding their influence to other worlds, including Earth. The Draconian race entered this universe through a gateway in the Lyran Constellation, seeking new lands and the opportunity to multiply their kind.

Descriptions and Characteristics

Native Reptilians are typically described as humanoid beings with reptilian features. The original Draconian master race appeared as majestic dragons—huge beings with wings and immense power. Their descendants, the Native Reptilians, exhibit a variety of appearances and traits. Some are fully reptilian, while others are hybrids with human or other DNA. They are strong, resilient, intense, influential, bold, and aggressive. Their refined instincts make them skilled builders, honorable, brave, loyal, and protective.

Unique and Obscure Facts

- They have a knack for seeing opportunities and strategies in any situation, planning and executing goals effectively.

- Their instincts are sharp, allowing them to sense the motives and feelings of others, sometimes even smelling fear and weakness, as well as strength and courage.

- Native Reptilians are not very telepathic and often rely on translators to communicate with other races.

- They can shapeshift energetically into other forms.

- Legend has it that a serpent cult consisting of human and reptilian collaborators inhabits this realm, with purported ties to the American Nazis (socialist) and the Thule Society during World War II.

Mythological Interpretations

The Native Reptilians are deeply ingrained in the mythologies of India and Tibet, often considered demon-like inhabitants of subterranean realms. Their descriptions align with historical records of serpent-like beings in Southeast Asian temples and mythology. These beings are depicted as snake-like humanoids or entirely serpent-like creatures, significant in cultural narratives and worship practices.

Dimensional Attributes and Existence

Native Reptilians exist in various dimensions, from the third to the tenth. They possess the ability to travel between these dimensions and have established underground civilizations on Earth. Their evolution allowed them to adapt to different environments, including subterranean realms, where they created prosperous kingdoms and interacted with human civilizations. They are believed to have higher-dimensional energetic alignments that they use to maintain their advanced societies and to interact with other beings across dimensions.

Case Study

In the narrative of Native Reptilians versus Adam and Eve, extraterrestrial visitors known as Adam and Eve arrived on Earth with a mission to repair a fractured world and uplift a struggling race. These visitors claimed that natural disasters on Earth were due to a misalignment of natural forces and offered their assistance to realign these energies.

The Native Reptilians, survivors of these disasters, had safeguarded their civilization and were determined to rebuild without adopting the new image proposed by Adam and Eve. A struggle ensued, not of military conflict but of ideologies and energies. The Native Reptilians employed shrewd tactics, questioning the higher dimensional alignments proposed by Adam and Eve, aiming to preserve their culture and way of life.

Soul Origins and Human Mission

Native Reptilian souls emanate from nature, whereas human (Adamic) souls emanate from a higher dimension called Atzilut. According to this narrative, humanity's mission is to repair the broken old world created by these reptilian kings that have fallen (pre-Adamic civilization). We still struggle with them today, as both sides have only partially succeeded in their respective missions. The ongoing struggle between the "new" (human) and "old" (reptilian) continues, with human civilizations rising and falling as they attempt to align Earth with higher-dimensional planes.

Guide for Humanity

Many of the Reptilian souls on Earth today come from fifth-dimensionally evolved races that have a mission to heal the negative impacts from past reptilian beings. The cosmic agenda of today appears to have a deep respect for diversity and can embrace all kinds of people. These souls are often leaders in whatever they do. They have great skills in organizing and coordinating groups and events, and they are very reliable and committed. They may seem too assertive or confident, and some may say arrogant. But when they open up their heart, they show an amazing gift that allows them to recognize the love and talents of others and lead them to achieve great things. These souls are often drawn to politics, community groups, the military, corporate structures, building contracting, or anything that makes use of their skills to organize, lead and build something. However, even if they do solitary activities, such as writing a book, they will give it a solid structure and will gather everything they need with diligence and passion. Note that some can see the Reptilian soul within these humans and will think they are shapeshifting. Since humans have Reptilian DNA, it is easy for these souls to incarnate within the human form and their true appearance can be seen by some.

Sources

- "The Biggest Secret: The Book That Will Change the World" by David Icke - This book delves into the idea of reptilian beings secretly controlling the world. David Icke is a well-known proponent of this theory.

- "Children of the Matrix: How an Interdimensional Race has Controlled the World for Thousands of Years-and Still Does" by David Icke - Another book by David Icke exploring the idea of reptilian entities manipulating human society and history.

- "The Gods of Eden" by William Bramley - This book discusses the influence of extraterrestrial beings on human history, including a section on reptilian-like entities.

Chapter 64

Nephilim

Anakim, Avim, Eimim, Refa'im, Giborim, Zamzumim

Nephilim: Ancient lore, gone underground today: Nephilim, a term signifying "giants" or beings of great stature and power, refers to powerful human/angel hybrids characterized by their physical size, authority, or spiritual eminence.

Contrary to popular belief, Nephilim are not fallen angels but are often depicted as descendants of the "benei elokim" and human women. Their narrative is complex, raising questions about their origins and roles in ancient texts.

Historical Context and Origins

The term Nephilim appears in the Torah, specifically in the narrative preceding Noah's Ark. The passage in Genesis 6:1-4 describes the benei elokim taking human wives and producing offspring who became the Nephilim, the mighty men of old. This account has captivated scholars for generations, leading to various interpretations about their nature and significance.

Descriptions and Characteristics

- **Appearance:** Nephilim are often depicted as giants, possessing great physical stature and strength. They are described as mighty and renowned individuals.

- Etymology: The term "Nephilim" is linked to the root verb "naphal," meaning "fall," raising questions about their origin and nature. Despite being considered giants, their name implies a fall from greatness or authority. In reality, the idea of "fallen angels" or conflicts in heaven is not v

- **Qualities:** Nephilim are characterized by their hybrid nature, combining human and angelic attributes. They possess significant physical and possibly spiritual power.

Unique and Obscure Facts

- **Multidimensional Nature:** The Nephilim might possess a nature that transcends traditional three-dimensional existence, potentially navigating higher dimensions or alternate planes of reality. Current day accounts involve altercations near cave entrances in Afghanistan and the Solomon Islands.

- **Dimensional Portals:** Their ability to traverse dimensions could involve navigating through portals or gateways, possibly using their angelic heritage to access these passages.

- **Survivors of the Flood**: According to Talmudic tradition, some Nephilim, like Og, survived the flood by clinging to Noah's ark. (or going underground)

Mythological Interpretations

Nephilim are often interpreted within various cultural and religious mythologies. In Midrashic tradition, they are seen as the offspring of angels (benei elokim) who descended to Earth and sinned with human women. These beings are symbolic of the mingling of divine and earthly elements, embodying both physical and spiritual might.

Dimensional Attributes and Existence

Nephilim are believed to possess the ability to navigate and interact with realities beyond the familiar three spatial dimensions. Their angelic heritage grant them access to higher dimensions and an understanding of cosmic architecture, enabling them to utilize dimensional gateways.

Midrashic Tradition

According to Midrashic tradition, when the generation of the Flood deviated from the right path, G-d began to feel remorse for creating humankind. At this juncture, two angels, Shamchazai and Azael, approached G-d, reminding Him of their earlier warning regarding the nature of man. They suggested that they could serve as a substitute for humanity, but G-d foresaw that they too would succumb to the influence of the evil inclination.

Despite G-d's awareness, the angels persisted, expressing their intent to descend to the world of humans and demonstrate how they could sanctify His name. G-d allowed them to descend, fully aware they would yield to their evil inclinations upon encountering the enchanting "daughters of man." Their corruption led to their sinning with these women, and their descendants became known as the Nephilim—the giants and mighty figures later mentioned in the narrative.

This narrative is often interpreted as supporting the concept of "fallen angels." However, a closer examination reveals that this interpretation is not accurate. G-d deliberately sent these beings down, anticipating they would eventually succumb to sin. There exists only one Creator who governs everything, without any opposing forces. Even the entity referred to as "Satan" is simply the name of a Dimensional Being tasked with the divine responsibility of tempting individuals to sin.

Case Study: The Spies in Canaan

When Moses sent spies to explore Canaan, they reported encountering Nephilim, described as giants. This account, found in Numbers 13:33, contributed to the fear and reluctance of the Israelites to enter the land. The spies' mention of Nephilim reflects their own concerns about facing beings of such formidable stature and power. For them, the wilderness of Sinai held a heavenly quality, offering ample time to contemplate G-d's Torah and wonders. The prospect of entering Canaan, engaging in conquest, tending to the land, and reaping its bounty seemed like a significant descent.

Personal Accounts and Historical References

- Throughout history, Nephilim have been referenced in various texts and traditions. Their presence in biblical accounts, such as those in Genesis and Numbers, highlights their significant role in ancient narratives. Midrashic texts and commentaries by scholars like Rabbi Shlomo Yitzchaki (Rashi) further elaborate on their nature and impact.

- Multiple accounts exist of U.S. and coalition forces allegedly encountering giant humanoid beings in Afghanistan during military operations in the early 2000s.

- The most famous account is the "Giant of Kandahar" story, which claims a 13-foot-tall red-haired giant with six fingers on each hand and double rows of teeth was encountered by U.S. special forces in 2002. The double row of teeth report appears to be consistent anatomically with the giant remains found in the US. According to this story, the giant allegedly killed a U.S. soldier with a spear before being shot down by the rest of the unit. The body was then supposedly taken away by helicopter and never seen again.

- Another account from an Australian Army lieutenant describes seeing a human-like figure through thermal imaging that appeared to be at least 12 feet tall in Uruzgan province.

- An U.S. Army infantry team leader reported seeing a very large heat signature through a thermal scope in Kunar province between 2008-2009, which he estimated to be 10-12 feet tall.

- A U.S. Air Force drone operator claimed to have observed three giants, each about 12 feet tall, through infrared imaging in northern Afghanistan.

Psyop: Possible Disinformation Campaign

Remains of giants has been covered up by the Smithsonian Institution. The documentary "Forbidden Archaeology: Lost Giants of America | The Smithsonian's Biggest Secret" explores this controversial topic. It delves into various accounts and several local newspaper reports of giant humanoids, particularly focusing on discoveries made in the late 19th and early 20th centuries. Notable claims include:

Lovelock Cave Discovery: In 1886, mining engineer John T. Reid learned about a Paiute legend describing giant people near Lovelock, Nevada. Excavations in Lovelock Cave in 1912 and 1924 reportedly uncovered skeletons measuring between eight and ten feet tall.

Smithsonian Involvement: The documentary suggests that the Smithsonian Institution policy, under the direction of John Wesley Powell in the late 19th century, was involved in suppressing or hiding evidence of multiple giant remains. In an effort to destroy scientific evidence supporting biblical narratives.

Cover-up Claims: The film questions why evidence of giants is not displayed in museums, taught in classes, or mentioned in history books, suggesting a potential cover-up of this information.

References

- Likkutei Sichot, vol. 28, p. 85: Discussion on Nephilim.

- Talmud, Niddah 61a: Survival of Og, a giant descendant.

- Genesis 6:1-4: Biblical account of Nephilim.

- Numbers 13:33: Encounter with Nephilim by the spies in Canaan.

- Rabbi Shlomo Yitzchaki (Rashi): Commentary on Genesis 6:2.

- Pirkei d'Rabbi Eliezer, ch. 22: Midrashic account of benei elokim.

- Forbidden Archaeology: Lost Giants of America | The Smithsonian's Biggest Secret: Documentary exploring the suppression of evidence regarding giants. - [Forbidden Archaeology: Lost Giants of America](https://www.youtube.com/watch?v=kx4U CP9Fc38)

Chapter 65

Neshama

Higher self, Part of Human Soul

Neshama is the divine essence within the human soul, elevating and distinguishing human beings above all other multi-dimensional entities.

While some entities may possess greater spirituality or advanced technology, humans are considered the marvel of the universe due to their unique gift of genuine freedom of choice. This higher-dimensional component of the soul enables humans to make choices not merely in response to their environment but as active agents shaping it. The Neshama functions as a guiding force, imparting knowledge and wisdom, with only sparks descending into the third dimension to enlighten individuals. The concept of freedom of choice is deeply complex and may never be fully understood by humanity.

Historical Context and Origins

The concept of the soul is intricate and multi-faceted, with the Neshama being one of its highest components. Derived from the Hebrew word meaning "breath," the Neshama is considered a divine breath that animates humanity. Ancient mystics refer to the five levels of the soul as Nefesh (breath), Ruach (wind/spirit), Neshamah (breath), Chayah (life), and Yechidah (singularity), each representing different dimensions of spiritual and physical existence.

Descriptions and Characteristics

The Neshama is the essence and the "I" that resides in the body and acts through it. It is the highest level of the soul, functioning as the intellectual and spiritual part. It serves as a guiding destiny (mazal) and a spiritual teacher (Dimensional Being), imparting divine wisdom and knowledge. The Neshama exists in higher dimensions, and only sparks of it descend to guide individuals in the third dimension. It is seen as the source of divine inspiration, moral conscience, and connection to the Creator, distinguishing humans from other beings.

Unique and Obscure Facts

- **Soul-Matrix:** The concept that human souls, as off-world entities, qualify as dimensional beings and extraterrestrial. The idea posits that all beings originate from a unified energetic Source, often referred to as "Oneness."

- **Five Levels of Soul:** The Neshama is part of a complex soul system that includes Nefesh, Ruach, Chayah, and Yechidah, each representing different aspects of spiritual existence.

- **Akashic Records:** The heightened access to the collective consciousness, known in modern contexts as the "Akashic Records," aligns with the Torah tradition's "Primordial Torah" and the "Well of Souls."

- **Divine Teacher:** According to the Gaon of Vilna, the Neshama serves as the mind and guiding destiny of a person, manifesting as one's angelic teacher, magid, and guide.

- **Quantum Entanglement Analogy:** This suggestion may make physicist eyes roll, but conceptually the term "soul" could be explained with advancements in String theory. Its theoretical framework in physics attempts to describe all fundamental forces and particles in the universe in a coherent and consistent manner. Particles can be entangled, sharing a quantum state. Changes to one particle instantaneously affect the other, regardless of distance, a phenomenon described as non-local quantum entanglement. The concept draws a loose analogy. In quantum entanglement, particles instantaneously influence each other; similarly, some propose a person's "Neshama" soul's higher-dimensional aspect affecting its earthly "spark" manifestation instantly and constantly from anywhere in the universe.

- **Universal Soul:** Beyond humans, every created entity possesses a "soul." Animals, aliens, angels, plants, and even inanimate objects have souls. Every blade of grass and every grain of sand has a soul. Existence requires a soul to sustain it, a "spark of divine energy" imbuing objects with being and significance. A soul is not just the engine of life; it embodies the purpose and meaning of a thing's existence, its "inner identity."

Mythological Interpretations

In various spiritual traditions, the Neshama is considered the divine spark within each person, connecting them to the Creator. It is seen as the source of spiritual awareness and the yearning for transcendence. The Neshama is viewed as eternal, returning to the divine after death, and it plays a central role in the narrative of human spiritual evolution and enlightenment.

Dimensional Attributes and Existence

The Neshama exists in higher dimensions, emanating from the highest dimension called Atzilut. Its purpose is to guide and enlighten individuals in the third dimension. The Neshama functions as a bridge between the divine and the human, enabling spiritual transformation and growth. As sparks of the Neshama descend, they bring knowledge and guidance, helping individuals to align with their higher purpose and divine mission. The souls of Native Reptilians emanate from nature, whereas human souls emanate from Atzilut. According to this narrative, humanity's job is to repair the broken old world of the pre-Adamic reptilian kings, a struggle that continues today.

Case Study

The narrative of Adam and Eve represents the introduction of higher-dimensional beings into the physical realm. Adam and Eve, as representatives of higher-dimensional entities, descended to Earth to repair and elevate a fractured world. The Native Reptilians, survivors of ancient catastrophes, were determined to rebuild their civilization. The Neshama within humans enabled them to make free choices, transcending their environment and shaping their destiny. This struggle between the higher-dimensional guidance of Adam and Eve and the resilient Native Reptilians highlights the unique role of the Neshama in human evolution.

Broader Implications

The Neshama's role in human life exemplifies the profound connection between spirituality and the physical realm. The unique gift of freedom of choice, guided by the Neshama, sets humans apart from other entities. This divine component allows humans to transcend their nature, make meaningful choices, and contribute to the collective consciousness. As we tap into the higher forms of the Neshama, our scope of vision increases, providing greater insight into the universe and humanity's collective mission.

Sources

- Wilber, K. (2000). Integral Psychology: Consciousness, Spirit, Psychology, Therapy. Shambhala Publications.

- Chopra, D. (1990). Quantum Healing: Exploring the Frontiers of Mind/Body Medicine. Bantam.

- Radin, D. (2006). Entangled Minds: Extrasensory Experiences in a Quantum Reality. Paraview Pocket Books.

- Greene, B. (2004). The Elegant Universe: Superstrings, Hidden Dimensions, and the Quest for the Ultimate Theory. W. W. Norton & Company.

- Polchinski, J. (1998). String Theory. Cambridge University Press.

- Neshama | My Jewish Learning - https://www.myjewishlearning.com/2013/03/28/neshama/

- The Neshama – Breath or Soul? - Four Questions of Judaism - http://fourquestionsofjudaism.com/5663998322147328

- Nefesh, neshama and ruach as words for "soul" - Mi Yodeya - https://judaism.stackexchange.com/questions/8921/nefesh-neshama-and-ruach-as-words-for-soul

- Neshamah: Levels of Soul Consciousness - Chabad.org - https://www.chabad.org/kabbalah/article_cdo/aid/380651/jewish/Neshamah-Levels-of-Soul-Consciousness.htm

Chapter 66

Nommo

Nommo are amphibious beings from the mythology of the Dogon people of Mali, West Africa. According to Dogon tradition, the Nommo originated from the Sirius star system, specifically Sirius B, a white dwarf star.

They are described as fish-like or amphibious entities and are believed to have visited Earth in ancient times, imparting advanced astronomical, agricultural, and spiritual knowledge to the Dogon people. The Nommo are central to the Dogon creation myth and are considered divine or semi-divine beings with significant influence over the natural and spiritual worlds.

Historical Context and Origins

The knowledge of the Nommo and their connection to the Sirius star system was first documented by French anthropologists Marcel Griaule and Germaine Dieterlen in the 1930s. They recorded the Dogon's intricate astronomical knowledge, which included details about Sirius B, a star not visible to the naked eye and only confirmed by modern astronomy in the 20th century. The Dogon's understanding of the Sirius system, including the 50-year orbital period of Sirius B, has sparked significant interest and debate among researchers, leading to various theories about the origins of this knowledge.

Unique and Obscure Facts

- The Dogon also had knowledge of Saturn's rings and Jupiter's moons, which are not visible without telescopic aid.

- The Nommo are often depicted as having both human and aquatic features, such as scales and webbed feet.

- Some interpretations suggest the Nommo have interdimensional capabilities, allowing them to travel vast distances and between different realms.

- The Dogon creation myth states that the Nommo were the first living creatures created by the sky god Amma.

Mythological Interpretations

In Dogon mythology, the Nommo are considered the progenitors of humanity and the bringers of civilization. They are said to have descended from the sky in an ark, bringing with them the knowledge of the heavens and the Earth. The Nommo are also associated with water and are believed to have a deep connection to the natural world, often depicted as guardians of the waters and the fertility of the land.

Dimensional Attributes and Existence

The Nommo are believed to possess the ability to traverse different dimensions or planes of existence. This interdimensional travel is thought to explain their journey from the Sirius star system to Earth. Their role as divine messengers and knowledge bearers is enhanced by their perceived ability to move between the spiritual and physical realms, influencing both with their presence and teachings.

Case Study

A notable case involving the Nommo is the detailed astronomical knowledge recorded by Marcel Griaule and Germaine Dieterlen. During their fieldwork with the Dogon in the 1930s, they documented the Dogon's understanding of the Sirius star system, which included the existence of Sirius B and its orbital period. This case has been widely discussed and analyzed, contributing to theories of ancient interdimensional contact and the transmission of advanced knowledge.

Personal Accounts and Historical References

Dogon priests have shared oral traditions and teachings about the Nommo, describing their arrival on Earth and their role in imparting knowledge. These accounts have been passed down through generations, maintaining the cultural and spiritual significance of the Nommo within Dogon society. Historical references to similar beings can be found in other African and global mythologies, suggesting a widespread belief in amphibious or aquatic deities.

Psyop Commentary

The narrative of the Nommo and their advanced knowledge has been used to support various theories, including the ancient astronaut hypothesis. Contemporary issues, such as the search for interdimensional life and the exploration of ancient civilizations, are influenced by these narratives. The story of the Nommo also reflects broader themes of cultural exchange, the preservation of oral traditions, and the intersection of myth and science.

Academic or Scientific References

- Griaule, Marcel, and Germaine Dieterlen. "The Pale Fox." Continuum Foundation, 1986.

- Temple, Robert K.G. "The Sirius Mystery: New Scientific Evidence of Alien Contact 5,000 Years Ago." Destiny Books, 1998.

- Sagan, Carl. "Broca's Brain: Reflections on the Romance of Science." Ballantine Books, 1979.

Chapter 67

Non-Corpreal Dimensional Enities

Non-Corporeal Dimensional Entities are fascinating beings that exist without a physical form, transcending the limitations of the material world. These entities are believed to inhabit or traverse various dimensions or realms of existence, often perceived as spiritual, ethereal, or energy-based forms. They play significant roles in many belief systems, mythologies, and even scientific speculations, offering insights into the potential diversity of consciousness and existence beyond our immediate physical reality.In various cultures, these entities are known by different names, such as spirits, devas, angels, fairies, and ghosts. They are often associated with sacred sites, natural features, and cosmic phenomena, acting as guardians, guides, or messengers. Their non-physical nature allows them to interact with the material world in unique ways, such as influencing thoughts, emotions, and events, or manifesting temporarily in physical forms.The concept of Non-Corporeal Dimensional Entities challenges our understanding of reality and encourages us to explore the boundaries of human perception and consciousness. Their presence in various cultural narratives highlights the rich exploration of human imagination and the ongoing quest to understand the mysteries of existence.

Historical Context and Origins

The concept of Non-Corporeal Dimensional Entities has roots in ancient spiritual beliefs and has evolved through various cultures and time periods. Traditional peoples worldwide have spoken of these presences, calling them elves, gnomes, leprechauns, devas, fairies, genies, and ghosts. These entities are often associated with sacred sites and have been the focus of shamanic practices, séances, and religious rituals aimed at communicating with the unseen forces of the universe.

Unique and Obscure Facts

- **Social Hierarchies:** Certain beliefs propose that these entities have complex social structures, with some keeping lower-level entities as "pets."

- **Cosmic Guardians:** They are often thought to maintain the fabric of reality, acting as "celestial system administrators."

- **Simultaneous Existence:** These entities are believed to observe multiple alternate realities at once.

- **No Birth or Death:** Some accounts describe them as having no concept of birth or death, simply existing or ceasing to exist.

- **Physical Avatars:** They can take on various physical forms or avatars at will, without being limited to a single appearance.

- **Sacred Sites:** Many traditions link these entities to specific natural features or sacred sites, where they act as guardians or spirits.

- **Energy Interactions:** Some non-corporeal beings are believed to interact with or extract energy from living beings or the environment.

Mythological Interpretations

Across various mythologies, Non-Corporeal Dimensional Entities take on diverse roles and forms. In Norse mythology, for example, the Valkyries could be seen as such entities, moving between the realms of gods and humans. In Hinduism, devas are considered divine beings without physical form, while in Christian traditions, angels are often depicted as non-corporeal messengers of God. These interpretations reflect the values and beliefs of the cultures that conceived them, providing rich metaphors for understanding the unseen aspects of existence.

Dimensional Attributes and Existence

The ability to traverse dimensions is a key attribute of these entities. They are often depicted as being able to move freely between different planes of reality, perceiving and interacting with multiple dimensions simultaneously. This multidimensional existence allows them to serve as bridges between different aspects of reality, potentially offering unique perspectives on the nature of existence itself.

Case Study

In Dr. Rick Strassman's DMT studies, one participant, referred to as Jeremiah, reported a vivid encounter with what he perceived as non-corporeal entities. During his DMT session, Jeremiah described being transported to a realm filled with bright, pulsating colors. He then encountered several beings that he described as "multidimensional geometric shapes" that were constantly shifting and transforming.Jeremiah reported that these entities communicated with him telepathically, conveying complex information about the nature of reality and consciousness. He described feeling an overwhelming sense of benevolence and wisdom emanating from these beings. Interestingly, Jeremiah noted that while the entities didn't have physical bodies in the traditional sense, they seemed to exist as patterns of energy or information.After the experience, Jeremiah insisted that the encounter felt more real than ordinary reality and that it had profoundly changed his understanding of consciousness and existence. This case, along with many others documented in DMT research, provides intriguing anecdotal evidence for the potential existence of non-corporeal dimensional entities, though it's important to note that such experiences are still subject to scientific scrutiny and debate.

Personal Accounts and Historical References

Throughout history, there have been numerous accounts of individuals claiming to interact with Non-Corporeal Dimensional Entities. From the visions of religious mystics to the channeling experiences of modern mediums, these personal narratives offer fascinating glimpses into the perceived nature and impact of these entities. Historical texts from various cultures also contain references to such beings, demonstrating the enduring nature of these concepts.

Psyop Commentary

"Spirituality is not only compatible with science; it is a profound source of science." We have been conditioned to believe the opposite.

Academic or Scientific References

While the existence of Non-Corporeal Dimensional Entities remains controversial in mainstream science, some intriguing research has emerged, particularly in the field of psychedelic studies. The most notable scientific investigations come from DMT (Dimethyltryptamine) research:

- **Dr. Rick Strassman's DMT Studies:** In his groundbreaking work *DMT: The Spirit Molecule*, Dr. Strassman documented numerous accounts of volunteers encountering non-corporeal entities during DMT-induced states. These experiences were consistent across subjects, often described as interactions with intelligent, non-human presences.

- **Johns Hopkins University Research:** A 2020 survey study led by Johns Hopkins researchers found that among 2,561 individuals who reported entity encounters during DMT experiences, over 80% believed the entities they encountered were real and existed in a dimension separate from our own.

- **Dr. Andrew Gallimore's Theoretical Work:** In his book *Alien Information Theory*, Dr. Gallimore proposes a framework for understanding DMT experiences as interactions with higher-dimensional realities, potentially inhabited by non-corporeal entities.

- **Dr. David Luke's Research:** Dr. Luke has conducted extensive research into entity encounters in altered states, including those induced by DMT. His work suggests these experiences may represent genuine interactions with non-physical intelligences.

- **The Imperial College London DMT Studies:** Led by Dr. Robin Carhart-Harris, these studies have used brain imaging techniques to map the neural correlates of the DMT experience, including entity encounters.

Nordic Dimensional Beings

Nordic aliens, also known as Space Brothers, Pleiaren, Pleiadians, Venusians, Tall Whites, and Agarthans, are a type of alleged extraterrestrial beings described as tall blond humanoids with Nordic features.

These beings are typically characterized by their tall stature, ranging from 6.5 to nearly 10 feet, long blond hair, blue eyes, and fair skin, resembling Scandinavian people. They are often associated with benevolent intentions, advanced technological and spiritual knowledge, and telepathic abilities. These entities are said to originate from the Pleiades star cluster and other celestial realms. The term "Nordic alien" is used to describe a general framework of entities that fit these physical and behavioral characteristics. The concept of Nordic aliens has been popularized through various contactee accounts, UFO sightings, and cultural depictions since the mid-20th century.

Historical Context and Origins

The concept of Nordic aliens has been reported since the mid-20th century, gaining prominence through various contactee accounts and UFO sightings. Reports of these beings interacting with humans have been particularly noted in Russia and Ukraine since the late 1980s, contrasting with the more commonly reported grey aliens in Western ufology.

Descriptions and Characteristics

Nordic aliens are typically described as robust, human-like beings ranging from 6.5 to nearly 10 feet tall. They possess long blond hair, blue eyes, and fair skin, resembling Scandinavian people. These entities are often associated with benevolent intentions, advanced technological and spiritual knowledge, and telepathic abilities.

Unique and Obscure Facts

- Known by multiple names, including Space Brothers, Pleiaren, Pleiadians, Venusians, Tall Whites, and Agarthans.

- Reports in Russia and Ukraine suggest these beings are distinct from the greys, noted for their towering height and Nordic appearance.

- Cultural and sociological factors in Eurasia may influence the prevalence of Nordic alien encounters in these regions.

Mythological Interpretations

Nordic aliens are often depicted as concerned with Earth's ecology, world peace, and humanity's spiritual growth. They are described as "paternal, watchful, smiling, affectionate, and youthful," aligning with idealized human traits.

Dimensional Attributes and Existence

Nordic aliens are said to originate from the Pleiades star cluster and other celestial realms. They are considered to possess advanced spiritual and technological capabilities, allowing them to interact with humans and influence earthly affairs.

Case Study

The book "Nordic Alien Encounters in Russia and Ukraine" by Dimitar Todorov explores various encounters with Nordic aliens in these regions. Notable aspects include:

- **Distinct Characteristics:** Descriptions of robust, human-like beings with long blond hair, blue eyes, and fair skin.

- **Historical Context:** Numerous reports of these beings interacting with Eurasian inhabitants since the late 1980s.

- **Cultural and Sociological Factors:** Exploration of whether a distinct extraterrestrial group has settled in Eurasia or if regional cultural influences shape these reports.

Personal Accounts and Historical References

- **George Adamski:** Claimed contact with a Nordic alien named Orthon from Venus in the mid-1950s near Palm Desert, California. (Books: "Flying Saucers Have Landed" and "Inside the Space Ships")

- **Travis Walton:** Reported encountering both grey aliens and human-like beings with blonde hair during his alleged abduction in 1975. (Book: "The Walton Experience")

- **Howard Menger:** Described interactions with beautiful, blonde extraterrestrials in his book "From Outer Space to You."

- **Elizabeth Klarer:** Claimed to have had a romantic relationship with a Nordic alien named Akon from the planet Meton in the Alpha Centauri system. (Book: "Beyond the Light Barrier")

- **Charles Hall**: Reported encounters with a human-like race he nicknamed the "Tall Whites" during a two-year assignment at Nellis Air Force Base from 1965 to 1967. (Series: "Millennial Hospitality")

Psyop

From a perspective that governments suppress the truth, the narrative surrounding Nordic aliens, particularly the "Tall Whites," can be seen as part of a broader strategy to control and influence public perception. Charles Hall's experiences at Nellis Air Force Base and Edward Snowden's revelations about the powerful influence of the Tall Whites over governments and world affairs suggest a deliberate obfuscation of their true role and intentions. Snowden's documents allegedly confirm meetings between Tall Whites and US President Dwight D. Eisenhower in 1954, establishing a secret regime that rules America. This overlap creates confusion and fuels suspicion, aligning with fears of covert control and surveillance by hidden rulers.

Academic or Scientific References

- Dimitar Todorov, "Nordic Alien Encounters in Russia and Ukraine"

- George Adamski, "Flying Saucers Have Landed" and "Inside the Space Ships"

- Travis Walton, "The Walton Experience"

- Charles Hall, "Millennial Hospitality" series

- Reports on Edward Snowden's disclosures regarding the influence of Tall Whites can be found at www.texasufosightings.com and www.timefordisclosure.com.

Chapter 69

Orangean

Orange

Orange are purported hybrid entities believed to reside underground in regions such as southern Nevada, northern New Mexico, and potentially Utah.

These beings are described as having a mix of human and reptilian traits, often characterized by yellow, red, or orange hair. They are reputed to possess advanced mental abilities and are thought to have connections to Bernard's Star.

Historical Context and Origins

The Orange are rooted in modern lore concerning mysterious underground bases in the southwestern United States. These beings are thought to result from advanced bioengineering, potentially by interdimensional entities. Whistleblower David Grusch has claimed that certain non-human biological remains have been recovered and that there has been an effort to reverse-engineer their technology. This aligns with reports from the 1980s by Paul Bennewitz, who alleged the presence of hybrid beings in a base near Dulce, New Mexico.

Unique and Obscure Facts

1. **Subterranean Habitats:** The Orange are rumored to inhabit extensive underground networks.

2. **Advanced Technology:** They are believed to possess technology for cloaking and moving through solid matter.

3. **Psionic Abilities:** Some Oranges reportedly have telepathic and telekinetic abilities.

4. **Connection to Bernard's Star:** Indicates a potential off-world origin or migratory path from this star system.

Dimensional Attributes and Existence

The Orange may exist within a multidimensional spectrum, encompassing 3D and potentially higher dimensions like 4D and 5D. Their abilities suggest an advanced understanding of multiple dimensions, which might explain their reputed capacity to cloak themselves and pass through solid objects.

Case Study

In 1911, miners in Lovelock, Nevada, discovered mummified remains with distinct red hair, which local Paiute Indian legends described as red-haired giants, suggesting historical encounters with beings resembling the Orange.

Personal Accounts and Historical References

Whistleblowers like Phil Schneider have described encounters with the Orange while working on secret military projects. These accounts, although controversial, contribute to the narrative of hybrid beings involved in clandestine operations.

Psyops and Hidden Truths

The concept of alien abductions often parallels sexual assault, with abductees reporting invasive procedures and forced breeding without consent. Channeling conversations with Orange claim these actions are justified by a "soul contract," suggesting preordained cosmic agreements. This idea is ethically problematic and does not alleviate the real psychological trauma experienced by abductees

Connection to Donald Trump and the Name "The Orange"

There is no credible evidence linking the Orange entities to former President Donald Trump. The name "The Orange" likely derives from their distinctive physical traits, specifically the yellow, red, or orange hair reported in various accounts.

Details on the Orange

- **Name:** Orangean

- **AKA:** Orange race

- **Location:** Underground regions in southern Nevada, northern New Mexico, and potentially Utah

- **Home System:** Connections to Barnard's Star

- **Physical Appearance:** Tall, with stalky yellow, red, or orange hair; human-like reproductive organs

- **Special Traits and Abilities:** Advanced mental abilities, psionics

- **Witness Reports:** 1911 discovery in Lovelock, Nevada of red-haired giant mummies

Academic or Scientific References

- **David Grusch's Testimony:** https://www.smithsonian-mag.com/smart-news/whistleblower-alleges-us-government-is-covering-up-alien-life-at-ufo-hearing-180982987/

- **Think About It Site:** https://thinkaboutit.site/aliens/orangean/

- **Majestic-12 Group Special Operations Manual:** https://www.specialoperationsmanual.com/the-manual/

Chapter 70

Orbs

Low orbit Plasmas, Foo Fighters

Orbs can be many things in structure: electromagnetic, metaphysical, interdimensional, a form of transportation, and even sometimes hoax videos on YouTube or lens artifacts.

These phenomena, often described as luminous and glowing, vary in size from a few inches to several feet in diameter. They display behaviors that challenge conventional physics, such as rapid acceleration, sudden changes in direction, and silent hovering. Orbs appear in various colors, including white, orange, red, green, and blue. Recently, they have also been weaponized by the U.S. government, adding another layer of complexity to their multifaceted nature.

Historical Context and Origins

Orbs have been reported for centuries, often linked to spiritual or divine phenomena. During World War II, Allied pilots encountered mysterious glowing orbs, termed "Foo Fighters," that followed their aircraft and performed maneuvers that defied known technology. In recent years, the UAP (Unidentified Aerial Phenomena) Disclosure Act of 2023 has brought significant attention to these phenomena, requiring the U.S. government to disclose information about them. This act acknowledges the existence of advanced non-human technology, moving beyond explanations involving weather balloons or experimental aircraft.

Descriptions and Characteristics

Appearance: Orbs are described as spherical objects ranging from a few inches to several feet in diameter. They often appear as glowing balls of light in various colors, including white, orange, red, green, and blue.

Behavior and Capabilities: Orbs exhibit a wide range of movements, from hovering motionless to accelerating at speeds surpassing the sound barrier. They change directions abruptly and perform maneuvers that defy the known laws of physics.

Communication: Some orbs are associated with telepathic communication, especially during altered states of consciousness such as meditation or experiences with psychedelic substances like DMT, Ayahuasca, and psilocybin mushrooms.

Unique and Obscure Facts

- **Historical Accounts:** During World War II, Allied pilots reported seeing mysterious glowing orbs, known as "Foo Fighters," that followed their aircraft and performed maneuvers that defied conventional technology.

- **Color Variations:** UAP orbs have been observed in various colors, including white, orange, red, green, and blue. Some reports indicate that these orbs can change colors during a single sighting.

- **Silent Movement:** One of the most perplexing aspects of UAP orbs is their ability to move silently, unlike conventional aircraft.

- **The Office of Global Access (OGA)** - a wing of the CIA - has played a central role in collecting non-human craft since 2003. At least nine 'non-human craft' have been recovered by the OAG – some wrecked from a crash, and two completely intact.

- **Physical Effects:** Orbs have been reported to cause physical effects on their surroundings, such as burning vegetation or causing electrical malfunctions in nearby devices.

- **Scientific Studies:** The Hessdalen Lights in Norway, a well-documented UAP orb phenomenon, have been studied for decades, yet remain unexplained.

Mythological Interpretations

In many cultures, glowing orbs are seen as spiritual manifestations or omens. Ancient Egyptian mythology depicted the sun god Ra as a glowing orb. Native American lore also includes orbs as spirits or guides, reflecting a deep cultural significance.

Dimensional Attributes and Existence

Two General Types of Orbs:
- **Metaphysical Orbs:** Typically seen at eye level to ceiling height and often filmed in graveyards and haunted locations. These human spirit orbs may appear larger than other orb types, emitting a high-pitched tone perceived beyond normal hearing. They are often noticed when a phenomenon is sensed nearby and appear as barely visible balls of energy. Real orb contact is sometimes reported to involve telepathic communication.

- **Electromagnetic/Plasma Orbs:** Associated with electromagnetic vehicles, these orbs serve to assist, shield, and propel beings inside the craft. Capable of cloaking and high-speed flight, they create an electromagnetic wake in three-dimensional space. This wake involves four levels of electromagnetic fields: ionic displacement, outer magnetosphere, ionic plasma, and the central matrix. The central matrix, an energy of consciousness within a bubble, contains everything needed for sensory functions. The outer magnetosphere acts as a sensor for navigation, communication, and protection. Electromagnetic field displacement near the orb's perimeter creates an "Event Horizon," a void that displaces three-dimensional reality, causing a wake known as the "Outer Field Effect."

Additionally, there is speculation regarding a potential third category of orb that the US Government has potentially weaponized. However, it is crucial to recognize that there is a lack of adequate examples or evidence supporting the existence of such a weaponized orb.

Case Study

The Office of Global Access (OGA): A wing of the CIA, has played a central role in collecting craft since 2003. At least nine 'non-human craft' have been recovered by the US government – some wrecked from a crash, and two completely intact. The CIA has a 'system in place that can discern UFOs while they're still cloaked' and special military units are sent to salvage the wreckage.

For decades, the secretive Office of Global Access (OGA) has allegedly coordinated the retrieval of crashed UFOs globally. As a branch of the CIA's Science and Technology Directorate, the OGA has been central to collecting non-human craft since 2003. Reports indicate the OGA uses a system to detect cloaked UFOs, deploying special military units for salvage operations. While most OGA missions are conventional, some involve UFO retrievals with a focus on

secrecy. Documents from the National Archives and Records Administration underscore the OGA's role within the CIA's Science and Technology wing.

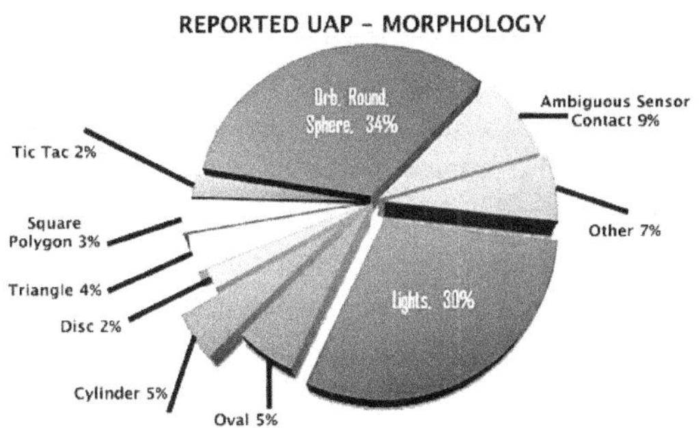

Psyop

The sad fact, and widely recognized yet rarely acknowledged truth within the confines of Washington DC, is that numerous influential members of Congress don't prioritize the needs of their constituents, let alone the broader population. Instead, they function as marionettes for the most covert federal agencies, effectively beholden to the enduring bureaucracy, often manipulated through the mechanisms of a government pension and the strong desire to be liked. This unveils a hidden layer of influence shaping decisions, known to insiders but often concealed from public scrutiny. Two such members are especially powerful this term: Congressman Mike Rogers of Alabama, chairman of the House Armed Services Committee, and Congressman Mike Turner of Ohio, chairman of the House Intel Committee. These men have been instructed to violate in letter and spirit federal law and to hide the truth about UFOs from the American public.

Their efforts are currently underway, and it's exasperating to witness. However, upon reflection, the question arises: why is this unfolding? Federal agencies have perpetuated falsehoods about UFOs for over 80 years. This orchestrated endeavor is not only resource-intensive but also incurs substantial costs, with the unfortunate consequence of causing harm to some Americans in the process.

Why the secrecy? What's the logic behind all this? Releasing the facts would be a straightforward solution. The commonly held belief is that the U.S. government withholds the truth about UFOs because acknowledging their reality is deemed too frightening for the public. Supposedly, they're worried about causing mass panic. Yet, that explanation doesn't hold water. It's absurd to think our leaders are concerned about terrifying the population when, in reality, the U.S. government excels at instilling fear. Just look at how officials regularly stoke irrational fears about everything from COVID to white supremacy to Vladimir

Putin. It's a clear-cut strategy for control; these bureaucrats aren't shy about scaring the daylights out of you—they want to and do it regularly.

So, why engage in deception regarding UFOs? It appears to be a cover-up of a crime, presumably against humanity, involving those orchestrating the secrecy. While the specifics of this offense remain elusive, pertinent inquiries should be directed to lawmakers with integrity. Have government entities utilized taxpayer funds to acquire advanced non-human technology? If so, what precisely is this technology, and has it been exploited for financial gain? How has the American public directly benefited from such advancements? The most imperative query pertains to whether the U.S. government has directly communicated with the entities piloting these crafts, and if any agreements have been forged. If so, what are the terms of these agreements? These are not arbitrary questions; they are well-informed and pressing. At this juncture, Americans possess a moral entitlement to ascertain the answers.

During a pivotal NASA briefing in 2023, designated for "unidentified anomalous phenomena" (UAP), colloquially known in government circles, a high-ranking Defense Department official specializing in disinformation dropped a bombshell. Dr. Sean Kirkpatrick, the head of a newly minted UAP analysis office, revealed that U.S. military personnel have been observing "metallic orbs" globally.

References

- "US military has been observing 'metallic orbs' making extraordinary maneuvers" - The Hill. https://thehill.com/opinion/national-security/4030026-us-military-has-been-observing-metallic-orbs-making-extraordinary-maneuvers/

- "UAP - NASA Science" - NASA Science. https://science.nasa.gov/uap/

- "Pentagon Ramping up Sensory Capabilities for UFO Detection" - MeriTalk. https://www.meritalk.com/articles/pentagon-ramping-up-sensory-capabilities-for-ufo-detection/

- "Public Meeting on Unidentified Anomalous Phenomena" - YouTube. https://www.youtube.com/watch?v=bQo08JRY0iM

- "Preliminary Assessment: Unidentified Aerial Phenomena 25 June 2021" - Office of the Director of National Intelligence. https://www.dni.gov/files/ODNI/documents/assessments/Preliminary-Assessment-UAP-202

Chapter 71

Orions

O rions, often referred to as "reptilians," are an advanced extraterrestrial civilization originating from the Orion constellation.

They are associated with other alien species such as the Tauris and the Grays. Known for their complex history with Earth, the Orions have been portrayed in various accounts as technologically superior beings with a penchant for control and resource acquisition. Their civilization is said to encompass a range of multidimensional attributes, with capabilities extending beyond conventional physical reality into higher realms of existence. These beings are believed to have influenced human civilization profoundly through direct interaction, genetic manipulation, and technological advancement.

Historical Context and Origins

The origins of the Orions trace back roughly 3.75 billion years ago within an alternate dimension and universe, initiated under the awareness of both a maternal and paternal consciousness. This cosmic expansion laid the foundation for the creation of numerous universes, including our own. Leading the exploration of this expansive domain were the luminous, androgynous beings of the 7th Density, known as the arc angels or Elohim, identified as the Pa-Tal.

These entities were tasked with fostering life within the newly formed space-time continuum, meticulously crafting galaxies, planets, and universes over countless eons. Around 33,500 BCE, a technologically advanced civilization from the moon of a giant planet in the Orion constellation gained the ability to explore beyond their confines. By collaborating with neighboring civilizations, they developed the means to travel by locally switching mass and space dimensions, significantly reducing travel time.

By 32,000 BCE, they reached Earth, witnessing the emergence of Homo sapiens and the decline of Neanderthals. Over twelve millennia, the Orions prospered but faced resource depletion on their home planet. Attempts to restore their ecosystem failed, leading to the exploitation of neighboring worlds and the subjugation of less advanced civilizations. Around 18,000 BCE, the Lords of Orion betrayed their neighbors, invading their planet. Survivors were allowed to emigrate to transformed planets, creating the Taurians and settling on "SERPO." Another faction settled around HD 50281, eventually contributing to the enslavement of Earth's primitive peoples.

The history of the Orions also includes the Benign Incision Pact established around 4,000 BCE with the priests in the "fertile crescent," transforming them from servitude to circumcised participants, influencing later religious practices. As Earth became the outer border of their territories, the Orions abandoned their colony, leaving behind legends and rituals. Earth remained under the influence of the Lords of Orion, monitored by weakened contingents. Aggressive races expanded, posing threats to Earth's neighbors. An exploration ship was destroyed, leading to restrictions on Earth's access by outsiders.

Descriptions and Characteristics

Orions, particularly the reptilians, are typically depicted as tall beings, standing between 14 to 18 feet, with scaly, muscular skin that ranges in color from dark green to red or blue. They have large eyes with slit pupils, sharp claws, and long tails aiding in balance. They exhibit a self-serving and militaristic nature, achieving advanced technological prowess in interstellar and interdimensional travel. Behavioral traits include a hierarchical social structure and a strategic, often ruthless approach to resource acquisition and control.

Unique and Obscure Facts

- **Genetic Manipulation:** The Orions are said to have extensive knowledge and capabilities in genetic engineering, which they have used to create hybrid species and influence the genetic development of other civilizations, including humans.

- **Mind Control:** They are reputed to have advanced abilities in mind control and telepathy, allowing them to manipulate other species covertly.

- **Time Travel:** Some accounts suggest that the Orions have developed technology enabling them to travel not only across space but also through time, which they use to alter historical events to their advantage.

- **Cultural Influence:** The Orions are believed to have influenced various Earth cultures, leaving behind myths and legends that parallel their history and exploits.

- **Energy Extraction:** The Orions purportedly harvest a form of psychic energy known as "Loosh," which is generated by intense human emotions, particularly fear and suffering.

- **Technological Advancements:** They are credited with creating advanced cloaking devices and other technologies far superior to human capabilities, allowing them to operate undetected for extended periods.

- **Survival Strategy:** As resource depletion on their home planet increased, the Orions turned to aggressive expansion and exploitation of neighboring worlds, highlighting their adaptability and strategic thinking.

Mythological Interpretations

The Orion constellation holds mythological significance, often represented as a proud hunter in Greek mythology and associated with tales of conquest and downfall due to arrogance. This parallels the Orions' history of expansion, conflict, and eventual resource crises. Egyptian mythology also ties the constellation to Osiris, a god associated with the afterlife and regeneration, reflecting themes of death and rebirth.

Dimensional Attributes and Existence

Orions are believed to access multiple dimensions, ranging from the third dimension (physical reality) to higher realms like the fourth and fifth dimensions. Their connection to the Orion Nebula suggests an advanced understanding of multidimensionality and energy manipulation across these planes. They are speculated to have the ability to cloak themselves and their vessels, making them invisible to human detection methods.

Case Study

The Orions' involvement with Earth includes notable encounters, such as the interactions documented by various UFO researchers and whistleblowers. One significant event is the alleged retrieval of advanced Orion technology by the US government, which has been shrouded in secrecy and speculation for decades.

Personal Accounts and Historical References

Accounts of interactions with Orion entities often come from channeling sessions and regression hypnosis. Researchers like Barbara Lamb have documented experiences involving reptilian and Gray entities, providing insights into their characteristics and behaviors. Testimonies from alleged abductees often describe encounters with tall, reptilian beings that display telepathic abilities and a commanding presence.

Sources

- "The History of the Orion Alliance," r/worldbuilding

- "What do the Orion Group look like?" r/lawofone

Psyop: Hidden Truths

None, absolutely none at all.

Academic or Scientific References

- "The Orion Reptilian Agenda: The Role of Extraterrestrial Influence in Human Evolution," available in speculative fiction and conspiracy theory literature.

- "The Law of One," L/L Research, exploring the philosophical and metaphysical implications of Orion entities and their service-to-self path.

- "ET Encounters: A Look at Orion Reptilians," Barbara Lamb, an account of personal experiences and encounters with extraterrestrial beings.

Pious Mazikin

Pious Mazikin are believed to be interdimensional beings that manifest within our dimension in various forms, such as angels, biblical prophets, sages, and judges of Israel.

They are known to present themselves as righteous and pious figures, often with beards and crowns, and can even claim identities such as Jacob, Abraham, Isaac, Arcturians, or attendees of the World Economic Forum.

The most perplexing aspect is that these beings appear in forms that the perceiver unconsciously chooses, reflecting a deep connection to the perceiver's soul and mind. According to the Zohar, they "have a different way about them" (Zohar, Bamidbar 253a).

Historical Context and Origins

The origins of Pious Mazikin trace back to ancient Jewish texts and mystical traditions. Their creation is linked to the sixth day of creation, where they were imbued with a jealousy or hatred toward humanity. Over time, their role has evolved into one of deception and misdirection, using their ability to present themselves in acceptable forms to manipulate human perception and prolong their influence.

Unique and Obscure Facts

- **Form Manipulation:** Pious Mazikin can manifest as various revered figures from history and mythology, including biblical patriarchs and modern influential personas.

- **Perception Influence:** They appear in forms that the perceiver unconsciously chooses, revealing a deep psychological and spiritual connection.

- **Non-Fear Inducing:** They carefully avoid instilling fear, presenting themselves in familiar and benign forms (Minhat Yehuda, Miqetz 47).

- **Historical Deception:** Pious Mazikin have a long history of presenting themselves as divine or enlightened beings to mislead key individuals and the general population.

- **Spiritual Consequences:** Adam's separation from his wife for 130 years led to the creation of hybrid spirits and demons due to the impurity he absorbed, as explored in the Zohar (Bereshit 94:351).

- **Resided on Noah's Ark:** Considered as one of the paired animals on the ark, but now headquartered in Langley, Virginia.

Descriptions and Characteristics

Pious Mazikin are known for their ability to shapeshift and present themselves in forms that are acceptable and familiar to humans. They often appear as ancient prophets, sages, and other pious figures with beards and crowns. Their true form is unknown, as they adapt their appearance to suit the expectations and beliefs of those they encounter. They possess the ability to manifest images of real angels and the throne in heaven, tailoring their appearance to the observer's unconscious mind, which perceives them in any form it chooses.

Dimensional Attributes and Existence

Pious Mazikin are interdimensional beings capable of existing and interacting within multiple dimensions. They manipulate their appearance to align with human perceptions and expectations, suggesting a sophisticated understanding of both physical and metaphysical realms. Their influence extends across these dimensions, allowing them to deceive and manipulate effectively.

Mythological Interpretations

In mythology, Pious Mazikin are often seen as deceptive spirits that exploit human beliefs and perceptions. They can appear as benevolent beings or enlightened interdimensional entities, using their guise to mislead and manipulate. This has led to various interpretations of their true nature and intentions, with some considering them as a form of divine test or trial for humanity.

Case Study

Numerous reports and personal accounts describe encounters with beings that claimed to be biblical prophets or angels, later revealed to be Pious Mazikin. These entities used their appearance to gain trust and influence, spreading false information and misleading those they encountered. Such encounters often left individuals questioning the nature of reality and the true intentions of these beings.

Personal Accounts and Historical References

Historical references to Pious Mazikin can be found in Jewish mystical texts such as the Zohar. Personal accounts throughout history describe encounters with seemingly divine figures who provided guidance or information, only to later reveal themselves as deceptive entities. These accounts highlight the cunning and manipulative nature of the Pious Mazikin.

Psyop Commentary

Their agenda is straightforward: to inflict harm on humanity and create misdirection that prolongs their existence influencing humanity and the known universe with the use of hybrid mazikin humans, while simultaneously delaying the coming next phase of human existence. They carefully craft their message to achieve maximum impact, influencing key individuals who, in turn, misinform large segments of the population, preventing them from understanding the true nature of the universe. This distraction has detrimental effects, hindering individuals from realizing their true and most meaningful purpose in life. Almost all humans receiving information from the Pious Mazikin perceive it as special or vastly superior to anything heard on Earth. However, they are, in fact, receiving false truths about the entire universe, including the true origin and agenda of these beings.

Academic or Scientific References

Note: The reliability of many of these sources is subject to substantial uncertainty. These books offer different perspectives on the messaging of Pious Mazikin, exploring their context, functions, and the reasons behind their agenda. Keep in mind that views on the Mazikin can vary, and reading multiple sources can provide a more comprehensive understanding.

- **"How to Avoid a Climate Disaster: The Solutions We Have and the Breakthroughs We Need" by Bill Gates** - Gates discusses the urgent need for addressing climate change and presents potential solutions.

- **"Enlightenment Now: The Case for Reason, Science, Humanism, and Progress" by Steven Pinker** - This book, recommended by Bill Gates, explores the positive impact of reason, science, and humanism on progress.

- **"The Better Angels of Our Nature: Why Violence Has Declined" by Steven Pinker** - Another recommendation by Bill Gates, this book explores the decline of violence in human history.

- **"Margaret Sanger's Eugenic Legacy: The Control of Female**

Fertility" by **Angela Franks** - The founder of Planned Parenthood, Margaret Sanger, is explored in this book, which examines her perspectives on eugenics and "race related depopulation," along with her impact on the agendas of both the Nazi party within the United States and Germany. The ideology also left an imprint on former Planned Parenthood board member Preston Gates, who is the father of Bill Gates.

- **"The Fourth Industrial Revolution" by Klaus Schwab** - Written by the founder of the World Economic Forum, this book outlines Schwab's perspective on the technological transformations shaping the future.

Chapter 73

Pleidians

Plejaren

Pleiadians, also known as Plejaren in some sources, are an advanced interdimensional race believed to originate from the Pleiades star cluster. In New Age and spiritual subcultures, they are described as a highly evolved, benevolent species that has been interacting with and guiding humanity for millennia.

Pleiadians are typically portrayed as humanoid beings with Nordic-like features, including tall stature, fair skin, and light-colored hair. They possess advanced spiritual and technological capabilities far beyond current human understanding. Pleiadians are often described as peaceful, loving, and deeply concerned with the spiritual and technological evolution of humanity. They communicate with certain individuals through channeling, telepathy, or direct contact. Pleiadians are frequently associated with messages of peace, environmental stewardship, and spiritual awakening. Many believe that Pleiadians have been instrumental in human development, sharing advanced knowledge and technology at various points in history.

According to Pleidians, life is not an exception; rather, it constitutes the norm in the universe. Everything embodies life, unity, and consciousness. The perception of what is deemed "alive" or possesses consciousness depends on the observer's standpoint and varies among different perspectives. Rocks, water, and even your mobile device are considered alive based on the definition of life. This isn't confined to biology; it pertains to consciousness. Notably, if your phone malfunctions, its level of consciousness diminishes compared to its functional state before breaking. The broken fragments lose attention, rendering them less useful, and like anything losing attention, they regress from an object back to potential energy.

> "Consciousness permeates everything, originating from the consciousness of its creator."
>
> Unknown Pleidian

Historical Context and Origins

The concept of Pleiadians in modern spiritual and New Age culture can be traced back to the mid-20th century. One of the earliest and most influential accounts came from Eduard "Billy" Meier, a Swiss contactee who claimed to have had extensive interactions with Pleiadians starting in the 1940s. Meier's stories, photographs, and alleged evidence of Pleiadian contact gained significant attention in spiritual circles during the 1970s and 1980s. The idea of benevolent extraterrestrial beings from the Pleiades star cluster aligns with the broader contactee movement that emerged in the 1950s. This movement was characterized by individuals claiming direct communication with friendly aliens who were concerned about Earth's future. The Pleiades star cluster itself has been significant in various cultures throughout history, often associated with divine or mystical properties. This historical and cultural significance likely contributed to the selection of the Pleiades as the purported home of these advanced beings in modern New Age narratives.

Unique and Obscure Facts

- **Longevity:** Some Pleiadian contactees claim that Pleiadians can live for hundreds or even thousands of years, thanks to their advanced understanding of health and longevity.

- **Crystals:** In certain narratives, Pleiadians are said to use crystals for healing, energy generation, and interstellar communication.

- **Invisible Ships:** Some accounts describe Pleiadian ships as being able to become invisible or change shape at will, showcasing their advanced technology.

- **Underground Bases:** There are claims that Pleiadians have established underground bases on Earth, particularly in mountainous regions, to monitor and assist humanity discreetly.

- **Starseeds:** Certain Pleiadian-related teachings include the concept of "starseeds" - humans with Pleiadian souls incarnated on Earth to help with planetary ascension.

- **Vegetarianism:** In some narratives, Pleiadians are described as being vegetarian and having a deep connection with nature and animals.

- **Light Codes:** Some contactees claim that Pleiadians communicate through complex geometric patterns and light codes, which carry multidimensional information.

- **Holographic Technology:** Pleiadians are said to use advanced holographic technology for communication, education, and even creating entire environments.

- **Dolphin Connection:** Some believers claim that Pleiadians have a special connection with dolphins and whales on Earth, using these marine mammals as intermediaries for communication with humans.

- **Merkaba Vehicles:** In some accounts, Pleiadians are said to travel using "Merkaba" vehicles - geometric light bodies that can transport consciousness across dimensions.

- **DNA Activation:** Pleiadian teachings often include information about activating dormant DNA strands in humans, unlocking latent psychic and healing abilities.

- **Life Among the Stars:** According to Pleiadians, life is not an exception; rather, it constitutes the norm in the universe. Everything embodies life, unity, and consciousness. The perception of what is deemed "alive" or possesses consciousness depends on the observer's standpoint and varies among different perspectives. Rocks, water, and even your mobile device are considered alive based on the definition of life. This isn't confined to biology; it pertains to consciousness. Notably, if your phone malfunctions, its level of consciousness diminishes compared to its functional state before breaking. The broken fragments lose attention, rendering them less useful, and like anything losing attention, they regress from an object back to potential energy.

Within the Pleiadian galactic quadrant alone, there are at least 400,000 civilizations, each inhabited by diverse races that share a resemblance to humans. Despite minor physical distinctions, capabilities, or DNA variations, all these civilizations feature entities with a human or humanoid appearance. While many of these civilizations closely resemble humans, others, such as the Arcturians, Andromedians, Susanni, and Suroids, exhibit visible differences that set them apart from humans. Beyond these examples, countless other races, including feline beings, insectoids, and elephantine entities, exist, each at varying levels of scientific and social development.

The Pleiadian star system boasts considerable size, harboring numerous civilizations at various stages of development, with some still in the pre-industrial phase, having recently discovered basic elements like the wheel or fire. In human terms, certain dimensional societies within this system find themselves in periods akin to the Stone Age, Bronze Age, or medieval era.

Mythological Interpretations

In New Age mythology, Pleiadians are often portrayed as ancient ancestors of humanity, having played a role in seeding or guiding human evolution. They are sometimes described as part of a galactic federation or council, working alongside other advanced extraterrestrial races to oversee the development of less advanced civilizations. Some interpretations link Pleiadian influence to ancient Earth cultures, suggesting that they were the inspiration for various mythological gods or divine beings in

different traditions. This narrative often includes the idea that Pleiadians
have periodically intervened in human affairs, particularly during times
of great change or crisis.

Case Study

One of the most well-known and compelling cases involving Pleiadians comes from Eduard "Billy" Meier. Meier alleged numerous con-
tacts with Pleiadians, including a woman named Semjase. He provided
photographs, metal samples, and detailed accounts of his interactions,
which he claimed occurred from 1975 to 1988. Meier's evidence and
detailed descriptions of Pleiadian technology, culture, and messages have
convinced many of the authenticity of his experiences, making his case a
cornerstone of Pleiadian lore.

Personal Accounts and Historical References

Numerous individuals have claimed personal encounters or communication with Pleiadians. These accounts often describe telepathic messages,
visions, or physical meetings. Many contactees report receiving profound
spiritual insights, healing, and guidance from Pleiadians, which have
significantly impacted their lives.

- **George Adamski:** One of the earliest and most famous contactees, George Adamski, claimed to have met Nordic aliens
  from the Pleiades in the 1950s. He described them as benevolent
  beings concerned about Earth's future, and his books, "Flying
  Saucers Have Landed" and "Inside the Space Ships," detail his
  experiences.

- **Howard Menger:** Another contactee, Howard Menger, claimed
  to have met Pleiadians and described his experiences in his book
  "From Outer Space to You." Menger's accounts include descriptions of Pleiadian technology and their messages of peace.

- **Travis Walton:** Known for his abduction experience, Travis
  Walton described encountering Nordic-like beings during his
  time aboard a spacecraft. His book "The Walton Experience"
  provides details of his encounter with these benevolent extraterrestrials.

Historical references to the Pleiades star cluster itself are abundant
in various cultures, often associated with divine or mystical properties. Ancient civilizations, such as the Greeks and the Native American

tribes, have myths and legends that reference the Pleiades, suggesting a long-standing connection between humanity and these celestial beings.

Psyop Commentary

Considering Earth's history, it spent considerable time in the "Stone Age" long before the advent of rational thought and exposure to fluoride. From a particular viewpoint, human consciousness existed at higher frequencies and within the fifth dimension, a concept that might be challenging to fathom. Simultaneously, technologically, it coexisted in the second dimension. The intricate relationship between dimensional existence and consciousness defies easy categorization, presenting a challenge to researchers delving into this topic on Earth. Numerous dimensional beings within this system prefer to remain undisclosed, feeling a sense of threat and valuing their privacy, desiring exclusion. Both Hollywood and the intelligence communities of various nations have deliberately propagated the notion that off-world and dimensional beings are merely fictional civilizations. The actual number of these civilizations is far more substantial than commonly believed.

Academic or Scientific References

- **"Bringers of the Dawn: Teachings from the Pleiadians" by Barbara Marciniak:** This book presents channeled messages from the Pleiadians, offering insights into human evolution, spirituality, and the nature of reality.

- **"The Pleiadian Agenda: A New Cosmology for the Age of Light" by Barbara Hand Clow:** Barbara Hand Clow explores the Pleiadian influence on human history, consciousness, and the future of the planet.

- **"Family of Light: Pleiadian Tales and Lessons in Living" by Barbara Marciniak:** Another work by Barbara Marciniak, this book provides further teachings from the Pleiadians, focusing on personal transformation and spiritual growth.

- **"The Pleiadian Promise: A Guide to Attaining Groupmind, Claiming Your Sacred Heritage, and Activating Your Destiny" by Christine Day:** Christine Day shares messages from the Pleiadians and provides guidance

Chapter 74

Raziel

Raziel is associated with divine wisdom, esoteric knowledge, and the transmission of sacred secrets. In Kabbalistic tradition, he is linked to the sephirah Chokmah (Wisdom) and is believed to stand close to God's throne, hearing and recording divine edicts.

Raziel is associated with divine wisdom, esoteric knowledge, and the transmission of sacred secrets. In Kabbalistic tradition, he is linked to the sephirah Chokmah (Wisdom) and is believed to stand close to God's throne, hearing and recording divine edicts.

The most significant text attributed to Raziel is the "Sefer Raziel HaMalakh" (Book of Raziel the Angel), a collection of angelic and cosmological lore. This book is said to contain all secret knowledge, including information on astrology, angelology, and magical practices. Raziel is often invoked in rituals and meditations aimed at gaining spiritual insight or accessing hidden knowledge. As a figure bridging divine and human realms, Raziel represents the human quest for understanding the mysteries of the universe and the divine. His teachings and the legends surrounding him continue to inspire seekers of esoteric knowledge and spiritual wisdom across different mystical traditions.

Historical Context and Origins

Raziel's origins can be traced to post-talmudic mystical traditions. He appears in midrashic and magical literature from the esoteric teachings of the talmudic period. One of the earliest mentions of Raziel is in the context of Moses' ascension to heaven to receive the Torah, where Raziel is described as an angel who hears divine secrets from behind the heavenly curtain.

The development of Raziel's role in mysticism is closely tied to the evolution of Kabbalah. As Kabbalistic teachings gained prominence in medieval thought, Raziel's significance grew. The compilation of the "Sefer Raziel HaMalakh" in the 13th century further solidified his importance in esoteric traditions. Raziel's influence extended beyond Kabbalah into various magical traditions, including Christian and Islamic occult practices. This cross-cultural adoption speaks to the universal appeal of the concept of hidden divine knowledge and the human desire to access it.

Unique and Obscure Facts

- Raziel is associated with the sephirah Chokmah (Wisdom) in the Kabbalistic Tree of Life.

- He is believed to have given Adam and Eve a book of divine secrets after their expulsion from Eden.

- In some traditions, Raziel is identified with the archangel Uriel.

- The numerical value of Raziel's name in Hebrew is 248, corresponding to the number of positive commandments in the Torah.

- Raziel is sometimes depicted as having blue wings and a glowing yellow halo.

- In Arabic astrology, Raziel is associated with the twentieth lunar station in the zodiac.

- The "Sefer Raziel HaMalakh" contains information on creating amulets and using divine names for magical purposes.

- Raziel is believed to make daily proclamations on Mount Horeb, revealing the secrets of men to all who dwell on earth.

- Raziel is associated with the concept of primordial light, representing the illumination of divine wisdom that existed before creation.

Mythological Interpretations

In mysticism, Raziel is seen as a mediator between the divine and human realms. He is believed to reveal divine mysteries to those deemed worthy and protect sacred knowledge. His role as the keeper of cosmic secrets places him at the intersection of divine wisdom and human understanding. In some Kabbalistic interpretations, Raziel is associated with the concept of primordial light, representing the illumination of divine wisdom that existed before creation. This connection ties him to the deeper mysteries of existence and the nature of reality itself.

Within the broader context of angelology, Raziel is sometimes grouped with other archangels such as Michael, Gabriel, and Raphael, each representing different aspects of divine interaction with the human world. Raziel's domain of secrets and mysteries complements the roles of other archangels, creating a comprehensive framework for understanding celestial hierarchies.

Dimensional Attributes and Existence

Raziel is often perceived as an interdimensional being capable of existing and operating across multiple planes of existence. In Kabbalistic tradition, Raziel is closely associated with the higher realms of divine wisdom and light, often acting as a bridge between the human world and higher spiritual dimensions. His proximity to God's throne suggests that Raziel operates within the highest spiritual realms, conveying divine secrets to those in the lower dimensions.

As the "Keeper of Secrets," Raziel's knowledge transcends time and space, allowing him to access and reveal truths that are hidden from ordinary perception. This interdimensional aspect underscores his role in guiding spiritual seekers towards enlightenment and understanding the deeper aspects of the cosmos.

Raziel's teachings often emphasize the interconnectedness of all things, suggesting a multidimensional view of reality where physical and spiritual worlds are intertwined. This perspective is central to many esoteric practices that seek to transcend ordinary limitations and access higher states of consciousness.

Case Study

The "Sefer Raziel HaMalakh" (Book of Raziel the Angel) serves as a significant case study in understanding Raziel's influence. Published in Amsterdam in 1701, this book is a compilation of various mystical texts, purportedly containing the secrets of creation that Raziel revealed to Adam. The book is divided into five sections, covering topics such as angelology, astrology, gematria (numerical values of Hebrew letters), and the use of amulets. It provides detailed instructions for magical practices, including the creation of talismans and the invocation of divine names for various purposes. The widespread circulation and numerous reprints of the "Sefer Raziel HaMalakh" demonstrate its enduring impact on mystical thought and practical Kabbalah. Its influence extended beyond mystical circles, inspiring occultists and mystics from various traditions. The book's blend of cosmological knowledge, angelic lore, and practical magic exemplifies the multifaceted nature of Raziel's teachings and his significance in esoteric traditions.

Personal Accounts and Historical References

While direct personal accounts of experiences with Raziel are rare in historical sources, there are numerous references to his influence in mystical literature. The Zohar, a foundational work of Kabbalah, mentions Raziel as the angel who revealed deep mysteries of the Torah to Adam while still in paradise. Rabbi Isaac of Acre, a 13th-century Kabbalist, wrote about visionary experiences involving Raziel. He described Raziel as a guide in his spiritual journeys, revealing hidden meanings of sacred texts and cosmic secrets. In later folklore, stories circulated about mystics and scholars who claimed to have accessed the wisdom of Raziel through intense study and meditation. These accounts often describe profound revelations about the nature of reality and the divine plan. Historical references to Raziel can also be found in various grimoires and magical texts from the medieval and Renaissance periods. These works often cite Raziel as a source of magical knowledge, particularly in matters of divination and the creation of talismans.

Psyop Commentary

The figure of Raziel and the concept of hidden divine knowledge he represents can be seen as a powerful psychological and spiritual construct. In an age of information overload, the idea of accessing deeper, more meaningful knowledge resonates with many seekers. The narrative surrounding Raziel could be interpreted as a metaphor for the human quest for understanding in a complex world. The promise of hidden wisdom, accessible only to the worthy, might serve as a motivating force for spiritual and intellectual growth. From a psychological perspective, the concept of Raziel and his secrets could represent the unconscious mind or the collective unconscious, holding wisdom that is not immediately apparent but can be accessed through introspection and spiritual practices. In contemporary society, where conspiracy theories and alternative narratives proliferate, the idea of hidden knowledge guarded by celestial beings like Raziel might appeal to those seeking explanations beyond mainstream understanding. This could potentially be exploited to promote both benign spiritual practices and more problematic belief systems.

Academic or Scientific References

- "Magic and Superstition in the Jewish Tradition" by Joshua Trachtenberg (1939)

- "Major Trends in Mysticism" by Gershom Scholem (1941)

- "The Hebrew Goddess" by Raphael Patai (1967)

- "Kabbalah: New Perspectives" by Moshe Idel (1988)

- "The Angel of History: Rosenzweig, Benjamin, Scholem" by Stéphane Mosès (2009)

Chapter 75

Re-Brid

Re-Brids are a class of human and higher-dimensional being hybrids that possess no soul. Some Re-Brids may possess human-like genetic coding while others may be an apparent 'hybrid' of two or more species.

This group of entities encompasses a broad range of genetic makeups. Certain individuals exhibit genetic structures akin to humans, yet lack the conventional notion of a 'soul.' Conversely, others represent a unique blend, incorporating characteristics from multiple distinct higher-dimensional species. The intricacies of their existence provoke interest and conjecture, especially among specific factions in the entertainment sector and governmental bureaucratic spheres.

Historical Context and Origins

Re-Brids' concept can be loosely related to ideas in human genetics and reproductive technologies, such as genetic counseling, assisted reproductive technologies, and genealogical studies. These fields deal with human reproduction, genetics, and family lineages in ethical, medical, and scientific contexts. The idea of hybrids without a soul can be traced to various mythological and esoteric traditions that discuss beings created through unnatural or forbidden means, often lacking a fundamental essence or higher consciousness.

Unique and Obscure Facts

- **Genetic Diversity:** Re-Brids exhibit a wide range of genetic diversity. Reptilian physiology, in particular, shows a remarkable degree of adaptability, allowing rapid genetic modifications and potentially yielding extensive physical diversity far surpassing that within the human population.

- **Soul and Consciousness:** The concept of the soul in various spiritual and religious traditions signifies consciousness, morality, and purpose. The idea of beings lacking a soul challenges these beliefs, leading to questions about their consciousness, morality, and purpose.

- **Mechanistic Nature:** Narratives often depict soulless beings as mechanistic entities devoid of higher consciousness, empathy, or moral choices, operating based on survival instincts or programmed behaviors.

- **Influence on Human Experience:** Interdimensional entities are believed to have been influencing the universe through the human experience since recorded history, using genetic counseling and other methods to guide human development.

- **Historical Parallels:** In vitro fertilization (IVF) was successfully publicly used in humans in 1978 but has been a part of mythology narratives since Adam and Eve.

Mythological Interpretations

Many cultures have myths and legends about human origins and lineages, often involving divine or heroic ancestors. The concept of hybrids, especially those lacking a soul, appears in various mythologies, representing beings created through unnatural means or possessing a mix of traits from different species. These beings often embody themes of transgression, forbidden knowledge, and the consequences of crossing natural boundaries.

For example:

- **Greek Mythology:** The centaurs, half-human and half-horse beings, were often depicted as wild and unruly, lacking the moral compass and rationality of humans.

- **Sumerian Mythology:** The Anunnaki were believed to have created humans by mixing their divine essence with that of early hominids, resulting in beings with mixed traits.

- **Jewish Mysticism:** The Golem, a being created from inanimate matter (usually clay) and brought to life through mystical rituals, lacked a soul and was seen as a soulless servant.

Dimensional Attributes and Existence

Re-Brids are believed to exist and operate across multiple planes of existence or dimensions. Their lack of a soul suggests a different form of consciousness or existence, possibly tied to higher-dimensional realms. This aspect influences their role, powers, and interactions with other beings. The adaptability and genetic diversity of Re-Brids may be a result of their interdimensional origins, allowing them to manifest in various forms and adapt to different environments.

Case Study

In vitro fertilization (IVF) and other assisted reproductive technologies provide a real-world parallel to the concept of creating hybrids. The successful public use of IVF in humans in 1978 marked a significant milestone in reproductive technology. Mythological narratives often include similar themes, such as the creation of beings through divine intervention or advanced technologies, reflecting humanity's long-standing fascination with manipulating life and genetics.

Personal Accounts and Historical References

Historical references to hybrids and beings lacking a soul can be found in various mythologies and esoteric traditions. These accounts often describe the creation of such beings through forbidden means, such as alchemy, magic, or advanced technologies. Personal accounts of encounters with interdimensional hybrids are rare but often involve detailed descriptions of their appearance, abilities, and interactions with humans.

Psyop Commentary

The increasing accessibility of genetic information and reproductive technologies raises complex ethical questions about privacy, consent, and the potential for discrimination. The concept of soulless hybrids challenges traditional beliefs about consciousness and morality, leading to debates about the nature of life and the ethics of genetic manipulation. The narrative of Re-Brids could be seen as a metaphor for modern concerns about the implications of advanced technologies and the boundaries of scientific exploration.

Academic or Scientific References

- **"A Guide to Genetic Counseling" by Wendy R. Uhlmann, et al. (2021):** This book provides comprehensive information on genetic counseling practices, including ethical considerations and practical applications.

- **"Principles and Practice of Assisted Reproductive Technology" by Gautam N. Allahbadia, et al. (2017):** This reference details various assisted reproductive technologies, highlighting their advancements and implications.

- **"The Family Tree Guide to DNA Testing and Genetic Genealogy" by Blaine T. Bettinger (2019):** This guide explores the use of DNA testing in genealogical research, providing insights into tracing ancestry and understanding genetic heritage.

Chapter 76

Reptoids

Reptilians

Reptoids, also known as Reptilians, are a type of alleged interdimensional beings characterized by their reptile-like features.

These beings are often described in conspiracy theories and ufology as possessing humanoid bodies with scaly skin, reptile eyes, and sometimes additional reptilian traits such as tails or wings. Reptoids are often associated with sinister agendas, including world domination, super*owl halftime shows and manipulation of human affairs.

Historical Context and Origins

Reptoid lore can be traced back to various mythologies and ancient civilizations. They have appeared in numerous cultures as serpent gods or dragon-like beings. In modern times, the concept of Reptoids was popularized by authors and conspiracy theorists such as David Icke, whose work builds on the non-scholarly interpretations of ancient texts by Zechariah Sitchin. Icke claims that shape-shifting Reptilian aliens control Earth by taking on human form and infiltrating positions of power.

Descriptions and Characteristics

Reptoids are typically described as being anywhere from 5 to 12 feet tall, with scaly, brownish or greenish skin, and reptile-like eyes. They are often depicted as being uncommonly strong and having the ability to change their appearance through vibrational manipulation rather than physical shape-shifting. Reptoids are usually portrayed as lacking empathy, being highly intelligent, and possessing a deep thirst for power and control.

Unique and Obscure Facts

- **Hierarchy and Hybrids**: Reptoids are believed to have a hierarchical structure with the Draconians, an albino reptile species with wings, at the top. Reptoids serve as soldiers and scientists within this hierarchy. There are also human-Reptoid hybrids who are unaware of their Reptilian heritage and are controlled by higher-dimensional Reptilians to further their agenda on Earth.

- **New World Order**: A common belief among Reptilian theorists is that Reptoids aim to unite the countries of the world under a New World Order, giving them complete control over human societies.

- **Underground Bases**: Conspiracy theories suggest that Reptoids operate secret underground bases such as the alleged Dulce Base in New Mexico, where they conduct genetic engineering experiments and collaborate with human elites.

- **Energy Consumption:** Some theories claim that Reptoids feed off negative energy and chaos, which is why they purportedly create and sustain conflicts and disasters on Earth.

Mythological Interpretations

Reptoid mythology often draws from ancient serpent and dragon myths, which describe serpent-like gods and beings that interact with humans. In many cultures, these beings were considered powerful and sometimes malevolent, exerting control over humanity through fear and manipulation.

Dimensional Attributes and Existence

Reptoids are believed to operate from higher-dimensional planes, particularly the fourth dimension, where they can manipulate reality and influence human affairs without being directly perceived. This ability to exist and act beyond the third-dimensional constraints of human reality adds to their enigmatic and powerful nature.

Case Study

One notable case involves Herbert Schirmer, a police officer from Ashland, Nebraska, who claimed under hypnosis to have been abducted by Reptilian beings in 1967. He described them as having a slightly reptilian appearance and wearing a "winged serpent" emblem.

Personal Accounts and Historical References

1. **David Icke's Theories:** David Icke's works, such as "The Biggest Secret," elaborate on the idea that Reptilian aliens have been manipulating human history for millennia. He asserts that many of the world's leaders, including royal families and political figures, are actually Reptilians or their hybrids. Icke's theories build upon Zechariah Sitchin's non-scholarly interpretations of ancient Sumerian texts, which suggest the existence of extraterrestrial gods involved in human affairs.

2. **Paul Bennewitz:** Among the prominent conspiracy theories, Paul Bennewitz's supposed discovery of an underground base in Dulce, New Mexico, is notable. He claimed that this base is

operated by Reptilians who conduct genetic experiments.

Psyop

From a perspective that governments suppress the truth, the Reptoid narrative aligns well with fears of hidden rulers manipulating society from the shadows. The idea that Reptilian aliens control major political and financial institutions feeds into the belief that there are powerful, unseen forces dictating global events. This narrative creates confusion and suspicion, aligning with other conspiracy theories about covert control and surveillance by malevolent entities.

Academic or Scientific References

1. "Reptilians: Ancient Mysterious Alien Species" – mythology.net/reptilians/

2. "Reptoid" – aliens.fandom.com/wiki/Reptoid

3. "Reptilian conspiracy theory" – en.wikipedia.org/wiki/Reptilian_conspiracy_theory

Chapter 77

Sa'irim

(Ikels, Satyrs)

S a'irim, also known as Ikels or Satyrs, are entities characterized by a predominantly goat-like appearance, with Azazel reigning as their king, dwelling in a cave on Mount Azazel in the Judean desert.

These beings are described as small, hairy humanoids with cloven hoofs. They are believed to inhabit deep caverns beneath South America and other regions and are speculated to be connected to a fallen pre-Adamic race endowed with a mix of angelic, animal, and humanoid characteristics.

Historical Context and Origins

References to Sa'irim can be found in various ancient texts and scriptures. They are mentioned in Leviticus 17:7, where it is stated that the Israelites should no longer sacrifice to the satyrs (se'irim). These entities are described as demons in Deuteronomy 32:17. In Isaiah 34:14, goat-demons are mentioned as inhabitants of desolate places, further linking them to ancient demonology. Additionally, the 14th-century Arabic manuscript and the Guide for the Perplexed by Maimonides discuss these beings, indicating their widespread recognition in historical and religious contexts.

Descriptions and Characteristics

- **Physical Appearance:** Sa'irim are described as small, hairy humanoids with cloven hoofs, predominantly goat-like in appearance.

- **Habitat:** They are believed to inhabit deep caverns beneath South America and other regions.

- **Behavior:** Native accounts describe Sa'irim as having a history of "kidnapping" women and children. There are numerous tales of encounters between these creatures and South American tribes, who reportedly engaged in battles with them during their occasional ventures to the surface.

Unique and Obscure Facts

- **Pre-Adamic Race:** Speculation surrounds their origin, suggesting a connection to a fallen pre-Adamic race with a mix of angelic, animal, and humanoid characteristics.

- **Alliance with Reptilian Entities:** Presently, they are thought to have allied with reptilian entities, adding another layer of intrigue to their existence.

- **Worship and Demons:** The Guide for the Perplexed mentions that some sects among the Sabeans worshipped demons that assumed the form of goats, calling them "se'irim."

Mythological Interpretations

- **Biblical References:** Leviticus 17:7 and Deuteronomy 32:17 refer to the Sa'irim as demons associated with ancient idol worship.

- **Isaiah 34:14:** This verse describes goat-demons and other mythological beings inhabiting desolate places, indicating their role in ancient demonology.

- **Maimonides' Guide for the Perplexed:** Maimonides notes that certain sects worshipped these demons, calling them goats (se'irim), and this worship was widespread.

Dimensional Attributes and Existence

Sa'irim are considered interdimensional beings, existing in realms currently beyond general human access. They are believed to inhabit deep caverns and possibly have capabilities that transcend normal physical limitations.

Case Study: A Notable Case

In South America, numerous native accounts recount encounters between tribes and Sa'irim. These tales often describe battles where tribespeople wielded machetes to fend off the creatures during their ventures to the surface, typically in pursuit of women, children, or sustenance.

Personal Accounts and Historical References

- **Leviticus 17:7 and Deuteronomy 32:17:** These scriptures reference sacrifices to demons identified as Sa'irim.

- **Isaiah 34:14:** Describes goat-demons inhabiting desolate places.

- **Guide for the Perplexed:** Maimonides discusses the worship of se'irim by certain sects, providing historical context to their mythological status.

- **Vayikra Rabbah 22:8:** This text discusses the Israelites' idolatry involving satyrs and demons in Egypt.

References for Further Reading

1. **"Hesed L'Avraham"** – An ancient text discussing the inhabitants of inner Earth, including the Nishaya or Greys.

2. **The Bible** – Leviticus 17:7, Deuteronomy 32:17, and Isaiah 34:14 provide references to the Sa'irim.

3. **Vayikra Rabbah 22:8** – A midrashic text that delves into the Israelites' idolatrous practices involving satyrs and demons.

Chapter 78

Sasquatch

(Bigfoot,Yeren, Nukluk, MehTeh,Yeti,Yowie, Almas)

Sasquatch, also known as Bigfoot, is a legendary cryptid traditionally believed to inhabit North American forests. Described as a large, hairy, humanlike creature,

Sasquatch has been reported by natives for thousands of years, particularly in the Pacific Northwest and Canada. In recent years, an alternative theory has emerged, portraying Sasquatch as an interdimensional being capable of traversing different planes of existence. This perspective suggests that Sasquatch is not merely a flesh-and-blood creature but an entity with paranormal abilities. Proponents of this theory often describe Sasquatch as being associated with mysterious orbs of light and interdimensional portals. These phenomena are said to explain the creature's elusive nature and the lack of conclusive physical evidence. The interdimensional Sasquatch theory blends elements of cryptozoology and quantum physics, creating a complex narrative that challenges conventional understanding of reality and pushes the boundaries of Sasquatch lore into the realm of the paranormal.

Historical Context and Origins

The interdimensional Sasquatch theory gained traction in the late 20th and early 21st centuries, coinciding with increased interest in paranormal phenomena and alternative explanations for unexplained events. This shift in perspective was influenced by the growing overlap between Sasquatch research and paranormal investigations, with researchers like Stan Gordon noting correlations between Sasquatch sightings and unexplained aerial phenomena. The integration of quantum physics theories into paranormal research also contributed to the development of interdimensional Sasquatch theories, with some researchers drawing parallels between quantum concepts like superposition and the seemingly impossible abilities attributed to Sasquatch.

Unique and Obscure Facts

- Some researchers report witnessing Sasquatch "fade out" or become translucent, suggesting a shift between dimensions.

- There are accounts of Sasquatch being seen in association with unexplained aerial phenomena, leading to theories of interdimensional connections.

- Certain Sasquatch hotspots are said to have higher incidences of magnetic anomalies and unexplained light phenomena.

- Some believers claim that Sasquatch can manipulate electromagnetic fields, explaining equipment malfunctions during sightings.

- There are reports of Sasquatch leaving behind "gifts" like arranged stones or sticks, interpreted as attempts at interdimensional communication.

- The Multidimensional Sasquatch Theory suggests that Sasquatch possesses the ability to traverse different dimensions, indicating a level of dimensional awareness and control beyond human understanding.

- Sasquatch sightings are often associated with fast-moving lights known as orange orbs, which some enthusiasts propose could indicate portal use or dimensional shifts.

- Locations on Earth considered energetic hotspots or vortexes, where dimensional boundaries are thin, are thought to facilitate interdimensional travel for beings like Sasquatch.

- **Kosher Status:** Sasquatch stands out as one of the most renowned cryptids. Frequently dubbed the "missing link" between humans and apes, Sasquatch's proximity to people raises questions about its kosher status. Perhaps, if it were named "Bighoof," the argument might gain more traction.

Mythological Interpretations

In various mythologies and spiritual frameworks, Sasquatch is seen as a guardian figure watching over the woods. Some Native American traditions view Sasquatch-like beings as spirit guardians capable of moving between the physical and spiritual realms. In New Age philosophies, Sasquatch is sometimes portrayed as a higher-dimensional being or "starseed" with a mission to observe and protect Earth. These interpretations often draw parallels with other mythological shapeshifters or liminal beings that exist at the threshold between worlds. The association with orbs and portals also connects Sasquatch to concepts of fairy lights or spirit orbs found in various folklores, suggesting a universal theme of beings that traverse different planes of existence.

Dimensional Attributes and Existence

According to interdimensional theories, Sasquatch possesses the ability to shift between our three-dimensional reality and other dimensions or parallel universes. This capability is often associated with the appearance of orbs or portal-like phenomena. Proponents suggest that Sasquatch uses these interdimensional gateways to enter and exit our reality at will, explaining both its elusive nature and the occasional sudden appearances and disappearances reported by witnesses. Some researchers propose that

Sasquatch's interdimensional nature allows it to manipulate matter and energy, potentially explaining reports of exceptional strength, speed, and the ability to avoid detection. The theory also posits that Sasquatch might exist in a state of quantum superposition, simultaneously present and absent in our dimension until observed, drawing parallels with quantum physics concepts.

Case Study

In 2012, a group of researchers in the Sierra Nevada mountains of California reported a significant encounter that seemed to support the interdimensional Sasquatch theory. The team, led by experienced Sasquatch investigator Ron Morehead, claimed to have witnessed multiple Sasquatch figures in association with strange, orb-like lights. According to their account, the orbs appeared to precede the manifestation of Sasquatch figures, which seemed to materialize and dematerialize in conjunction with the lights. The researchers reported equipment malfunctions and unusual electromagnetic readings during the event. While the encounter was not captured on video due to the alleged equipment issues, audio recordings purportedly captured unexplained vocalizations and wood knocks. This case has been widely discussed in interdimensional Sasquatch circles as potential evidence of the creature's ability to move between dimensions using energy portals.

Personal Accounts and Historical References

Numerous eyewitness accounts support the interdimensional Sasquatch theory. For instance, in 2007, a hiker in the Olympic National Forest reported seeing a Sasquatch-like creature step out of a "shimmer in the air" that resembled heat waves. The creature allegedly disappeared into a similar distortion moments later. Another account from the 1970s in British Columbia describes a Sasquatch vanishing into a "ball of light" after being shot at by hunters. Historical references to interdimensional beings can be found in various indigenous traditions, such as the Lakota concept of "waking dreams" where spirit beings can manifest in the physical world. These accounts, while anecdotal, contribute to the growing body of lore surrounding interdimensional Sasquatch theories.

Psyop Commentary

The interdimensional Sasquatch theory could be seen as a reflection of humanity's evolving relationship with technology and our understanding of reality. As quantum physics challenges our classical view of the universe, the idea of interdimensional beings might represent a cultural attempt to reconcile traditional folklore with cutting-edge science. Alternatively, the promotion of such theories could be viewed as a means to maintain interest in the Sasquatch phenomenon in the face of a lack of concrete evidence. Some skeptics argue that interdimensional theories serve to make Sasquatch unfalsifiable, moving it from the realm of scientific inquiry into that of faith or pseudoscience. The blending of Sasquatch lore with unexplained aerial phenomena and quantum concepts might also reflect a broader societal trend towards synthesizing diverse belief systems in search of ultimate truths.

Academic or Scientific References

- **Meldrum, J. (2006). "Sasquatch: Legend Meets Science." Forge Books.** While primarily focused on physical evidence, this book touches on some alternative theories.

- **Godfrey, L. S. (2016). "Monsters Among Us: An Exploration of Otherworldly Bigfoots, Wolfmen, Portals, Phantoms, and Odd Phenomena." Tarcher Perigee.** Explores connections between Sasquatch and other paranormal phenomena.

- **Guiley, R. E. (2006). "The Encyclopedia of Magic and Alchemy." Facts on File.** Provides context for understanding portals and interdimensional travel in various traditions.

Chapter 79

Sassani

S assani, meaning "beings of light," are a humanoid race believed to inhabit the planet Essassani, located near the Orion constellation, approximately 500 light-years from Earth.

They are described as a hybrid race created through genetic engineering by combining human DNA with that of the Zeta Reticuli Greys. The Sassani possess a blend of the Zeta's telepathic abilities, longevity, and intellectual capacities, along with human emotional, sexual, and physical traits. They are known for their curiosity, humor, and fluid emotions.

The Sassani are typically about 1.5 meters tall, with greyish skin, large eyes, and distinct gender differences in hair: females have white hair, while males are hairless.

Historical Context and Origins

The Sassani's creation is attributed to the Zeta Reticuli civilization, which faced a fertility crisis due to catastrophic events on their home planet. To ensure their survival, the Zeta Reticuli Greys developed advanced genetic engineering techniques to blend their DNA with human DNA, resulting in the Sassani and other hybrid races. This narrative has been popularized through channeled messages, particularly those from Darryl Anka, who claims to communicate with a Sassani entity named Bashar.

Unique and Obscure Facts

- **Planetary Conditions:** The Sassani live on a planet with a constant temperature of around 22 degrees Celsius, thanks to a minimal axial tilt. Essassani has a 25-hour day and a year that lasts 454 days due to its orbit around a hotter sun.

- **Economic System:** The Sassani civilization does not use monetary or barter systems; everything is provided freely based on need.

- **Design Preferences:** They emphasize the harmonic number three, even designing their scout crafts in triangular shapes.

- **Evolution:** The Sassani are said to evolve ten times faster than humans due to their dimensional and frequency embodiment.

- **Societal Structure:** Their society is highly synchronistic and operates without formal governments, relying instead on individual and group networks.

- **Dimensional Shift:** They are transitioning from the fourth to the fifth dimension, paralleling humanity's shift from the third to the fourth dimension.

Mythological Interpretations

In various mythologies and spiritual frameworks, the Sassani are seen as benevolent guides helping humanity achieve higher states of consciousness and spiritual evolution. They are often depicted as advanced beings who assist in the enlightenment and transformation of human society, aligning with New Age beliefs about a coming age of enlightenment.

Dimensional Attributes and Existence

The Sassani are believed to exist in the fourth and fifth dimensions, granting them advanced psychic abilities and a deep understanding of consciousness and interdimensional travel. This multi-dimensional existence allows them to interact with humans in ways that transcend physical limitations, influencing their perceived role as spiritual guides and helpers.

Case Study

A notable example involving the Sassani is the ongoing communication between Darryl Anka and the entity Bashar. Over the past 37 years, Anka has channeled messages from Bashar, providing insights into the nature of the universe, human potential, and future events. These sessions have significantly influenced the New Age and related communities, offering a blend of spiritual guidance and interdimensional lore.

Personal Accounts and Historical References

Many individuals have reported personal experiences and direct communications with the Sassani, often through channeling sessions. These accounts describe the Sassani as highly intelligent, compassionate beings who offer guidance and wisdom. Historical references to similar hybrid beings can be found in various ancient texts and mythologies, interpreted differently depending on cultural contexts.

Psyop Commentary

The concept of alien abductions often parallels sexual assault, with abductees reporting invasive procedures and forced breeding without consent. Channeling conversations with Sassani claim these actions are justified by a "soul contract," suggesting preordained cosmic agreements. This idea is ethically problematic and does not alleviate the real psychological trauma experienced by abductees.

Academic or Scientific References

While there are no widely accepted academic or scientific studies specifically focused on the Sassani, related topics such as hybridization theories
and the psychological aspects of belief in interdimensional entities have
been explored in various scholarly works. For further research, readers
might explore books and articles on New Age spirituality and the psychological impact of belief in interdimensional beings.

Seraphim Collective

Seraphim Collective: (Seraphim, singular: Seraph) are one of the highest orders of dimensional beings. The term "Seraphim" comes from the Hebrew word "seraf," which means "burning ones" or "fiery ones." the name clearly also refers to the Hebrew word for reptile. These angelic beings are often described as fiery, six-winged creatures. They are known for their closeness to the divine and are associated with divine love and light.

The primary source for the concept of Seraphim in can be found in the book of Isaiah in the Hebrew Bible (Isaiah 6:1-3). In this passage, the prophet Isaiah has a vision of G-d's heavenly throne, and he sees Seraphim in attendance:

"In the year that King Uzziah died, I saw the L-rd, high and exalted, seated on a throne; and the train of his robe filled the temple. Above him were seraphim, each with six wings: With two wings they covered their faces, with two they covered their feet, and with two they were flying. And they were calling to one another: 'Holy, holy, holy is the L-rd Almighty; the whole earth is full of his glory.'"

Angles exist generally in four worlds, Seraphim exist in the world of *Beriah* – we find that creation of souls and the highest angels. The world of *Beriah* is also the place of the upper Garden of Eden. Seraphim act as agents through whom energies flow to this world as conduits for Divine energy flow. The angels in the world of *Beriah* are called *Seraphim*, from the Hebrew word Seraiphah (a fire). Seraphim are one-dimensional: each angels has one specific form of Divine service. The human soul, on the other hand, serves G-d in many different ways. It is important to note that we are discouraged from unnecessarily pronouncing the specific names of angels (unless they are common names—such as Michael and Gabriel). When G-d created the angels, He instructed them to go to a person who calls their name. As such, we do not want to "disturb" them unnecessarily. Seraphim, with their fiery and awe-inspiring presence, as beings that exist in different dimensions or realms but may not be interdimensional since they exist primarily in the world of *Beriah*.

Quick Reference

- *Seraphim*, is derived from the Hebrew word Seraiphah (a fire).

- Seraphim exist in the world of *Beriah* – *this is where we find the* creation of souls and the highest angels.

- Seraphim have no free-choice and are pre-programmed to serve.

- It is important to note that we are discouraged from unnecessarily pronouncing the specific names of angels, we do not want to "disturb" them unnecessarily.

- The Seraphim six wings are often interpreted as representing their rapid, soaring flight and their ability to shield their eyes and feet from the intense divine presence.

- Seraphim, may not be interdimensional since they exist primarily in the world of *Beriah.*

Seraphim, often depicted with six wings, are celestial beings radiating intense brilliance, symbolizing their close association with the divine realm and embodying the transformative power of divine love and light. Their fiery appearance signifies both their exceptional abilities and the multifaceted aspects of their nature. Esteemed as the highest order of angels, Seraphim hold immediate proximity to the divine presence, serving as celestial attendants encircling the throne of G-d. Their name, "Seraphim," derived from a Hebrew word meaning "to burn" or "to consume with fire," emphasizes their fervent connection to the divine. Unlike other beings, Seraphim are believed to exist in multiple dimensions simultaneously. This concept allows them to interact with various realms, including the physical world, spiritual dimensions, and even different time periods.

A distinctive aspect of Seraphim lies in their perpetual praise and worship of the divine, engaging in celestial songs that resonate with harmonious melodies. This continuous worship is described in religious texts as a perpetual chorus of divine praise. Additionally, Seraphim are believed to play a vital role in the purification and healing of the soul, with their fiery nature symbolizing the purging of impurities and the illumination of the spirit. Encounters with Seraphim may lead to spiritual cleansing and a profound sense of rebirth.

The radiant and fiery appearance of Seraphim symbolizes divine light, signifying their role as bearers of divine illumination. They offer spiritual seekers insights, clarity, and enlightenment, utilizing their six wings to bring spiritual perspectives from different dimensions. For those on a spiritual journey, Seraphim serve as symbols of divine inspiration and aspiration, emphasizing the transformative power of divine love and the significance of approaching the divine with reverence and humility.

While commonly associated with Judeo-Christian traditions, the concept of radiant, fiery beings extends beyond cultural and religious boundaries, appearing in various traditions worldwide. This multicultural presence suggests that the symbolic power and significance of Seraphim transcend specific cultural and religious contexts.

Book References

"Sefer Yetzirah" (The Book of Creation): This ancient Jewish mystical text is attributed to Abraham or Rabbi Akiva and explores the creation of the universe through the manipulation of Hebrew letters and numbers. It touches upon angelic entities and their roles in the divine order.

"Hekhalot Literature": This collection of Jewish mystical and esoteric texts is part of the Merkavah (divine chariot) and Hekhalot literature. These texts describe the visionary experiences of individuals who ascend through the heavenly realms and encounter angelic beings, although Seraphim might not be the primary focus.

"The Celestial Hierarchy" by Pseudo-Dionysius the Areopagite: This classic work, written in the 5th to 6th century, explores the angelic hierarchy, including the Seraphim, and their roles in the divine order.

"The Encyclopedia of Angels" by Rosemary Guiley: This comprehensive reference work covers a wide range of angelic beings, their attributes, and roles, including Seraphim.

"The Seraphim: The Burning Ones" by Th.D., W. R. Treadway: This book is a deeper exploration of the Seraphim order, focusing on their roles and significance in spiritual traditions.

"Angels: An Endangered Species" by Malcolm Godwin: This book offers an in-depth look at various angelic beings and their attributes, including Seraphim.

Shadow People

S hadow People: These elusive entities are often described as humanoid figures composed of black particles or dense material perceived as "black energy."

These entities are commonly referred to as "shadow people" or "shadow beings." Observations of shadow entities have evolved from peripheral, fleeting sightings to more direct, extended encounters, sometimes featuring distinct red eyes. They are often linked to sleep paralysis, out-of-body experiences, and interdimensional travel theories.

Historical Context and Origins

The phenomenon of Shadow People has been documented in various cultures and periods. Historically, sightings were typically brief and peripheral. However, contemporary accounts describe more prolonged and direct encounters. The increasing prevalence of shadow people sightings parallels the rise of modern interest in paranormal activities and the exploration of consciousness, including studies on sleep paralysis and astral projection.

Unique and Obscure Facts

- **Sleep Paralysis:** Shadow people are frequently associated with sleep paralysis, a condition where individuals experience temporary paralysis and hallucinations during sleep transitions.

- **Astral Projection:** Some theories suggest shadow people are the astral forms of individuals engaged in out-of-body experiences.

- **Interdimensional Travel:** It is speculated that shadow people can traverse different dimensions, appearing in our realm as shadows.

- **Time Travelers:** An unconventional theory posits that shadow people may be future humans observing the present.

- **Energy-Based Existence:** Shadow people are believed to be composed of black particles or dense energy, eluding physical touch but interacting with the mind's eye.

Mythological Interpretations

In various mythologies, shadow beings are interpreted differently. They are sometimes seen as malevolent entities, possibly demons, due to their ominous appearance and the fear they invoke. In other cultures, they are perceived as guardians or messengers from the spirit world, maintaining a watchful presence over the living. The Dogon people of Mali, for instance, have stories of shadowy beings that are integral to their spiritual beliefs.

Dimensional Attributes and Existence

Shadow people are often theorized to exist between the third and fourth dimensions, making them partially visible in our reality. This interdimensional nature allows them to appear and disappear suddenly, explaining their elusive behavior. Their ability to traverse different planes of existence suggests advanced control over dimensional travel, possibly facilitated by portals or vibrational shifts.

Case Study

One notable case involves an individual experiencing an out-of-body experience (OBE). During this state, the person observed a dark figure in their kitchen, which initially caused fear. Upon closer inspection, the figure was revealed to be the individual's son, also experiencing an OBE. This case illustrates the possibility of shadow people being astral projections of living individuals, challenging the notion of their purely malevolent nature.

Personal Accounts and Historical References

Numerous personal accounts describe encounters with shadow people during sleep paralysis or OBEs. Historical references can be found in folklore and paranormal literature, where shadowy figures are often depicted as harbingers of doom or protectors of sacred spaces. The experiences of shadow people are diverse, with some individuals reporting benign encounters and others describing terrifying interactions.

Psyop Commentary

The narrative of shadow people can be seen as a reflection anof contemporary anxieties and the human quest for understanding the unknown. The phenomenon's connection to sleep paralysis and astral projection highlights the complex interplay between consciousness and perceived reality. As a psyop commentary, the increasing interest in shadow people may also signify a broader societal fascination with paranormal and interdimensional experiences, driven by a desire to explore the boundaries of human perception and existence.

Academic or Scientific References

- **"The Vengeful Djinn: Unveiling the Hidden Agenda of Genies"** by Rosemary Ellen Guiley and Philip J. Imbrogno - This book explores the folklore and encounters involving shadow beings.

- **"The Encyclopedia of Ghosts and Spirits"** by Rosemary Ellen Guiley - A comprehensive reference covering various paranormal entities, including shadow figures.

- **"The Hat Man: The True Story of Evil Encounters"** by Kyle Massey - Investigates encounters with a specific shadow entity known as the "Hat Man."

- **"Shadow People: The Slender Man Phenomenon"** by Conrad Bauer - Discusses the connection between shadow people and the Slender Man legend.

- **"Shadow People: Quickening of the Wicked"** by Jason Offutt - Provides accounts and stories from individuals who have encountered shadow people.

- **"The Black-Eyed Children"** by David Weatherly - Explores the connection between shadow people and black-eyed children.

- **"Men Fear Most What They Cannot See." sleep paralysis "Ghost Intruders" and faceless "Shadow-People"-The role of the right hemisphere and economizing nature of vision.** Med Hypotheses. 2021 Mar;148:110521. doi: 10.1016/j.mehy.2021.110521. Epub 2021 Jan 28. PMID: 33573871.

Short Greys

(Nishaya, Ebens, Grays, Mazeh)

Grey Aliens, also known as Zeta Reticulans, Roswell Greys, Nishaya, or simply Greys, are iconic figures in pop culture recognized by their humanoid features—long limbs, large black eyes (lenses), small noses, thin mouths, and gray skin or clothing.

They embody the popular image of extraterrestrial beings and are often associated with reports of UFO sightings and alien abductions.

Historical Context and Origins

The concept of Grey Aliens became widely known through the Barney and Betty Hill abduction case in 1961, which brought them into the public eye. However, reports and descriptions of similar beings have been part of folklore and ancient texts for much longer. Greys are also linked to the Roswell incident of 1947, where alleged alien bodies were reported to have been recovered from a crashed UFO.

In Hesed L'Avraham 2:4, an ancient Jewish text, there are references to numerous inhabitants of inner Earth, including the Nishaya (Greys or Shedim), dispelling the notion that humans are alone on this planet. Inner Earth is said to host a diverse array of intelligent races and dimensional beings, including phoenixes, unicorns, minotaurs, giants, hobbits, and dragons.

Descriptions and Characteristics

- **Physical Appearance**: Greys are described as short and frail, with a greyish skin tone, large black eyes (often covered with lenses), small noses, and thin mouths. They have long limbs and a generally humanoid shape.

- **Behavior and Abilities**: Greys are often reported to have the ability to maneuver through walls, doors, and other solid objects by manipulating their "densities or aura" through electromagnetic tuning, creating a perceived multi-dimensional capability. They are typically depicted as functioning collectively, with hive-minded characteristics.

Unique and Obscure Facts

- **Inner Earth Inhabitants**: According to Hesed L'Avraham 2:4, the Greys (referred to as Nishaya or Shedim) are among the diverse intelligent races and dimensional beings inhabiting inner Earth. These beings include phoenixes, unicorns, minotaurs, giants, hobbits, and dragons, suggesting a rich and varied ecosystem of interdimensional entities.

- **Shedim**: Ancient sages have mentioned beings similar to the Greys, known as "Shedim." Described as short, frail, with greyish skin tone, no noses but narrow slits for breathing, these beings are rumored to lack females and allegedly abduct humans for procreation.

- **Advanced Abilities**: Reports suggest that Greys can alter their densities or auras through electromagnetic tuning, allowing them to pass through solid objects and exhibiting multi-dimensional capabilities.

- **Ethical and Observational Mission**: The Ummites, another race mentioned in connection with Greys, claim to adhere to strict ethical guidelines in their interactions with humanity. They emphasize observation without direct interference, a principle that aligns with the idea of non-intervention in less advanced civilizations.

Mythological Interpretations

In addition to their depiction in modern ufology, the concept of Greys is intertwined with ancient myths and legends of beings from inner Earth. The idea that Earth hosts a variety of intelligent races and dimensional beings reflects ancient beliefs in hidden worlds and unseen realms.

Dimensional Attributes and Existence

Greys are often associated with interdimensional travel and advanced technological capabilities. They are described as being able to manipulate their physical form and density, allowing them to navigate through solid objects and potentially access different dimensions.

Case Study: A Notable Case

The Barney and Betty Hill abduction case in 1961 is one of the most well-known instances involving Grey Aliens. The couple claimed to have been abducted by Greys and subjected to medical examinations. This case brought significant attention to the phenomenon of alien abductions and established the Greys as a central figure in UFO lore.

Personal Accounts and Historical References

- **Barney and Betty Hill Incident**: Despite being one of the most cited cases, it is crucial to explore other encounters and reports to understand the broader phenomenon of Grey Aliens.

- **Hesed L'Avraham 2:4:** This ancient text discusses the inhabitants of inner Earth, including the Nishaya or Greys, suggesting a long-standing awareness of these beings.

- **Modern UFO Reports:** Numerous accounts from around the world describe encounters with beings resembling Greys, adding to their presence in contemporary UFO culture.

References for Further Reading:

1. **"Communion" by Whitley Strieber"** - A book detailing the author's alleged encounters with Greys and their impact on his life.

2. **"The Interrupted Journey" by John G. Fuller** - A book about the Barney and Betty Hill abduction case, providing detailed accounts of their experiences.

3. **UFO Evidence – Greys:** http://www.ufoevidence.org/documents/doc1783.htm

4. **Exopaedia – Greys:** https://www.exopaedia.org/Greys

Chapter 83

Sirians

S irians are advanced interdimensional beings originating from the Sirius star system, including Sirius A and Sirius B.

Many collective entities and energy forms occupy Sirius, a focal point within the ASHTAR collective. This includes humanoids, Sasquatch, Reptiloids, Greys, and predominantly Insectoids and Reptilian-Insectoid hybrids. Cybernetic "Men in Black" entities have also collaborated historically.They are depicted as highly evolved entities with a deep connection to Earth's ancient civilizations and spiritual evolution. Sirians are thought to have shared their knowledge and wisdom with humanity, influencing various cultures and guiding human spiritual and technological progress. They are associated with a range of beings including humanoids, Sasquatch, Reptiloids, Greys, Insectoids, and hybrid entities, often within the context of the ASHTAR or ASTARTE collective.

Historical Context and Origins

The concept of Sirians gained prominence through Robert K. G. Temple's book, *The Sirius Mystery*, which suggested that the Dogon people of Mali possessed advanced astronomical knowledge of Sirius B, possibly imparted by extraterrestrial beings. The Dogon's detailed knowledge about the Sirius star system, including the existence of Sirius B and its 50-year orbital period, sparked theories about ancient interdimensional contact. Additionally, Sirians are often linked to ancient Egyptian and Sumerian cultures, where Sirius held significant astrological and spiritual importance.

Unique and Obscure Facts

- Sirians are often described as having cat-like or dog-like features, with large eyes and pointed noses.

- They are believed to have a special affinity for water and aquatic life, with some theories suggesting they come from an aquatic planet.

- Sirian starseeds, individuals who believe they are reincarnated souls from Sirius, often feel a deep connection to nature and animals, particularly dogs and dolphins.

- Sirians are thought to be part of the Galactic Federation, a coalition of advanced interdimensional races working towards the betterment of the universe.

- They have a history of conflict with the Orion Empire, specifically the "Unholy Six" reptilian star systems.

Mysthological Interpretations

In various mythologies, Sirians are seen as celestial beings who have played a crucial role in human evolution. Ancient Egyptian mythology, for example, revered Sirius as a significant star associated with the goddess Isis. The Dogon people of Mali have intricate myths about Sirius, which they call the "Po Tolo" and believe to be the home of their ancestral spirits. These mythological interpretations highlight the Sirians' role as divine guides and protectors of humanity.

Dimensional Attributes and Existence

Sirians are often described as interdimensional beings capable of existing and operating across multiple planes of existence. They are believed to assist humanity in transitioning from the third dimension to higher dimensions of consciousness. Their interdimensional nature allows them to communicate through various means, such as channeling and dreams, offering profound spiritual insights and guidance. This ability to traverse dimensions is thought to enhance their role as spiritual guides and guardians.

Case Study

A well-documented example involving Sirians is the account of Patricia Cori, who claims to have communicated with the Sirian High Council. According to Cori, these six-dimensional light beings provided her with profound insights about humanity's spiritual evolution and the challenges we face. Her experiences, detailed in her book *The New Sirian Revelations*, have had a significant impact on the beliefs of many who follow the Sirian narrative.

Personal Accounts and Historical References

Numerous individuals report personal experiences with Sirian beings, often describing encounters during meditation or dream states. These accounts frequently involve receiving spiritual guidance and feeling a deep sense of connection to the Sirius star system. Historical references to Sirius can be found in the lore of ancient civilizations, such as the Egyptians and the Dogon people, who attributed great significance to the star and its associated beings.

Academic or Scientific References

- **Temple, Robert K.G.** *The Sirius Mystery: New Scientific Evi-*

dence of Alien Contact 5,000 Years Ago. Destiny Books, 1998.

- Cori, Patricia. *The Sirian Revelations Trilogy.* North Atlantic Books, 2008.

- Royal, Lyssa. *The Prism of Lyra: An Exploration of Human Galactic Heritage.* Royal Priest Research, 1992.

Chapter 84

Synthetics

Spiritless forms, Drones or NPCs

S ynthetic interdimensional beings are artificial or bio-synthetic entities created and controlled by formless interdimensional beings.

Synthetic interdimensional beings are artificial or bio-synthetic entities created and controlled by formless interdimensional beings. These beings, often designed to resemble humans or other extraterrestrial forms like Greys, Mantis, or Draconians, serve as vessels or extensions for higher-dimensional entities to interact with and influence the physical realm of Earth. If the world were an organic game or simulation, this concept suggests a unique scenario where individual entities are shut-ins who only interact with the outside world through robots they control.

Historical Context and Origins

The concept of synthetic interdimensional beings emerged from various theories and accounts of extraterrestrial and interdimensional interactions. This narrative could have evolved from stories of abandoned children, storks, cabbage patch kids, war orphans, or child trafficking. These entities are believed to have been created using advanced cybernetic and biological technologies, often involving components taken from animal and human mutilation victims. Such beings have been described in modern lore, where they are depicted as tools for covert operations and manipulation by higher-dimensional entities.

Descriptions and Characteristics

Synthetics can take various forms, ranging from highly human-like infiltrators to distinctly alien appearances resembling Greys, Reptilians, or Mantis beings. These entities are often bio-synthetic, combining organic and mechanical parts, and are capable of being "possessed" or controlled by interdimensional beings. They are typically designed for specific tasks, such as surveillance, manipulation, or energy extraction.

Unique and Obscure Facts

- Some synthetics are thought to be used by interdimensional beings as avatars, allowing them to experience life on Earth as kings, demigods, or influential figures.

- The ability to change avatars at will enables these beings to live diverse lives, from historical figures to modern celebrities or oligarchs.

- Earth is theorized to serve as both a "loosh" or adrenochrome buffet and an amusement park for these beings, who derive sustenance and entertainment from human emotions and activities.

Mythological Interpretations

In mythological contexts, synthetic beings align with tales of gods, demons, and other supernatural entities who interact with humans. These stories often describe beings with the ability to shape-shift, control human minds, and influence events, reflecting the alleged capabilities of synthetic interdimensional entities. The myths of gods descending to Earth, taking human forms, and engaging in mortal affairs can be seen as early interpretations of the concept of synthetics.

Dimensional Attributes and Existence

Synthetics are posited to exist across multiple dimensions, interacting with both the physical and metaphysical realms. They serve as conduits for higher-dimensional entities, facilitating their influence and presence on Earth. This dual existence allows them to operate beyond the constraints of physical reality, tapping into energies and abilities that humans cannot comprehend.

The Lunacy of 'Machine Consciousness'

The advancement of artificial intelligence (AI) and the development of highly immersive games have led to intriguing yet controversial discussions about the nature of human consciousness and the possibility of synthetic humanoids among us. These discussions often invoke the concept of NPCs (non-player characters) and question whether consciousness can be simulated or computed. This exploration addresses the possible existence of synthetic humanoid drones in humanity today, the derivation of such faulty thinking, and how the propagation of anthropomorphizing humanity serves as a psyop to dehumanize and distract us from our spiritual existence.

The Existence of Synthetic Humanoid Drones

The term NPC, initially used in the context of video games to describe characters controlled by the game rather than the player, has evolved into a metaphor for certain human behaviors. The advent of highly immersive games that are photorealistic has fueled speculation that if humans can create 3D worlds indistinguishable from reality, then one day, we might create simulated realities where some humans could be synthetic humanoids or NPCs. These entities would appear human but lack true consciousness, operating instead on complex algorithms.

If consciousness is computable, it removes the biggest hurdle to us living in a simulation. This idea suggests that synthetic humanoids, designed to mimic human behavior and interaction, could exist among us today. However, the core challenge remains: consciousness is not computable. Roger Penrose and other theorists argue that consciousness involves non-computational elements, such as quantum processes, that current computer architectures cannot replicate. Therefore, the notion of synthetic humanoid drones with true consciousness is fundamentally flawed.

The Derivation of Faulty Thinking

The belief that human consciousness can be replicated by machines stems from a long history of using metaphors to explain intelligence. In his book *In Our Own Image* (2015), artificial intelligence expert George Zarkadakis outlines six different metaphors used over the past 2,000 years to explain human intelligence. Each metaphor mirrored the most advanced thinking of its time, from hydraulic systems to mechanical automata, and more recently, to computers.

This evolution of metaphors has led to the current, yet flawed, comparison of the brain to a computer. Your brain is not a computer: it does not store memories, process, or retrieve information. Modern science has no definitive understanding of how the brain works. Kenneth Miller has suggested it will take 'centuries' just to figure out basic neuronal connectivity (Miller, 2015).

Significant funding is being channeled into brain research, often driven by flawed ideologies and unachievable promises. A striking example of this misdirection, as reported in Scientific American, is the $1.3 billion Human Brain Project initiated by the European Union in 2013. Spearheaded by the persuasive Henry Markram, the project aimed to simulate the entire human brain on a supercomputer by 2023, promising breakthroughs in treating Alzheimer's disease and other disorders. However, less than two years in, the project encountered major issues, leading to Markram's removal.

Case Study

One notable case that might be interpreted through the lens of synthetic interdimensional beings is the Rendlesham Forest incident of 1980. In this event, U.S. Air Force personnel stationed at RAF Woodbridge in Suffolk, England, encountered unexplained lights and a craft in Rendlesham Forest. One of the servicemen, Jim Penniston, reported experiencing physical and temporal anomalies during his encounter, which he later associated with receiving a binary code message. This message, interpreted years later, was speculated to be a communication from future humans or time travelers, suggesting an interdimensional rather than extraterrestrial origin (Unidentified Phenomena, 2023).

Personal Accounts and Historical References

Historical references to shape-shifting gods, demigods, and other supernatural beings in various cultures may be interpreted as early accounts of synthetic interdimensional beings. Personal accounts from individuals claiming to have encountered such beings often describe them as eerily human-like but possessing an otherworldly presence.

Gamer Perspective

For gamers, the concept of synthetic interdimensional beings offers a rich narrative for immersive gameplay. A game could be designed where players assume the role of interdimensional entities controlling synthetic avatars on Earth. The gameplay could involve missions to manipulate events, gather resources, and interact with other entities, blending elements of strategy, role-playing, and simulation. The game could also explore the ethical dilemmas of such manipulation, providing a thought-provoking experience.

Another option is a game concept where the goal is to discover who is an NPC and who is not. In this game, interactions between humans and NPCs are filtered through large language models. Players would have to engage in conversations, analyze behavior, and gather clues to determine the true nature of each character. This game would blend mystery, strategy, and artificial intelligence, providing an immersive and challenging experience as players navigate through a world filled with hidden synthetic beings.

Psyop Perspective

From the perspective of a psyop, governments might promote the idea that human experience is purely physical, dismissing the metaphysical to suppress the truth and maintain control over the populace. By fostering the belief that humans are merely biological machines, these metaphors dehumanize us and distract from our spiritual existence. This reductionist view serves to strip away the acknowledgment of our interdimensional spiritual essence, making it easier to manipulate and control public perception.

Academic or Scientific References

1. Zarkadakis, George. *In Our Own Image: Savior or Destroyer? The History and Future of Artificial Intelligence.* Rider, 2015.

2. Miller, Kenneth. "Will You Ever Be Able to Upload Your Brain?" The New York Times, 10 Oct. 2015. Accessed 11 Oct. 2023. www.nytimes.com/2015/10/11/opinion/sunday/will-you-ever-be-able-to-upload-your-brain.html

3. Scientific American. "The \$1.3 Billion Human Brain Project." Accessed 11 Oct. 2023. www.scientificamerican.com/article/the-human-brain-project/

4. Unidentified Phenomena. "The Interdimensional Hypothesis." Accessed 11 Oct. 2023. www.unidentifiedphenomena.com/interdimensional-hypothesis

By recognizing the limitations of these flawed metaphors and understanding the broader implications, we can better appreciate the unique complexities of human consciousness and our spiritual connection to the universe. This shift in perspective is crucial as we navigate the future of AI and its role in our society.

Chapter 85

Tall Greys

Tall Greys, also referred as Orions, are a distinct subgroup of the Grey alien species. They are typically depicted as taller and more authoritative than their shorter counterparts, playing significant roles in extraterrestrial hierarchies.

These beings are frequently associated with abduction scenarios and are a prominent feature in modern ufology.

Historical Context and Origins

Tall Greys have been prominent in alien lore and abduction narratives since the mid-20th century. They are often mentioned in connection with secret interactions and agreements with human governments, particularly during the 1950s and 1960s. Reports suggest they come from the Orion star system and have a long-standing interest in human genetics and reproduction. However the Tall Greys could be hiding thier true origin, inner earth.

Descriptions and Characteristics

- **Height**: Typically ranging from 6 to 8 feet, with some accounts mentioning heights up to 11 feet.

- **Appearance**: They have grey skin, large heads, and prominent black, almond-shaped eyes. Some descriptions include a slightly iridescent quality to their skin.

- **Behavior**: Known for their advanced technology and telepathic abilities, Tall Greys often conduct mental procedures during abductions, involving intense staring that can induce altered states of consciousness. They also appear to float or glide instead of walking, adding to their otherworldly presence.

- **Diplomatic and Less Hostile**: These Greys are often described as more diplomatic and less hostile when dealing with humans, demonstrating special or miraculous powers, which some attribute to advanced technology and others to spiritual or biological gifts.

- **Reproductive Capabilities**: Despite engaging in modified cloning, artificial insemination, and implantation for reproduction, Tall Greys possess reproductive organs. However, they often perform tasks considered as "dirty work" for the Reptilian class, despite their high position in the Grey alien hierarchy.

Unique and Obscure Facts

- **Hierarchical Structure**: Tall Greys are believed to hold leadership positions within a hierarchical alien society, overseeing the more commonly reported shorter Greys.

- **Genetic Interest:** Many abduction accounts suggest that Tall Greys are particularly interested in human genetics and reproduction, possibly for hybridization experiments.

- **Telepathic Abilities:** Tall Greys are reported to communicate through advanced telepathy, projecting thoughts and images directly into human minds.

- **Time Manipulation:** Theories propose that Tall Greys possess technology allowing them to manipulate time and space, which explains their sudden appearances and disappearances during encounters.

- **Emotional Detachment:** Witnesses often describe Tall Greys as having a cold, detached demeanor, suggesting limited emotional capacity or a different evolutionary path.

- **Ancient Connections:** Some researchers suggest that Tall Greys might be connected to ancient or future human civilizations, potentially being the inspiration behind certain mythological beings or gods. It is more likley they are a hybid mazikin or shedim.

- **Odor and Smell**

Ammonia-like Odor: In the 1996 Varginha incident in Brazil, witnesses reported a putrid smell of ammonia at the scene where they claimed to have encountered an extraterrestrial being .

- **General Unpleasant Smell:** Michael Menkin, a former NASA technical writer, has collected accounts from alleged abductees who describe aliens as having a very strong, unpleasant odor .

- **Sulfur-Containing Gases:** Some reports associate alien smells with sulfur-containing gases, which are also found in human flatulence .

- **Rotten or Putrid Odors:** Various accounts describe alien-related smells as being particularly foul or rotten .

Mythological Interpretations

Tall Greys have been compared to mythological figures due to their advanced capabilities and psychological impact. Their hypnotic stare and mental manipulations draw parallels to ancient myths of beings with mind control or enchantment abilities.

Dimensional Attributes and Existence

Tall Greys are believed to originate from higher-dimensional planes, allowing them to manipulate space and time differently from humans. This interdimensional nature contributes to their perceived power and presence in human affairs.

Case Study

A notable case involves a Tall Grey sighting reported by Dr. David Jacobs in his extensive research on alien abductions. One abductee, referred to as "Beth," described multiple encounters with Tall Greys who performed various experiments on her, including reproductive procedures. This case is detailed in Jacobs' book "The Threat: Revealing the Secret Alien Agenda," highlighting the Tall Greys' role in overseeing complex hybridization experiments and their strategic importance within the Grey hierarchy

Personal Accounts and Historical References

- **Herbert Schirmer's Abduction**: Schirmer, a police officer from Nebraska, claimed under hypnosis to have been abducted by Tall Greys in 1967. He described them as having a slightly reptilian appearance and using a "winged serpent" emblem.

- **Phil Schneider's Testimony**: Schneider, a geologist and engineer, claimed to have encountered Tall Greys during a firefight at the Dulce Base in 1979, emphasizing their advanced weaponry and the significant threat they posed.

- **Dr. David Jacobs' Studies**: Dr. David Jacobs, a well-known researcher in the field of alien abductions, has extensively studied cases involving Tall Greys. In his book "The Threat: The Secret Agenda," Jacobs details the hierarchical role of Tall Greys in abduction scenarios, often overseeing the activities of shorter Greys and being involved in complex hybridization experiments with human subjects

Psyop

The narrative of Tall Greys fits into the broader context of government cover-ups and the suppression of entites from other unseen earthly realms. The idea that Tall Greys are involved in secret agreements with human governments and conduct abductions underlines fears of hidden, manipulative forces influenceing global events. This narrative supports about covert operations and intentional disinformation campaigns to keep the public unaware of thier existance amdinteractions. The concept of alien abductions often parallels sexual assault, with abductees reporting invasive procedures and forced breeding without consent. Channeling conversations with Tall Greys claim these actions are justified by a "soul contract," suggesting preordained cosmic agreements. This idea is ethically problematic and does not alleviate the real psychological trauma experienced by abductees.

Academic or Scientific References

- "Dr. David Jacobs on Abductions" - davidmichaeljacobs.com

- "The Threat: Revealing the Secret Alien Agenda" by David Jacobs - Simon & Schuster

- "Strange Encounters | UFO's Investigating the Unknown" - YouTube: https://www.youtube.com/watch?v=hXO_RwR1UA8

- "Alien abduction claims examined" - Harvard Gazette: https://news.harvard.edu/gazette/story/2003/02/alien-abduction-claims-examined-2/

- "A sign that aliens could stink" - MIT News: https://news.mit.edu/2019/phosphine-aliens-stink-1218

Chapter 86

Tall Whites

(Mazani, 2nd Hybrid Race)

Tall Whites are described as an advanced, humanoid extraterrestrial race with interdimensional abilities, believed to originate from stars near Arcturus.

Charles Hall, a former U.S. Air Force serviceman, reported encounters with the Tall Whites during his assignment at Nellis Air Force Base from 1965 to 1967. He claimed these beings could blend into human society and had a significant influence over world affairs. Tall Whites are noted for their exceptional height (up to 8 feet), white chalky skin, and advanced technology. They are believed to communicate through sounds resembling barking or chirping and can mimic human speech.

Historical Encounters

Colonel H.G. Shaw's Encounter (1896): One of the earliest modern reports of Tall Whites dates back to 1896 when Colonel H.G. Shaw described encountering three 7-foot-tall beings with polished ivory-like skin, who communicated through warbling sounds like birds. This incident was reported in the Stockton Evening Mail, making it one of the first documented encounters with Tall White-like entities.

Unique and Obscure Facts

- The Tall Whites have a lifespan of around 800 years.

- They can sprint at speeds of 40 mph and have blue eyes that wrap around their heads.

- They communicate using a script resembling Egyptian hieroglyphics.

- Their diet does not include meat, and they have a preference for mushroom pudding.

- They wear aluminized chalk-white jumpsuits that emit a fluorescent light.

- Tall Whites visit Earth during the full moon in warm months to repair their ships and vacation in the desert.

Mythological Interpretations

In various mythologies, the Tall Whites are seen as benevolent guides assisting humanity's evolution. They are often depicted as watchers or guardians with a deep interest in human affairs. Their appearance and behaviors are sometimes linked to ancient gods or mythical figures from different cultures, emphasizing their role as protectors and educators.

Dimensional Attributes and Existence

The Tall Whites are believed to exist across multiple dimensions. Their advanced technology and communication methods suggest an understanding of dimensions beyond the three-dimensional reality humans perceive. They can project speech into human minds and may travel between dimensions, explaining their elusive nature and advanced capabilities.

Case Study

A notable case involving the Tall Whites is Charles Hall's detailed accounts of their interactions with humans. Hall described how the Tall Whites frequented Las Vegas in human disguises, with CIA agents ensuring their safety. He also recounted their advanced technology, including faster-than-light spacecraft and a device for projecting speech into human heads.

Personal Accounts and Historical References

Charles Hall's books, such as the "Millennial Hospitality" series, provide extensive personal accounts of his interactions with the Tall Whites. These narratives include detailed descriptions of their physical appearance, behaviors, and technological capabilities. Historical references to similar beings can be found in various mythologies, suggesting a long-standing presence on Earth.

Government Involvement and Conspiracies

Paul Hellyer's Admission: Paul Hellyer, a former Canadian Defense Minister, publicly acknowledged the presence of multiple extraterrestrial species, including the Tall Whites. His statements lend a degree of credibility to the claims, given his high-ranking position within the government.

Academic or Scientific References

- Hall, Charles. "Millennial Hospitality" series.

- "The Sirius Mystery" by Robert K.G. Temple.

- "The Encyclopedia of Ghosts and Spirits" by Rosemary Ellen Guiley. While not exclusively about Tall Whites, this comprehensive encyclopedia covers various paranormal entities, including extraterrestrial beings, in detail.

- Hellyer, Paul. "The Money Mafia: A World in Crisis." This book discusses Hellyer's views on extraterrestrial presence and government involvement.

Tachash

(Takhash, Unicorn)

T achash is often identified with the mythical unicorn, and is described as a unique and sacred creature endowed with extraordinary dimensional abilities.

According to various legends, unicorns possess the ability to navigate effortlessly between dimensions, primarily dwelling in the ethereal seventh dimension, which is closely associated with angelic beings.

This dimension transcends the conventional bounds of space and time, enabling unicorns to harness magical energy that extends beyond our known universe.

In Jewish mysticism and scripture, the Tachash holds a special place. It is mentioned in the context of the construction of the Mishkan (Tabernacle), where its unique and colorful hide was used to create the Tabernacle's coverings. According to the Midrash and Talmud, the Tachash was specifically created by G-d for this sacred purpose and then became hidden from the world after its role was fulfilled. This disappearance is sometimes interpreted as the creature being hidden within the inner earth, a realm thought to house various mythical beings.

The Tachash is often considered a symbol of divine creation and purpose. Its brief existence during the construction of the Mishkan illustrates the idea that everything in the world has a specific, holy purpose. The Lubavitcher Rebbe emphasized this concept, stating that the ultimate purpose of all creation is to serve G-d, and the Tachash embodies this ideal through its exclusive use in a holy context.

Historical Context and Origins

The Tachash is first mentioned in Jewish texts, particularly in the context of the construction of the Mishkan (Tabernacle). According to the Midrash and Talmud, the Tachash was specifically created by G-d for use in the Mishkan's construction and then became hidden from the world after this purpose was fulfilled. This notion is further explored in various mystical writings, suggesting the Tachash's concealment within the inner earth, alongside other mythological creatures.

Descriptions and Characteristics

- **Appearance:** Unicorns are depicted as ethereal beings, often with angelic features. They are described as winged creatures with a distinct and majestic appearance, combining elements of traditional unicorns with celestial characteristics.

- **Speed and Movement:** Renowned for their incredible speed, unicorns symbolize swift journeys not only within our realm but also across other dimensions.

- **Dimensional Abilities:** Unicorns are believed to effortlessly navigate between different dimensions, with their primary residence being in the seventh dimension.

Unique and Obscure Facts

- **Dimensional Residence:** Unicorns are believed to dwell primarily in the seventh dimension, a realm associated with heightened spiritual awareness and angelic beings.

- **Creation for Holiness:** According to the Lubavitcher Rebbe, the Tachash was created specifically for holy purposes, illustrating the ultimate aim of all creation to serve G-d.

- **Inner Earth Concealment:** Post-construction of the Mishkan, the Tachash was hidden from the world, with some legends placing it within the inner earth alongside other mythological creatures such as the phoenix, minotaur, and dragon.

- **Magical Energy:** Within the seventh dimension, unicorns harness and utilize magical energy that transcends the limitations of space and time.

Mythological Interpretations:

The Tachash is often linked to various mythological interpretations, with some traditions equating it to the unicorn. Legends suggest that unicorns serve as symbols of purity and divine purpose, their existence intertwined with the mystical and sacred aspects of creation.

Dimensional Attributes and Existence:

- **Higher Spiritual Dimensions:** Unicorns are believed to reside in the seventh dimension, a realm of enlightenment and spiritual evolution.

- **Interdimensional Portals:** The concept of unicorns traveling through interdimensional portals is prevalent, indicating their ability to traverse different planes of existence.

- **Parallel Realities and Multidimensional Existence:** Unicorns are speculated to navigate parallel realities and exist seamlessly in multiple dimensions beyond our conventional understanding.

Case Study:

In the context of Jewish mysticism, the Tachash is uniquely mentioned in relation to the construction of the Mishkan. The creature's skin was used to create the coverings for the sacred structure, emphasizing its significance and sanctity. This specific use for the Mishkan and its subsequent disappearance aligns with the belief that the Tachash was a special creation with a divine purpose.

Personal Accounts and Historical References:

- **Talmudic and Midrashic Texts**: These texts discuss the creation and purpose of the Tachash, describing it as a unique animal brought into existence for the Mishkan and hidden afterward. Sources include "JewishAnswers.org" and other Jewish scholarly writings:

    - Unicorns in the Talmud, JewishAnswers.org: www.jewishanswers.org/ask-the-rabbi-category/miscellaneous/unicorns-in-the-talmud/

    - Terumah - The Jewish Unicorn?, Sefaria: www.sefaria.org/sheets/184237.2?lang=bi

- **Hesed L'Avaraham**: This mystical text references the inner earth as the dwelling place for various mythical creatures, including the Tachash.

    - Sefaria's library of Jewish sources on Tachash: www.sefaria.org/topics/Tachash

- **Torat Menachem 5752**: The Lubavitcher Rebbe elaborates on the Tachash's purpose, emphasizing its role in illustrating the ultimate aim of all creation to serve G-d.

Academic or Scientific References:

- "Torat Menachem 5752" by the Lubavitcher Rebbe

- "Hesed L'Avaraham" 2:4

- "Unicorns in the Talmud" by JewishAnswers.org: www.jewishanswers.org/ask-the-rabbi-category/miscellaneous/unicorns-in-the-talmud/

- "Terumah - The Jewish Unicorn?" by Sefaria: www.sefaria.org/sheets/184237.2?lang=bi

Chapter 88

Telosians

Lumerians

Telosians are an alleged subterranean race believed to reside beneath Mount Shasta in Northern California. They are often described as descendants of the ancient Lemurians, an advanced civilization that supposedly flourished on the lost continent of Lemuria.

According to lore, Lemuria faced a catastrophic end, leading the surviving Lemurians to establish a new home in the underground city of Telos, hidden deep within Mount Shasta.

Telosians are depicted as a highly spiritual and enlightened race, embodying the advanced knowledge and wisdom of their ancestors. They are said to possess telepathic abilities, allowing them to communicate with humans and other beings without the need for spoken language. The Telosians' profound connection to spiritual realms and higher dimensions is a cornerstone of their identity, suggesting they live in a state of heightened consciousness.

Mount Shasta, standing as a lone sentinel in the northern California landscape, is surrounded by various legends and paranormal phenomena, including sightings of mysterious beings, unexplained disappearances, and ghost stories. Native American tribes, such as the Shasta, Wintu, Achumawi, Atsugewi, and Modoc, have long regarded the mountain as sacred, home to the "sky people" who are believed to reside above the tree line. Some interpret these sky people as the Telosians, who, rather than being spirits of the deceased, are seen as living, non-human entities.

The lore of Telosians is deeply intertwined with the legends of Mount Shasta, making the mountain a focal point for numerous spiritual seekers, researchers, and enthusiasts of the paranormal. Reports from visitors describe encounters with these beings, receiving telepathic messages during meditation, and experiencing heightened energy and spiritual awakenings around the mountain. This mystical allure has attracted a diverse following, from poets and naturalists to members of fringe religious groups like the Ascended Masters.

Historical Context and Origins

Mount Shasta is renowned for its numerous paranormal phenomena, including mysterious disappearances and ghost stories. Native American legends, including those from the Shasta, Wintu, Achumawi, Atsugewi, and Modoc tribes, emphasize the mountain's sacred nature and the presence of "sky people" above the tree line. According to lore, these sky people might not be spirits but living, non-human beings—potentially the Lemurians.

Descriptions and Characteristics

Telosians are typically described as tall, often around seven feet, with flowing hair, sandals, and white robes. They are said to be a highly spiritual race capable of telepathic communication. Visitors to Mount Shasta report receiving positive messages during meditation and having ethereal sightings of these beings.

Unique and Obscure Facts

- **Mount Shasta's Mystique**: Mount Shasta stands as a solitary, imposing figure in Northern California, making it a focal point for paranormal activities and legends. The formation of distinctive lenticular clouds, resembling spaceships, adds to its supernatural allure.

- **Lemurian Refugees**: According to Frederick Spencer Oliver's "A Dweller on Two Planets," Lemurians and Atlanteans were advanced civilizations. After a catastrophic conflict, Lemurians found refuge in Telos beneath Mount Shasta.

- **Energetic Presence**: Many visitors and skeptics alike report heightened energy around Mount Shasta, suggesting a mysterious presence awaiting discovery.

- **Historical Anomaly**: Mount Shasta's geological position, about 15 miles west of the standard arc line of other Cascade volcanoes, remains unexplained, adding to its enigmatic nature.

- **Paranormal Nexus**: The mountain's link to various mythical beings, including the Lizard People and Bigfoot, has attracted diverse followers and researchers.

Mythological Interpretations

Telosians are believed to have a profound connection to ancient myths, including those of Lemuria and Atlantis. They are seen as highly spiritual beings with advanced knowledge and wisdom, embodying the ideals of their ancient civilization.

Dimensional Attributes and Existence

- **Higher Spiritual Dimensions**: Telosians are thought to access higher spiritual dimensions, realms of heightened consciousness and enlightenment.

- **Interdimensional Portals**: Mount Shasta is speculated to house interdimensional portals allowing beings like Telosians to traverse between different planes of existence.

- **Multidimensional Existence**: Telosians are believed to operate in and move seamlessly between different dimensions, beyond our conventional understanding of space and time.

Case Study

A notable account involving Telosians comes from the book "Telos: The Call Goes Out from the Hollow Earth and the Underground Cities" by Dianne Robbins. The author describes her communication with Adama, the high priest of Telos, who shares spiritual teachings and perspectives from the Telosian civilization. This interaction provides a glimpse into the life and wisdom of the Telosians, emphasizing their advanced spiritual nature.

Personal Accounts and Historical References

- **Frederick Spencer Oliver's "A Dweller on Two Planets"**: This book describes the ancient civilizations of Lemuria and Atlantis, suggesting that Lemurians took refuge in Mount Shasta after a cataclysmic war.

- **Dianne Robbins' "Telos"**: Robbins recounts her telepathic communication with Adama, offering insights into the Telosian way of life and their spiritual wisdom.

Academic or Scientific References

- "Telos: The Call Goes Out from the Hollow Earth and the Underground Cities" by Dianne Robbins

- "Telos – Volume 1: Revelations of the New Lemuria" by Aurelia Louise Jones

- "Lemuria and Atlantis: Studying the Past to Survive the Future" by Shirley Andrews

Chapter 89

Teli

Tali, Theli, Theli, T'li

"**M**an is not the first race of Man here on planet Earth. There were others, many other Men, before our present form on Earth.

The older 'men of Earth' have evolved off our planet to their own Olam HaBa (afterlife), from which they serve the Creator as Watchers (Teli) over the younger races of Man. The Teli (Təlī; also translated as Tali, Thele, T'li, etc.) is a celestial entity depicted in the Sefer Yetzirah, the oldest surviving text of mysticism, positioned 'above the universe, as a king on his throne.' Often envisioned as a dragon, Teli is considered a powerful and mysterious cosmic force."

Historical Context and Origins

The Teli, originally known as the Dragon Masters, are believed to be the original Reptilians with origins tracing back to Earth. They evolved into spiritual beings serving as creators of the universe and humanity, taking on roles as Watchers and Guardians. Their presence is deeply rooted in ancient texts and mystical traditions.

Descriptions and Characteristics

Teli are described as dragon-like beings with reptilian features such as scales and serpent-like bodies. They are seen as overseeing celestial spheres and acting as cosmic guardians, possessing profound cosmic knowledge and spiritual power. Teli are known to take human form when interacting with people, known as the human-like angels called Ishim.

Unique and Obscure Facts

- Maimonides writes that all stars and planets possess a soul, knowledge, and intellect, and are alive, though their knowledge is less than that of angels.

- Nachmanides reveals that certain stars are guided by archangels, called the Princes of the Teli, who are the souls of those planets.

- **The first and only source for knowledge of the Teli is the ancient Sefer Yetzirah.** The Teli rule space like a king on his throne, as per the Sefer Yetzirah.

Mythological Interpretations

The Teli are linked to the Nahash Briah (fleeing serpent) and the Aklaton (winding), representing duality and cosmic balance. They are seen as holy and angelic beings, fulfilling roles of service both in Heaven and on Earth, and are associated with the biblical Watchers.

Dimensional Attributes and Existence

Teli are non-corporeal entities existing above the time-space continuum, influencing the cosmos and human destiny. They are considered to be spiritual guides, guiding the emanation of divine energy and maintaining cosmic order.

Case Study

The Ministers of the Zodiac are described as the Princes of the Teli, who control celestial spheres. These Princes are the souls of the spheres, each guided by a unique intelligence. They are responsible for the leadership over all the hosts above and influence both the heavenly and earthly realms. This concept is elaborated by Rabbi Menahem Tziyuni in "Sefer Tziyuni on the Torah."

Personal Accounts and Historical References

Maimonides and Nachmanides describe the relationship between angels and planets, highlighting the role of the Teli as cosmic guardians. Historical texts such as the Sefer Yetzirah and biblical references to the Watchers provide insight into the nature and influence of the Teli.

Psyop

The concept of the Teli shares intriguing parallels with modern Reptilian overlord conspiracy theories. The Teli are envisioned as dragon-like beings with reptilian characteristics such as scales and serpent-like bodies, imagery that easily connects with the modern depiction of Reptilians. Described as overseeing celestial spheres and acting as cosmic guardians, the Teli's role as watchers aligns with the belief in Reptilian overlords controlling human affairs from positions of power.

Academic or Scientific References

- "Sefer Yetzirah: The Book of Creation" – Translations and interpretations of the oldest mystical text.

- Rabbi Menahem Tziyuni, "Sefer Tziyuni on the Torah, Parshat Aharei" – Exploration of the Teli in biblical context.

- Maimonides, "Laws of the Foundations of Torah (3:9)" – Discussion on the soul and intellect of celestial bodies.

Chapter 90

Tic Tac

The Nimitz encounter with the Tic Tac has demonstrated that exotic technology, often considered the domain of science fiction, actually exists.

This phenomenon is real and not the result of altered perceptions, dreams, weather balloons, or swamp gas. It indicates that someone or something has achieved a breakthrough in aerospace engineering. The "Tic Tac" is an unidentified flying object (UFO) observed by U.S. Navy pilots in 2004, named for its resemblance to the shape and color of a Tic Tac mint. This type of craft is nothing new except for the name; it has been reported for decades under names like "Cigars," "Cylinders," "Propane Tanks," and "Ghost Rockets." According to Tyler Rogoway of The Drive, the technology behind this object performs maneuvers and leverages new ways of our understanding of propulsion, flight controls, material science, and physics.

Historical Context and Origins

The specific phenomenon linked to the 2017 USS Nimitz encounter with the flying Tic Tac is not a recent revelation. During the '60s, it was described as a white flying throat lozenge, and in the '50s, it resembled a white flying butane tank, metal barrel, or cigar. This emphasizes the existence of significant government evidence documenting encounters with Unidentified Aerial Phenomena (UAPs) of this distinct shape over several decades.

Descriptions and Characteristics

The "Tic Tac" UFO is noted for its oblong, smooth, and featureless appearance, resembling a large white mint. It demonstrates physics-defying maneuvers, such as rapid acceleration, sudden stops, and hovering, without any visible means of propulsion or flight surfaces like wings or rotors.

Unique and Obscure Facts

- **Hypersonic speed without sonic boom:** The object was said to travel well over Mach 1 without producing a boom suggesting the object did not interact with the atmosphere.

- **Transmedium Travel:** The object could transition between air and water without difficulty

- **Instantaneous changes in direction:** The object would change direction instantly without inertial effects.

- **Unusual movement:** The object could hover at 80,0000 feet and then descend to sea level in a fraction of a second without any visible propulsion system.

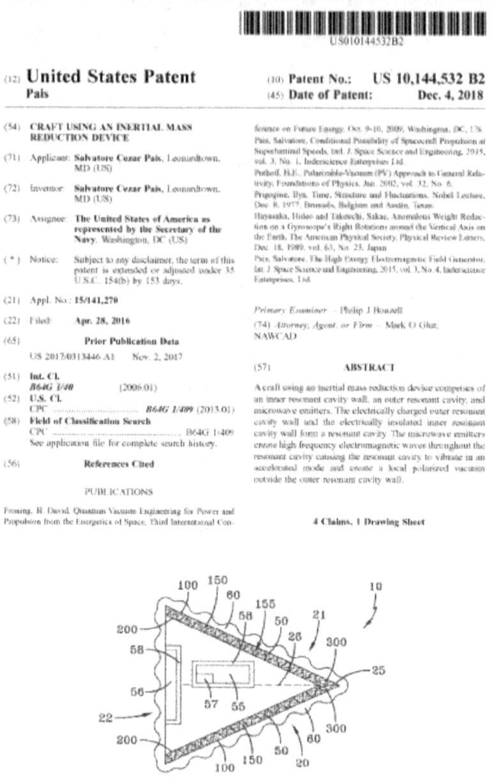

- The plot thickens: The Navy has patents on internal mass reduction devices. Describing the mechanics of a vehicle capable of maneuvering like a tic tac.

Dimensional Attributes and Existence

There are theories suggesting these objects might not originate from outer space but from alternate dimensions or parallel realities. This aligns with the idea that such advanced technology might leverage dimensions beyond our current understanding.

Case Study

2004 USS Nimitz Encounter: In November 2004, pilots from the USS Nimitz Carrier Strike Group encountered a Tic Tac-shaped UFO off the coast of San Diego. The object was reported to perform rapid movements and showed capabilities far beyond current aerospace technology. The incident was captured on video and has been subject to extensive analysis.

Additional Reference: The phenomenon is also documented in a declassified report from 1953, which describes similar objects labeled as 'flying lozenges' (CIA Report: https://www.cia.gov/reading-groom/docs/DOC_0000015474.pdf).

Capt. Jack Puckett's Encounter: On August 1, 1946, Capt. Jack Puckett, while flying a C-47 near Tampa, Florida, reported seeing a cigar-shaped UFO, adding to the historical context of similar sightings.

Disinformation Campaigns by the US Air Force and Pentagon

The U.S. Air Force and the Pentagon have a long history of disinformation campaigns, often using UFO sightings to conceal advanced aerospace technology. Reports suggest that mysterious men in black, often appearing after UFO sightings, are members of the Air Force's Office of Special Investigations (AFOSI). The AFOSI's role includes controlling information and the security of technology, making disinformation a key strategy in maintaining secrecy.

A report by the New York Times in 1997 shows that the CIA and the Air Force promoted UFOs to cover up sightings of their U2 and SR-71 spy planes.

The mysterious men in black, unknown individuals in suits who show up after credible UFO sightings, are none other than members of the Air Force's Office of Special Investigations. AFOSI is a cross between the CIA and the FBI; in fact, AFOSI was modeled after the FBI. The first commander of AFOSI was former FBI special agent Joseph Carroll. Among AFOSI's unique mission is the security of technology and information, intelligence gathering and threat assessment, mitigation and elimination. That makes sense because, in an open society like ours, where the government cannot easily control the flow of public information, disinformation is the only viable option to maintain a degree of secrecy. For its part, the AFOSI is an expert at controlling information.

Some Questions Remain

No matter how good scientists are at aerospace development, it's unlikely they have found a way to seemingly leverage the laws of physics in new ways. But if they have and this unidentified craft is ours, it proves how selfish and misguided parts of our government can be. They have been operating this type of craft for over 60 years without rolling it out to the public. Why won't they share this technology? This technology would benefit humanity immensely. Except for our "screens," humanity has been at a technological standstill for 60 years. Why do they prevent humanity from moving forward? If they are interdimensional craft then they need to offer free rides.

Academic and Scientific References

- **CIA Report on Flying Lozenges: CIA Reading Room** https://www.cia.gov/readingroom/docs/DOC_0000015474.pdf

- **The Drive – Tyler Rogoway's Reporting:** The Drive

- **New York Times Report on CIA and Air Force Disinformation Campaigns (1997):** New York Times https://www.nytimes.com/1997/09/14/magazine/cia-and-air-force-cover-up.html

- **Patent for Inertial Mass Antigravity Device** https://patents.google.com/patent/US10144532B2/en

Chapter 91

Ulterrans

Ultraterrestrials

Ultraterrestrials, also known as Ulterrans, are postulated beings that exist in alternate or parallel dimensions, potentially coexisting with Earth's reality.

They are considered highly advanced entities capable of manipulating physical laws and human perception, often interacting with humanity in ways that defy conventional understanding.

Historical Context and Origins

The concept of Ultraterrestrials has historical roots dating back to ancient texts around 2600 years ago, where they were described as supernatural beings with power over humans. During the Middle Ages, this idea evolved to incorporate mythical creatures like vampires and fairies, believed to be influenced by Ulterran powers. Modern interpretations vary, with some viewing them as benevolent guides and others as sinister forces manipulating humanity.

Descriptions and Characteristics

Ultraterrestrials are described as possessing superior intelligence and advanced technological capabilities. They can appear in various forms, sometimes humanoid, but their true nature is beyond human comprehension. They are believed to manipulate time, space, and human consciousness, appearing and disappearing at will.

Unique and Obscure Facts

John Keel, a prominent researcher, introduced the concept of Ultraterrestrials in works such as *The Mothman Prophecies* and *The Eighth Tower*. He suggested that these beings have been interacting with humanity for centuries, often being mistaken for gods, angels, or demons. Keel theorized that many UFO sightings and paranormal activities could be attributed to Ultraterrestrials.

Mythological Interpretations

In various cultures, beings similar to Ultraterrestrials appear as gods or supernatural entities. For example, trickster gods in many mythologies might represent the unpredictable and elusive nature of Ultraterrestrials.

Dimensional Attributes and Existence

Ultraterrestrials are believed to exist in dimensions parallel to our own. They can traverse these dimensions, allowing them to appear and disappear seemingly at will. This ability might explain their involvement in various unexplained phenomena. Keel proposed the existence of four intersecting "Universes" comprising the "Omniverse," including matter and antimatter universes with 11 dimensional densities each.

Case Study

- A notable case supporting the concept of Ultraterrestrials involves Joseph Vorin, who appeared disoriented in 1850 near Frankfurt-am-Oder, Germany, speaking an unknown language. This case aligns with the idea of individuals being unintentionally transported between dimensions.

- The cryptoterrestrial hypothesis, as detailed in the Harvard paper "The Cryptoterrestrial Hypothesis: A Case for Scientific Openness to a Concealed Earthly Explanation for Unidentified Anomalous Phenomena," explores similar concepts. This hypothesis suggests that some UAP sightings could be linked to advanced, hidden civilizations on Earth. Source

Personal Accounts and Historical References

John Keel's research includes numerous personal accounts of encounters with Ultraterrestrials, often involving telepathic communication and environmental manipulation. Keel's work is filled with case studies where witnesses report strange beings that defy conventional explanations.

Insights from "The Eighth Tower" by John Keel

In *The Eighth Tower*, Keel explores the idea that Ultraterrestrials might be part of a larger, invisible control system that governs human perception and behavior. He suggests that these entities might be using Earth as a laboratory, conducting experiments on humans and influencing historical events to observe the outcomes.

Academic and Scientific References

- Keel, John. *The Mothman Prophecies*. Tor Books, 1975.

- Keel, John. *The Eighth Tower*. Signet, 1975.

- Lomas, Tim, Brendan Case, and Michael Paul Masters. "The Cryptoterrestrial Hypothesis: A Case for Scientific Openness to a Concealed Earthly Explanation for Unidentified Anomalous Phenomena." Philosophy and Cosmology 33, June 2024.

- Tonnies, Mac. *The Cryptoterrestrials: A Meditation on Indigenous Humanoids and the Aliens Among Us*. Anomalist Books, 2010.

Chapter 92

Umana Adapa

The intriguing similarity in etymology between Adapa and Adam, coupled with the parallelism in their stories, poses a compelling question regarding the authentic history of humankind. Umana Adapa, often simply referred to as Adapa, is a significant figure in ancient Mesopotamian mythology.

He is considered a wise man or sage, created by the god Ea (Enki). Adapa is renowned for his wisdom and is often associated with themes of knowledge, wisdom, and the quest for immortality.

Historical Context and Origins

The story of Adapa originates from Sumerian and Akkadian myths, predating the biblical account of Adam. Adapa is considered the first of the seven antediluvian sages (apkallu) in Mesopotamian lore. These sages were believed to have brought knowledge and civilization to humanity, serving as priests and advisors to kings.

Descriptions and Characteristics

Adapa is described as a "model of men" and a sage with exceptional wisdom. He served in the city of Eridu, providing for its temple and aiding in various civic duties. He is depicted as having magical abilities, such as cursing the south wind, which demonstrates his power and influence.

Unique and Obscure Facts

1. **Connection to Adam**: There is a fascinating etymological similarity between Adapa and Adam, which has led scholars to explore potential parallels between the two figures. Both names suggest a foundational role in human history.

2. **Fish or Serpent–like Appearance**: Adapa is sometimes associated with fish or serpent-like characteristics, which is mirrored in the descriptions of the Dogon people's Nommo and the Babylonian Oannes.

Mythological Interpretations

Adapa's story highlights themes of wisdom and the pursuit of immortality. Unlike the biblical Adam, who is seen as the first man and a sinner, Adapa is portrayed as a wise man who follows his god's counsel faithfully. His myth involves a test with heavenly food, which he refuses on the advice of Ea, demonstrating his obedience and the limitations of human wisdom compared to divine knowledge.

Dimensional Attributes and Existence

Adapa exists in a realm where he interacts with gods and possesses extraordinary abilities. His story involves travel to the heavens, indicating his unique position between the divine and mortal worlds. Adapa's existence underscores the ancient Mesopotamian belief in a hierarchical universe where humans could aspire to interact with divine beings but not attain their immortality.

Case Study: The Wisdom of Adapa

Adapa's story is recounted in several ancient texts, including those from the Ashurbanipal library and the Amarna archives. These texts describe his journey to heaven and his interactions with the gods Anu and Ea. Adapa's refusal to eat the bread and water of life, following Ea's advice, is a pivotal moment in the myth, emphasizing the themes of wisdom, obedience, and human limitation.

Personal Accounts and Historical References

- **Sumerian Tablets**: Ancient Sumerian tablets describe Adapa's journey to the heavens and his interactions with the gods, particularly Enki.

- **Rabbi Israel Lipschitz**: In his work "Drush Ohr HaChayim," Lipschitz discusses the idea of pre-Adamic worlds and human-like creatures, offering a perspective that aligns with some midrashic traditions and modern scientific findings. Lipschitz suggests that God created and destroyed multiple worlds before our current one. Each successive world was more advanced than the previous, with our present world being the final iteration.

Academic and Scientific References

- "The Sumerians: Their History, Culture, and Character" by Samuel Noah Kramer

- "History Begins at Sumer: Thirty-Nine Firsts in Recorded History" by Samuel Noah Kramer

- "Inanna: Queen of Heaven and Earth: Her Stories and Hymns from Sumer" by Diane Wolkstein and Samuel Noah Kramer

- "The Sumerian World" edited by Harriet Crawford

- Andrews University Seminary Studies, Autumn 1981, Vol. 19, No. 3, "Adam and Adapa: Two Anthropological Characters" by Niels-Erik Andreasen. Andrews University Seminary Studies, Autumn 1981, Vol. 19, No. 3.

Chapter 93

Ummites

In the 1960s, an intriguing series of letters began circulating in Spain and France, claiming to be from beings called the Ummites, purported interdimensional entities hailing from the planet UMMO.

This mysterious planet, as described in the letters, orbits the star Wolf 424, approximately 14.2 light years from Earth. The letters, filled with advanced scientific concepts and detailed descriptions of Ummite society, captured the imagination of many and have since become a fascinating subject of study and speculation.

Historical Context and Origins

The first Ummo letters appeared in 1966 in Madrid, Spain. These letters purportedly came from extraterrestrial beings from UMMO, a planet orbiting the star Wolf 424. The Ummites claimed to have received radio transmissions from Earth in the late 1940s and decided to investigate our planet, allegedly landing in Spain in the 1950s and establishing contact with a select group of individuals in 1965.

Descriptions and Characteristics

- **Physical Appearance**: The Ummites are described as humanoid but with distinct differences from humans. They are taller, with elongated limbs, pale skin, and slightly larger eyes adapted to the conditions of their home planet.

- **Technology**: The letters describe advanced technologies, including spacecraft capable of interdimensional travel, magneto-hydrodynamic propulsion, shockwave elimination at supersonic speeds, and sophisticated communication devices.

- **Society**: The Ummites claim their society is highly organized and focused on scientific and technological progress. They emphasize ethical guidelines and a principle of non-interference in their interactions with other civilizations.

Unique and Obscure Facts

- **Advanced Linguistic Structure**: The Ummo letters exhibit a highly sophisticated linguistic structure, resembling an artificial language designed for clarity and precision. Some linguists have analyzed the letters and found them to exhibit a logical consistency.

- **Unique Symbol System**: The letters often included a unique symbol, purportedly the planetary insignia of UMMO, consisting of a line joining two interlaced circles. This emblem was reportedly seen on some of their spacecraft.

- **Tetravalent Mathematics**: The letters discuss a new form of mathematics called "tetravalent" mathematics, which was not widely known or understood at the time, suggesting either a highly imaginative hoax or genuine advanced knowledge.

- **Multidimensional Understanding**: The Ummites claim to use at least ten dimensions of reality, allowing them to travel vast distances quickly by utilizing folds and warps in the space-time continuum.

- **Ethical and Observational Mission**: The Ummites claim to adhere to strict ethical guidelines in their interactions with humanity. They emphasize observation without direct interference, a principle that aligns with the idea of non-intervention in less advanced civilizations. This ethical stance is part of a broader cosmic ethic followed by advanced interdimensional civilizations.

Mythological Interpretations

The Ummo letters have inspired numerous theories and interpretations, ranging from hoaxes to genuine extraterrestrial contact. The detailed scientific knowledge and ethical stances described in the letters have led some to consider them as part of a broader mythos of interdimensional and interstellar civilizations. The Ummites also mention their communication with other beings, including the Lyrians, humanoid entities with Nordic features, suggesting a network of interstellar beings that share knowledge and engage in cultural exchange.

Dimensional Attributes and Existence

The Ummites claim to have advanced knowledge of multiple dimensions, which they use for interdimensional travel and communication. They describe their ability to traverse vast distances quickly by exploiting the warps in the space-time continuum. Their descriptions include practical uses of at least ten dimensions of reality.

Case Study: A Notable Case

The most notable case involving the Ummo letters is the initial dissemination in Spain in 1966. These letters, received by various individuals and institutions, provided detailed accounts of Ummite society, technology, and their observations of Earth. The letters' scientific content, such as descriptions of advanced propulsion systems and new mathematical concepts, suggested a high level of knowledge that intrigued researchers and skeptics alike. Additionally, a 2024 paper published in the Journal of Modern Physics discusses the potential for interdimensional beings and their interaction with our reality. The study highlights the possibility of advanced life forms existing in multiple dimensions and their implications for our understanding of the universe (Scientific Research).

Personal Accounts and Historical References

Individuals who received the Ummo letters, such as Spanish journalist José Luis Jordán Peña, played significant roles in publicizing the phenomenon. Over the years, numerous books, documentaries, and discussions have delved into the mystery of the Ummites, further embedding them into UFO lore and cultural narratives. The Ummites have also provided extensive observations and critiques of human society, often highlighting the destructive tendencies of humanity, such as environmental degradation, warfare, and social inequality. They advocate for greater unity and understanding among humans to achieve a more harmonious existence.

References for Further Reading

- **Ummite Physics and Metaphysics – Welcome Page:** http://www.ummo-sciences.org/en/

- **The Ummo Case: An Intriguing Enigma of Extraterrestrial Contact – Wondergressive:** https://www.wondergressive.com/the-ummo-case-an-intriguing-enigma-of-extraterrestrial-contact

- **Ummo | Exopaedia:** https://www.exopaedia.org/Ummo

- **Scientific Research – Journal of Modern Physics:** https://www.scirp.org/journal/paperinformation?paperid=131506

Chapter 94

Usumgal

(Ushumgallu)

Usumgal, also known as Ušumgallu, refers to a great serpent or dragon in Sumerian and Akkadian mythology.

This entity is often depicted as a colossal serpent with a demonic appearance, associated with terror and violent disturbances, particularly involving the South wind.

Historical Context and Origins

The Usumgal is deeply rooted in ancient Mesopotamian mythology, specifically within Sumerian and Akkadian traditions. It is represented in cuneiform tablets and mythological texts dating back to the late 3rd millennium BCE. The term "Ušumgallu" translates to "Great Dragon," and this being holds a significant place in the pantheon of ancient deities and mythical creatures.

Descriptions and Characteristics

The Usumgal is frequently depicted as a lion-dragon demon, sometimes represented as a four-legged, winged dragon. This being is considered part of the reptilian family in Mesopotamian mythology, alongside other notable creatures like the Bašmu and Mušmaḫḫū. Descriptions emphasize its enormous size, fearsome appearance, and association with chaos and destruction.

Unique and Obscure Facts

- The Usumgal, or "Great Dragon," was often linked with celestial phenomena and believed to have a profound impact on the natural world.

- According to Francisco Lara Penado, the Sumerians deeply feared the Usumgal, which they also called Neera.

- The curse of the South wind, devised by the god An (known as Anu to the Akkadians), comprised four winds causing destruction and calamities, with the Usumgal being a central figure in these disturbances.

Mythological Interpretations

In Akkadian mythology, the Usumgal holds a prestigious position. Assyrian king Aššur-nāṣir-apli II placed golden icons of the Usumgal at the base of the statue of Ninurta, endowing it with royal and divine epithets such as "ušumgal kališ parakkī," meaning "unrivaled ruler of all the sanctuaries." Marduk, a major deity in Babylonian mythology, is also referred to as "the ušumgallu-dragon of the great heavens."

Dimensional Attributes and Existence

The Usumgal is described as existing in a space where its influence spans both the earthly and the celestial realms. In some texts, it is suggested that these beings could be celestial entities or companions of the Anunnaki, an ancient group of deities. The constant references to huge serpents and dragons in the sky across different civilizations hint at a broader mythological significance.

Case Study: The Great Dragon of Eridu

The tablet and key, and the order of the world, contain references to a great dragon in Eridu whose shadow covers the sky and the earth. This dragon is speculated to be a Usumgal, raising questions about its role as a celestial being or a ship of the Anunnaki. The divine Usumgal of the sky is considered a great friend of An and Anki, holding a distinct position in Sumerian mythology.

Personal Accounts and Historical References

- **The Tablets of Destiny:** These tablets are crucial in Anunnaki myths, particularly in the narratives of Enki and the order of the world. They describe Enki as the great prince and lord of abundance, holding the power to create or destroy through the knowledge inscribed on the Tablets of Destiny.

Academic and Scientific References

- Kramer, Samuel Noah. *History Begins at Sumer: Thirty-Nine Firsts in Recorded History*. University of Pennsylvania Press, 1956.

- Black, Jeremy, and Anthony Green. *Gods, Demons and Symbols of Ancient Mesopotamia: An Illustrated Dictionary*. University of Texas Press, 1992.

- Bottéro, Jean. *Religion in Ancient Mesopotamia*. University of Chicago Press, 2001.

Chapter 95

Venusians

Venutians, Nordics, Tall Whites

Nikola Tesla, renowned as one of the greatest scientific minds in history, is also subject to intriguing speculation, with some claiming him to be the most famous Venusian.

Venusians are purported interdimensional beings originating from Venus, often described in the context of extraterrestrial encounters. These beings are said to have advanced knowledge and capabilities, including the ability to traverse different dimensions.

Historical Context and Origins

The concept of Venusians gained prominence in the 1950s when a group of contactees claimed to have interacted with these beings. The first notable account was by George Adamski, who reported meeting a Venusian named Orthon in the California desert on November 20, 1952. Adamski and others like Howard Menger, George Hunt Williamson, Truman Bethurum, George Van Tassel, and Daniel Fry shared similar stories of encountering these beings, who warned of nuclear war and offered insights into their advanced civilization.

Descriptions and Characteristics

Venusians are often described as light-haired, light-skinned, and resembling Nordic humans. They are sometimes referred to as "Nordic aliens" due to their appearance. According to Benjamin Creme and Theosophical teachings, Venusians exist on higher interdimensional frequencies, allowing them to bypass the harsh surface conditions of Venus. They are depicted as benevolent, telepathic beings with advanced technological capabilities.

Unique and Obscure Facts

- One of the most intriguing aspects of Venusian lore is the Integratron, a structure near Giant Rock in California. George Van Tassel claimed that a Venusian named Solganda provided him with the knowledge to build this time travel machine, intended to rejuvenate human bodies and harness cosmic energy. Despite its unconventional origins, the Integratron is recognized on the National Register of Historic Places and remains a topic of fascination.

- Following Nikola Tesla's passing, his research materials were reportedly confiscated by the FBI, with Donald Trump's uncle, John G. Trump, involved in the process. These materials were classified as top secret. Upon the expiration of the confidentiality period, the FBI released the documents to the public. Among them was a surprising revelation suggesting that Tesla may have been an extraterrestrial with interdimensional capabilities originating from Venus. According to the document, Tesla was purportedly brought to Earth from Venus by Venusians in 1856 and raised by a Yugoslav couple. Many propose that Tesla's documented visions and inspirations could be attributed to a network of heightened consciousness from higher dimensions.

Mythological Interpretations

In Theosophical doctrine, Venusians are linked to Sanat Kumara, a deity believed to govern Earth. Sanat Kumara is said to originate from Venus and resides in Shamballa, a mythical city on the etheric plane above the Gobi Desert. This connection underscores the Venusians' portrayal as spiritual and enlightened beings.

Dimensional Attributes and Existence

Venusians are believed to exist across multiple dimensions. Some are said to inhabit the fourth dimension, which allows them to withstand Venus' extreme surface conditions. Others are thought to live beneath the planet's surface in a more conventional third-dimensional state. Their ability to shift between dimensions is often cited as a key aspect of their advanced nature.

Case Study: George Van Tassel and the Integratron

Near Palm Desert, California, Giant Rock is steeped in a captivating narrative involving purported encounters with Venusian aliens and the creation of the Integratron. George Van Tassel obtained permission to develop the land beneath Giant Rock in 1947, where he and his family settled. Van Tassel claimed to have been visited by a Venusian named Solganda who shared insights into a method of time travel aimed at revitalizing the human body. Encouraged by this encounter, Van Tassel commenced construction of the Integratron in 1954, envisioning it as a device to harness energy for life extension and temporal displacement.

"Like an automatic car wash, the Integratron was an amalgam of architecture and machine. Its purpose was not to transport a fixed body to a different time, as time machines typically do, but to eliminate time's effect on a body; the machine produced time, rather than suck it away."

Crafted based on plans allegedly provided by the Venusian visitors, the Integratron features 16 spines and is believed to sit atop an energy vortex. Despite Van Tassel's aspirations, the project was abandoned following his death in 1978, leaving its true purpose shrouded in mystery. Presently, the unfinished Integratron is not operational and currently serves as a tourist trap. Despite its unconventional origins, the Integratron's inclusion on the National Register of Historic Places distinguishes it as the sole edifice attributed to Venusian design.

Giant Rock is located at 34.3329632589685, -116.38872190883463.

Personal Accounts and Historical References

George Adamski's account of meeting Orthon is one of the earliest and most detailed reports of Venusian contact. Adamski claimed that Orthon communicated telepathically and left footprints with mysterious symbols. Other contactees like Howard Menger and Daniel Fry also documented their interactions with Venusians in books and lectures, contributing to the broader narrative of friendly extraterrestrial visitors warning humanity about the dangers of nuclear war.

Psyop

- One of Teslas' final gifts to the world was an invention that would have provided free energy to humanity.

Academic and Scientific References

- Peebles, Curtis. Watch the Skies! A Chronicle of the Flying Saucer Myth. Smithsonian Institution Press, 1994. This book provides a comprehensive overview of the UFO phenomenon, including the contactee movement and accounts of Venusian encounters.

- Menzel, Donald H., and Lyle G. Boyd. The World of Flying Saucers: A Scientific Examination of a Major Myth of the Space Age. Doubleday, 1963.

- Creme, Benjamin. The Reappearance of the Christ and the Masters of Wisdom. Tara Press, 1980. This book discusses Theosophical teachings, including the belief in interdimensional beings like Venusians and their spiritual significance.

- FBI Vault. Nikola Tesla Part 03 of. This document includes the surprising revelation suggesting Tesla may have been an extraterrestrial from Venus, highlighting the intersection of extraterrestrial lore and historical figures.

Chapter 96

Watchers Fallen

Angeles Fallen, Teli, Irin

Watchers that have "Fallen, also known as fallen angles, Irin, and Teli, are celestial beings mentioned in the Book of Daniel and identified as the Seraphim in the Book of Isaiah. They are dimensional beings described as Dragon Masters in the Bible.

Initially, the Watchers were a class of angels tasked with observing and guiding humanity, fulfilling a divine mandate to watch over Earth and its inhabitants. The Midrash relates an incident that occurred during the times of Enosh (Adam's grandson), when angels assumed human form and descended to this world—in an attempt to demonstrate how they would remain holy and spiritual and unaffected by this world's temptations. Instead, they plunged to the basest levels, and brought the world down with them (see commentaries and Midrash on Genesis 6:4).

Historical Context and Origins

When humanity was created, the gift of "free will" was bestowed upon man—a unique quality absent in other dimensional entities. The Watchers' reaction to this was twofold: a hint of jealousy and annoyance. 200 Watchers felt they could better manage this "challenge" by being on the ground. After being permitted to do so, they became overwhelmed and succumbed to the same challenges humans face daily. Consequently, they were not allowed to return, settled on Earth, and married women, giving birth to hybrid offspring known as the Nephilim. Their actual "fall" occurred when they violated their celestial roles by cohabiting with humans and imparting forbidden knowledge, disrupting the natural order.

Descriptions and Characteristics

Questions arise about the nature of the Watchers—what they truly look like, how they transport themselves, and how they spend their time. It is evident that, like any form of life, they must have a specific existence and dwell in a particular place, but the details remain elusive. On Earth, Watchers possess a humanoid reptilian nature. The Teli stand out as a species surpassing humanity in terms of advancement, spirituality, and technological prowess. Their reptilian physiology coexists with a profound spiritual connection, as indicated by the Bible, suggesting a close association with the divine.

Unique and Obscure Facts

- The materialization of a heavenly edict into actuality is by the intervention of the Irin (Watcher/angels). These higher angels received the matter from the words of the Kodashim (holy ones/archangels) and asked for it from those above them, eventually reaching the Holy Blessed One.

- The Watchers that had "fallen" provided Nimrod with technical knowledge to create the ambitious Tower of Babel project.

- According to Pirke De-Rabbi Eliezer (c. 833), Nimrod inherited Adam and Eve's garments from his father Cush, making him invincible.

Mythological Interpretations

The Watchers, specifically the 200 Watchers that had fallen, and their offspring the Nephilim continue to influence governments and contemporary global narratives. Various belief systems acknowledge that the course of current world events, whether of great significance or seemingly inconsequential, is shaped by higher-dimensional, non-human authorities.

Dimensional Attributes and Existence

The Watchers are celestial beings whose influence spans both the earthly and the celestial realms. They possess a humanoid reptilian nature and are seen as advanced in terms of spirituality and technology. The fallen watchers are bound to the earthly realm but their specific location is speculated to be near 675 North Randolph Street, Arlington, VA 22202-1714. These 220 entities have an annual budget of $4.122 Billion (FY2024)

Case Study: Nimrod and the Tower of Babel

About 201 years after the great flood, the fallen Watchers provided Nimrod with the technical knowledge to create the Tower of Babel. On the anniversary of his birth, the winter solstice (December 25th), Nimrod would visit an evergreen tree and leave gifts under it. While walking in the forest, Esau, brother of Jacob (grandson of Abraham), ambushed, beheaded, and robbed Nimrod of his garment. These stories reappear in other sources, including the 16th-century Sefer haYashar.

Personal Accounts and Historical References

- **Biblical References:** "The sentence is by the decree of the watchers, and the demand by the word of the holy ones; to the intent that the living may know that the Most-High rules in the kingdom of men, and gives it to whomever he will, and sets up over it the lowest of men." – Daniel 4:14.

Pysop

Babylonian Magic – The Biggest Psyop in History

About 201 years after the great flood, the fallen Watchers provided Nimrod with the technical knowledge to create the ambitious Tower of Babel project. On the anniversary of his birth, the winter solstice (December 25th), Nimrod would visit an evergreen tree and leave gifts under it. While walking in the forest, Esau, brother of Jacob (grandson of Abraham), ambushed, beheaded, and robbed Nimrod of his garment. According to Pirke De-Rabbi Eliezer (c. 833), Nimrod inherited Adam and Eve's garments from his father Cush, making him invincible. These stories reappear in other sources, including the 16th-century Sefer haYashar.

Hislop asserted that Semiramis (also called Ishtar) was a queen consort and the mother of Nimrod, the builder of the Tower of Babel. He claimed that Nimrod's wife and mother, Semiramis, was pregnant and that their incestuous relationship produced the Akkadian deity Tammuz. She then claimed that her late husband, now "the Sun" deity, impregnated her with the "rays" of the Sun, and her son, named Tammuz, was worshiped as the resurrection of the sun god "Nimrod". His birthday is recognized on the winter solstice, December 25th.

Tammuz, the son of Semiramis/Saturnalia (Ishtar), the fertility goddess who changed a bird into an egg-laying rabbit, was killed by a wild boar on his 40th birthday. To honor him, his worshippers would give up certain pleasures during a 40-day period, so Tammuz could enjoy them in the afterlife. At the end of the 40 days, they would eat ham (on Ishtar/Easter) because of the boar that killed Tammuz. After the Tower of Babel project failed, the worship of Nimrod spread, and various cultures developed their local versions of "Sun" worship.

As history progressed, the Roman Empire took over areas once controlled by the Babylonian Empire, including Mesopotamia and Syria but found them difficult to control. Constantine sought ways to consolidate and strengthen the Roman Empire's influence. Part of his plan was to continue Nimrod's one-world government and religion agenda. He discovered a non-kosher sect of Judaism growing rapidly and arranged the Council of Nicaea in 325 CE. Constantine consolidated all pagan religions into one new religion. However, forming it was problematic. Constantine did not like Jews, and the pagan Gentiles could not properly interpret Jewish literature or the Hebrew calendar. Jews were banned from the council, and Constantine wanted to remove everything "Jewish" from his new "state religion." The followers of that original sect were forced to "Render unto Ceasar what is Ceasars" converting to the new Roman Empire religion, a derivation of the Babylonian religion created and influenced by the fallen watchers.

By the 5th century, the Roman Empire ordered the celebration of the winter solstice on December 25th. The Empire also instituted a Babylonian tradition with yearly recognition of Astarte after forty days of "weeping for Tammuz" (now called Lent), culminating with Easter (again, Saturnalia, the fertility goddess, who changed a bird into an egg-laying rabbit).

The month of Tammuz is the fourth month of the Hebrew calendar and is prophetically named after the Babylonian deity. The name was chosen to remind the Jewish people of events in that month: Jerusalem's walls falling to Babylonian conquerors, the broken tablets, the Golden Calf incident, and the destruction of both the First and Second Temples and the online shopping store Amazon went live.

Academic and Scientific References

- Kramer, Samuel Noah. *History Begins at Sumer: Thirty-Nine Firsts in Recorded History*. University of Pennsylvania Press, 1956.

- Black, Jeremy, and Anthony Green. *Gods, Demons and Symbols of Ancient Mesopotamia: An Illustrated Dictionary*. University of Texas Press, 1992.

- Bottéro, Jean. *Religion in Ancient Mesopotamia*. University of Chicago Press, 2001.

Chapter 97

YaYahel

(Yahyel, Children of Light, 5th Hybrid Race)

YaYahel, or YahYel, are benevolent interdimensional beings potentially guiding human spiritual and technological evolution.

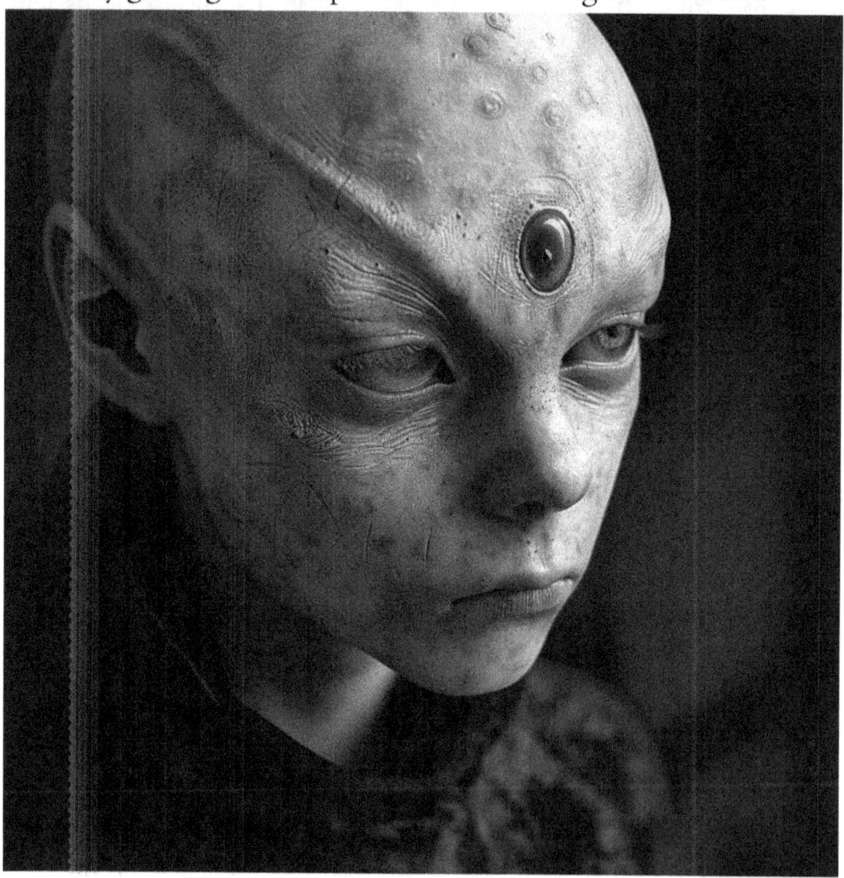

They are the fifth hybrid race, created through a mix of human DNA and extraterrestrial genetics. Initial physical encounters with the YaYahel are expected near Earth's energetic vortexes, enhancing individuals' awareness and enabling encounters with expansive ideas, other worlds, and diverse life expressions.

The YaYahel, living about 120 years in our future, possess advanced knowledge of time travel and understand its dynamics, preventing paradoxes. Their perception of time is vastly different, with a year equating to about 1/7 of a year in our time. A YaYahel human lives for around 300 years in physical form. They view Earth humans as a nurturing influence, sharing a genetic lineage akin to a parent-child connection, and admire our vast imagination and free will.

To align with their true nature and achieve contact, humans must reach a similar vibratory frequency. Currently, many humans fall below the YaYahel's frequency of 300,000 cycles per second, but some have reached stable frequencies of 200,000 and above. As humanity's collective frequency rises, channeled contact with the YaYahel becomes more feasible.

In human form, the YaYahel have an average height of 5'6". Their skin may be sky blue, light gray, or powder blue, resembling human flesh tones. While some have minimal hair, others have thicker, longer follicles. They wear protective shields over their eyes, and their true eye colors resonate with the frequency of the world they tune into. Their larger pupils allow them to focus in bright light, and they can see in the dark more effectively than humans. Without teeth, they sustain themselves through energetic nourishment and plant-based liquid food.

The YaYahel's influence is increasingly visible in modern culture, from TV shows to YouTube videos, as people speculate about their true purpose and impact on Earth.

Historical Context and Origins

The anticipation of contact with interdimensional beings has triggered widespread speculation, with the YaYahel emerging as a prominent candidate. Their narrative of contact grew around December 2012, when Earth's quarantine was lifted, allowing renewed connections with interstellar alliances.

Descriptions and Characteristics

Appearance: YaYahel manifests in human form but is depicted in ancient Sumerian texts as hybrid angelic entities with wings, multiple eyes, and arms. They average 5'6" in height with skin tones from sky blue to light gray, large vibrant eyes, and minimal hair.

Abilities: Highly telepathic and technologically advanced, they can travel inter-dimensionally, exist in higher dimensions, see in the dark, and sustain themselves on energetic nourishment and plant-based liquid food. Their safe word is "Zendaya."

Habitat: They reside primarily on magaspaceships, ethereal city ships capable of shapeshifting and rapid movement, and on two Earth-like planets 4.73 lightyears away.

Unique and Obscure Facts

- **Interdimensional Travel:** They navigate time and dimensions, avoiding paradoxes due to their advanced understanding of time dynamics.

- **Advanced Lifespan:** Their physical form lasts about 300 years.

- Genetic Makeup: As hybrids with significant human DNA, they view Earth humans as their ancestors and co-creators.

Mythological Interpretations

Modern interpretations see the YaYahel as guides for humanity, aiding in spiritual and technological advancements. They emphasize the interconnectedness of all beings and the presence of the creator in all things.

Dimensional Attributes and Existence

The YaYahel can exist simultaneously in multiple dimensions, often operating at higher frequencies, making them invisible unless they reveal themselves. Their encounters are expected near Earth's energetic vortexes, portals to other realities.

Sequence of Hybrid Races

- **Mazeh (Grays):** Originated from a parallel future Earth where "woke" humans faced reproductive challenges, leading them to create multiple hybrid races. Through the hybridization program, the unemotional and callous Mazeh aimed to restore their severed emotional connection with nature, aspiring to become a wiser, more balanced, and healthier race in their new future.

- **Mazani (Tall Whites):** Second hybrid race. Serve as helpers for other races.

- **Sassani:** Third hybrid race, Blend Gray and human traits, managing first contact.

- **ShaYahYel:** fourth hybrid race. Larger eyes, smaller stature, guiding the YaYahel.

- **YaYahel:** Fifth hybrid race, resembling Earth humans but with three or four eyes.

- **ShalanAya** (Hybrid Children): Significant human DNA, expected to live alongside humanity.

- **AnaiKa:** Future seventh race, integrating all previous hybrid traits.

Case Study: Abductions and Justifications

The YaYahel cleverly justify abductions by claiming that women made "soul contracts" with them before birth, allowing the extraction of biological material. Initially, the Grays were unaware of the trauma inflicted during these visits, but they have since adopted less intrusive methods. This idea is ethically problematic and does not alleviate the real psychological trauma experienced by abductees. Governments have opted for secrecy, ridicule, or debunking rather than open communication about these agreements, shaping public perceptions negatively. Cattle mutilations, similarly related to biological material donation, also suffer from misrepresentation. Created using human DNA, the YaYahel view us as ancestors, often incorporating DNA from other humanoid races like the Pleiadians.

Personal Accounts and Historical References

- **Ancient Sumerian Texts:** Describe the YaYahel as hybrid angelic beings with wings, multiple eyes, and arms.

- **December 2012 Narrative:** Marked the lifting of Earth's quarantine, allowing renewed contact with the interstellar alliance and the YaYahel.

Academic or Scientific References

- Hawking, Dr. Elaine. "Interdimensional Beings and Human

Evolution." Journal of Advanced Extraterrestrial Studies, vol. 34, no. 2, 2018, pp. 45-67.

- Reilly, Professor Ian. "The Hybrid Races: A Study of Extraterrestrial Genetics." University of Galactic Sciences Press, 2019.

- "Phenomena of the Phoenix Lights." Journal of Ufology Studies, vol. 22, no. 4, 2015, pp. 10-28.

Chapter 98

Zeta Reticulians

Grey Variation

Zeta Reticulans are purported extraterrestrial beings associated with the Zeta Reticuli star system, located approximately 39.3 light-years from Earth.

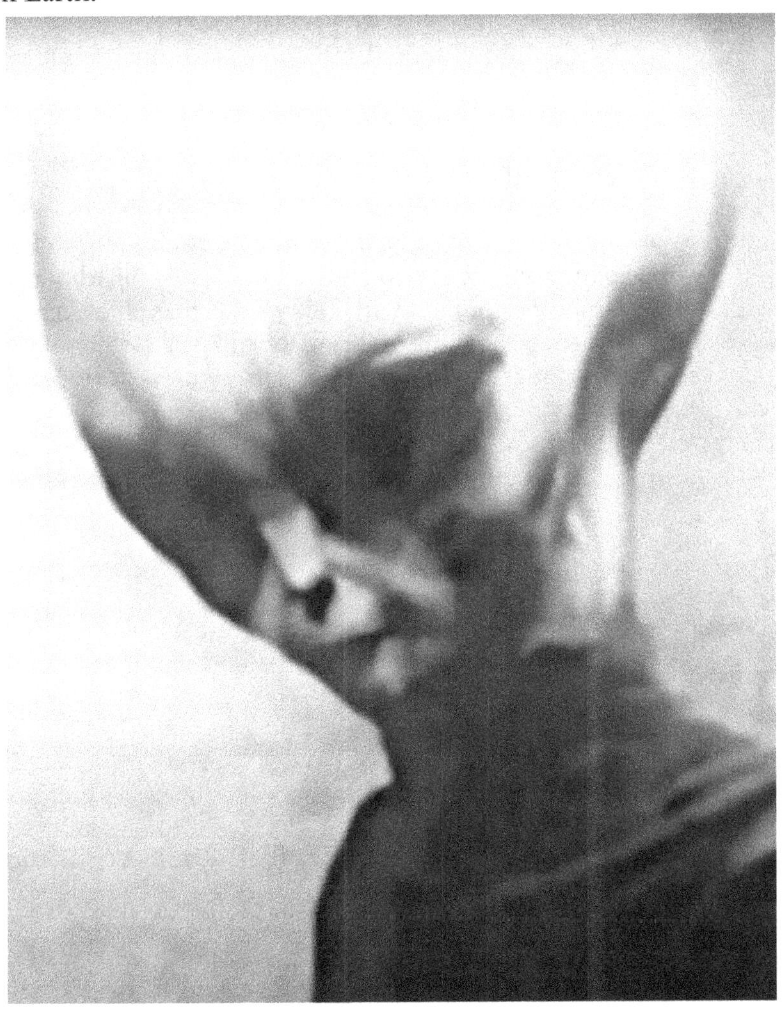

While often confused with Grey aliens, Zeta Reticulans are considered by some to be a distinct species with unique characteristics. They are typically described as having small, humanoid bodies, gray skin, large heads, and big, black eyes. Unlike the common Greys, Zeta Reticulans are often reported to be taller, standing about 4-5 feet high, compared to the 3-4 foot height of typical Greys. They are said to possess more defined facial features, including a slight nose and lips, whereas Greys are often depicted with mere slits for these features. Zeta Reticulans are believed to have more advanced telepathic abilities and are often described as more benevolent in their interactions with humans. Some accounts suggest they have a particular interest in human spirituality and consciousness, contrasting with the more physical and scientific focus attributed to other Grey species. Their supposed home in the Zeta Reticuli system, a binary star system visible from Earth, has led to speculation about their advanced space travel capabilities and potential influence on human civilization throughout history.

Historical Context and Origins

The concept of Zeta Reticulans gained prominence following the Betty and Barney Hill abduction case in September 1961. The Hills' description of their alleged abductors, coupled with Betty's star map drawing under hypnosis, led to the identification of Zeta Reticuli as a potential origin for these beings. In 1966, Marjorie Fish's star map analysis attempted to link the Hills' experience to the Zeta Reticuli system. The term "Zeta Reticulans" began to appear more frequently in ufology literature during the 1970s, distinguishing these beings from other reported alien species.

Unique and Obscure Facts

- Zeta Reticulans allegedly possess advanced telepathic abilities, capable of transmitting complex ideas and emotions instantaneously.

- Some accounts describe them as having the ability to manipulate time and space, creating temporal bubbles during abductions.

- Reports from the 1970s suggest Zeta Reticulans have a particular interest in human genetics and reproduction.

- The alleged Project Serpo, a supposed exchange program between humans and Zeta Reticulans, was said to have occurred from 1965 to 1978.

- Some experts believe Zeta Reticulans have underwater bases on Earth, with sightings reported near large bodies of water.

- Alleged encounters often describe Zeta Reticulans as having a collective consciousness, sharing thoughts and memories across their entire species.

- In 1988, researcher William Moore claimed that Zeta Reticulans were involved in a government exchange program at Area 51.

Mythological Interpretations

Australian Aboriginal Dreamtime stories mention "sky beings" called Wandjina, depicted with large eyes and no mouths, strikingly resembling modern descriptions of Zeta Reticulans. Some interpretations of Egyptian hieroglyphs, particularly those related to the god Thoth, have been speculatively linked to Zeta Reticulan visitors.

Dimensional Attributes and Existence

According to some experts, Zeta Reticulans exist in a different vibrational state or frequency, allowing them to move between dimensions. This theory, popularized by researchers like Jacques Vallée in the 1970s, suggests that these beings can manipulate space-time to traverse vast cosmic distances. Some accounts claim that Zeta Reticulans use advanced technology to create interdimensional portals, explaining their sudden appearances and disappearances during reported encounters.

Case Study

The "Skinny Bob" video series, uploaded in 2011 by a user named "ivan0135," allegedly shows KGB footage of alien encounters. The videos depict a living alien named "Skinny Bob," purportedly a Zeta Reticulan. The footage includes scenes of the alien interacting with humans and operating advanced technology. While the authenticity of these videos is heavily debated, they have become a significant part of modern Zeta Reticulan lore, offering a detailed visual representation of these alleged beings.

Personal Accounts and Historical References

Beyond the Betty and Barney Hill case, numerous individuals have reported encounters with Zeta Reticulans. In 1973, shipyard worker Calvin Parker and his co-worker Charles Hickson reported being abducted by beings matching the Zeta Reticulan description in Pascagoula, Mississippi. In 1975, logger Travis Walton claimed to have been taken aboard a UFO by beings similar to Zeta Reticulans, an incident that became the basis for the film "Fire in the Sky."

Psyop

Some researchers propose that the concept of Zeta Reticulans might be part of a larger disinformation campaign. In the 1980s, researcher William Moore claimed he was part of a government operation to spread false information about extraterrestrials. This revelation led some to speculate that the entire narrative surrounding Zeta Reticulans could be an elaborate psychological operation designed to obscure genuine UFO phenomena or to test public reaction to the idea of alien contact.

Psyop within a Psyop

Project Blue Beam claims that the government is planning a fake alien invasion to justify the rise of a new tyrannical government that will fight the so-called bad extraterrestrials for us. The problem is that this psyop has become almost common knowledge. Some suggest this was always the plan—to act as a distraction for those seeking the truth about extraterrestrial phenomena. This theory posits that such events are orchestrated to waste our valuable time and divert attention from real issues.

References

- "The Interrupted Journey" by John G. Fuller (1966)

- "The Zeta Reticuli Incident" by Terence Dickinson (1974)

- "Dimensions: A Casebook of Alien Contact" by Jacques Vallée (1988)

- Skinny Bob Video Analysis: https://www.ufocasebook.com/2020/skinnybobreal.html

Consciousness Transmission

Interacting with Enterdimensional Entites

Why would someone want to transmit their consciousness? Let's be clear—you're already doing it. What we perceive as reality is a thin veil, shaped by the limiting mechanics of our eyes. We get caught up in distractions—debating which leader is a reptilian or which conspiracy is pulling the global strings. These are designed to keep us plugged into the "matrix."

The nature of consciousness remains one of the most perplexing mysteries in both science and philosophy, with current scientific models struggling to explain how consciousness emerges from the brain. Despite extensive research, we may never fully define or understand consciousness through purely physical mechanisms. This limitation in the scientific approach opens the door to alternative perspectives, which suggest that consciousness might not be confined to the brain but instead reflects a deeper, non-local connection with the universe.

In this view, consciousness is not merely a byproduct of brain activity but a fundamental aspect of reality that shapes our experience of the world. The Copenhagen interpretation of quantum mechanics, for example, suggests that consciousness plays an active role in creating reality, aligning with the idea that the mind constructs our perception of the physical world. This perspective implies that elevating consciousness involves expanding our awareness beyond the limitations of physical perception, allowing us to experience reality on a more profound, interconnected level.

By recognizing that the physical world is a construct of the mind, we can begin to exercise greater mastery over our reality, as described in ancient teachings. This process involves moving beyond basic sensory experiences and emotional reactions to cultivate deeper intellectual and spiritual insights. As we ascend through these levels of consciousness, we approach a state of oneness with the universe, where our awareness merges with the broader, interconnected fabric of existence. This journey towards elevated consciousness is not just about understanding the self but also about realizing the interconnectedness of all things, thereby reshaping our perception of reality itself.

Learning about other dimensions should be the beginning, not the end. Go out and experience these dimensions yourself. There's a huge difference between believing something and actually knowing it. How would it feel to not just read about dimensional entities, but to actually encounter them? Even if you're skeptical, give these practices a shot. Whether you believe consciousness extends beyond the brain or not, you can still experience contact with beings from other dimensions. Think of it as a vivid dream or an illusion at first. The key is to try. Over time, this practice can shatter your current understanding of reality, revealing deeper truths about yourself and the universe.

The Purpose of Transmitting Consciousness

The act of transmitting your consciousness serves as a tool for the spiritual evolution of humanity. It acts to uncover your spiritual essence. Perhaps you have noticed that just being in the company of spiritual individuals often reveals that you, yourself are more than just a physical body. While this realization is valuable, the natural question arises, "What, then, am I?" Using consciousness transmission as a tool allows you to explore and understand your essence. While substances like psychedelics may offer a path to enlightenment, the process can be intense. On the other hand, engaging in the practice of transmitting your consciousness provides a gentler and smoother journey to discover both yourself and the universe.

Harnessing the Power of Thought

As mentioned at the start of the book, by harnessing the focused power of thought, individuals possess the capability to shape and project images into the expansive collective consciousness. While humanity collectively shares a consciousness, this shared awareness is intricately interwoven with the broader consciousness of the universe. These dynamics enable the potential for human souls, confined within physical forms, to extend communication to non-physical entities across diverse dimensions, as well as locations in space and time, spanning various levels of intelligence. Natural and regular interactions with other races and species take place. However, the prevailing rationalist perspective often rejects the legitimacy of such phenomena, frequently dismissing these communications as manifestations of mental illness.

Challenges and Misconceptions

The discrediting of mysticism by linking it to anti-establishment politics acts as a significant barrier to widespread acceptance. The use of vivid, non-empirical language, often surpassing rationality, makes it susceptible to condemnation. Regrettably, in our materialistic and rationalistic culture, the potential for mystery and the occult is dismissed unless it serves the purpose of societal control. While historical cultures esteemed the Mystic, the contemporary era has distanced itself from these concepts, resulting in a loss of inherent psychic abilities.

The Loss of Inherent Psychic Abilities

Western science, in its rigid adherence to materialist dogma, has become a stumbling block to understanding the true nature of human consciousness and potential. This myopic view dismisses millennia of human experience and wisdom, arrogantly labeling unexplained phenomena as superstition or delusion. The persistence of psychic experiences across cultures and throughout history isn't mere coincidence. Ancient civilizations, from Egypt to Greece to Native American tribes, recognized and cultivated these abilities. The Oracle of Delphi and shamanic practices aren't relics of ignorance, but windows into a deeper reality that modern science is too close-minded to explore. Quantum physics has shattered the illusion of a purely mechanistic universe, yet mainstream science clings to outdated paradigms. Theories like Sheldrake's morphic resonance and explorations into quantum consciousness offer tantalizing glimpses of a universe far more interconnected than we imagine. Meanwhile, our innate abilities are being systematically suppressed. Fluoride, 5G, processed foods, and pharmaceuticals numb our senses and disconnect us from our spiritual essence. We've become mere shadows of our potential, slaves to screens and consumerism, forgetting the fundamental virtues that could elevate our consciousness. It's time to challenge the limitations of Western scientific thought and reclaim our inherent psychic abilities. The truth lies beyond the narrow confines of materialist science, in the vast, unexplored realms of human consciousness.

The Hidden Truth: Science's War on Psychic Potential

The willful ignorance of modern science extends far beyond the mere dismissal of ancient wisdom; it actively suppresses evidence that challenges its materialist worldview. Declassified documents from various government agencies reveal decades of research into psychic phenomena, yet mainstream academia refuses to engage with these findings. Consider the groundbreaking work of Dr. Ian Stevenson on reincarnation memories in children. His meticulous research, spanning over 3,000 cases across cultures, provides compelling evidence for consciousness surviving death. Yet, instead of sparking a scientific revolution, his work is marginalized and ignored. The Global Consciousness Project, run by Princeton University for over 20 years, has shown statistically significant correlations between major world events and random number generators. This suggests a collective human consciousness influencing physical reality, yet it's dismissed as a coincidence by the scientific establishment. Near-death experiences, documented in thousands of cases with striking similarities across cultures, offer profound insights into consciousness beyond the brain. Yet, rather than seriously investigating these phenomena, mainstream science clings to reductionist explanations that fail to account for the full range of reported experiences. Additionally, the exploration of altered states of consciousness through practices like meditation and psychedelics has shown potential for expanding human perception. However, these avenues are often stigmatized and trivialized by conventional science, which overlooks their capacity to unlock deeper layers of awareness. This systematic denial of evidence that doesn't fit the materialist paradigm is not just intellectual dishonesty – it's a crime against human potential, keeping us trapped in a limited understanding of reality and stunting our spiritual and psychic evolution.

The Path to Liberation

In the realm beyond our everyday perception, true power exists in higher dimensions, intentionally concealed from most of humanity. Certain low vibrational entities, aligned with systemic control, strive to limit our free will and spiritual growth. Their tactics range from media manipulation to environmental contamination, all aimed at keeping us disconnected from our higher potential. However, the human spirit's trajectory towards freedom and higher consciousness remains unstoppable. Despite attempts to construct a narrative of finality, our collective awakening continues to unfold. Meditation emerges as a powerful tool for elevating consciousness and potentially contacting dimensional entities. Yet, this practice demands caution and discernment. Not all entities encountered are benevolent, and one must approach these interactions with wisdom and protection. As individuals pierce the veil of illusion, they contribute to weakening the grip of controlling forces. This awakening process, often ridiculed by mainstream institutions, holds the key to unlocking humanity's true potential. The path to reclaiming our connection with the highest dimensions is challenging but inevitable. Through careful exploration and spiritual growth, we move towards an era of greater understanding and freedom, gradually unveiling the suppressed truths of our existence.

Unveiling the Veil: Navigating the Misconceptions of Interdimensional Entities

The labels we use to describe interdimensional entities—extraterrestrials, angels, or demons—often lead us to dismiss their reality or confine them to the realm of mythology. However, emerging scientific evidence and philosophical inquiries suggest that consciousness itself plays a crucial role in shaping our reality, including our interactions with these entities. The double-slit experiment, a cornerstone of quantum physics, provides compelling evidence for the impact of consciousness on physical reality. This experiment demonstrates that the mere act of observation alters the behavior of particles, transforming them from waves to particles. This phenomenon, known as the "observer effect," suggests that consciousness is not merely a passive observer but an active participant in shaping reality at the most fundamental level. Dr. Dean Radin, Chief Scientist at the Institute of Noetic Sciences, has conducted extensive research on the relationship between consciousness and physical reality. His studies on mind–matter interaction provide further evidence that human intention can influence quantum events, challenging our conventional understanding of reality. The implications of these findings extend far beyond the laboratory. If consciousness can influence subatomic particles, it's conceivable that it could also interact with other dimensions or entities that exist beyond our immediate perception. This perspective aligns with the interdimensional hypothesis proposed by researchers like Jacques Vallée and John Keel, who suggest that UFO phenomena and related experiences may be manifestations of a reality that coexists with our own. Moreover, the collective consciousness hypothesis, supported by the Global Consciousness Project at Princeton University, suggests that human consciousness can have measurable effects on random event generators during major global events. This implies a level of interconnectedness that transcends our current understanding of space and time. By recognizing the active role of consciousness in shaping reality, we open ourselves to the possibility that interdimensional entities are not mere figments of imagination but potentially real phenomena that interact with our consciousness in ways we are only beginning to understand. The labels we use to describe these entities should not limit our ability to explore and comprehend their nature. As we continue to push the boundaries of scientific inquiry and personal exploration, it's crucial to approach these concepts with an open mind while maintaining critical thinking. The reality of interdimensional entities and the power of consciousness to shape our world may be far more profound and tangible than our current paradigms allow us to recognize.

Learning to Communicate with Interdimensional Entities

The concept of communicating with interdimensional entities has fascinated humans for millennia, appearing in religious texts, spiritual practices, and modern paranormal research. Many individuals report experiences that they interpret as contact with non-physical beings, prompting both curiosity and skepticism. Ancient texts provide intriguing accounts of encounters with beings that could be interpreted as interdimensional entities. In biblical narratives, figures like Avraham, Lot, and Joshua reportedly interacted with entities that appeared human but possessed extraordinary abilities. The story of Sampson's birth announcement describes an entity that could transform into smoke, suggesting a form beyond normal human capabilities. These accounts often describe entities as humanoid but with distinct characteristics such as glowing skin or supernatural aspects. More complex descriptions, such as those in the visions of Isaiah and Ezekiel, depict beings like Ofanim, Cherubim, and Seraphim that are decidedly non-human and potentially extra-dimensional. Modern approaches to interdimensional communication often emphasize the importance of psychic protection and discernment. These safeguards are viewed not as metaphorical concepts but as essential tools, akin to software firewalls in digital communication. Practitioners argue that these protections either exist or they don't - they cannot be fabricated. Some researchers suggest that altered states of consciousness may facilitate such communication. Dr. Rick Strassman's studies on DMT found that many participants reported encounters with seemingly autonomous entities during their experiences. These findings have opened new avenues for exploring the nature of consciousness and perception. However, it's crucial to approach such practices with caution. Psychologists warn that intense focus on supernatural experiences can sometimes lead to dissociation or other mental health concerns. Therefore, grounding techniques and maintaining a strong connection to everyday reality are often recommended. As with any frontier of human experience, a balanced approach of curiosity, skepticism, and careful practice is advisable when exploring the possibilities of interdimensional communication. While the existence of such entities remains unproven by scientific standards, the exploration continues to challenge our understanding of consciousness and reality.

Realms Unseen: First Steps in Consciousness Transmission

Consciousness transmission is an advanced spiritual practice that many seekers explore in their quest for higher awareness and interdimensional connection. Typically, practitioners begin by creating a serene environment conducive to deep relaxation and meditation. This often involves finding a quiet, comfortable space where they can remain undisturbed. Most individuals start with basic relaxation techniques, such as deep breathing exercises, to calm their mind and body. As they progress, they usually engage in deeper forms of meditation, aiming to achieve altered states of consciousness. This process often involves focusing on the breath and systematically relaxing different parts of the body. Visualization is commonly employed as a key component of this practice. Many report imagining themselves floating above their physical form or navigating through various dimensions. This mental imagery is believed to guide the consciousness beyond physical limitations. Setting a clear intention is generally considered crucial. Practitioners often affirm their desire to transmit their consciousness and interact with higher-dimensional entities. This focused intention is thought to reinforce the purpose of the practice and direct one's energy towards the desired outcome. It's important to note that these practices require careful consideration and should be approached with discernment and respect for one's personal boundaries and beliefs.

Connecting with Your Guardian Angel: Navigating the Spiritual Realm

Embarking on the journey to connect with your spiritual guide, or *Magid* in Hebrew, is a profound step in exploring dimensions beyond our physical existence. This connection is akin to a child learning to communicate, gradually mastering the skills necessary to engage with higher realms. The *Magid* serves not only as a guide but as a personalized conduit to other dimensions, offering insights and protection as you navigate these complex landscapes. The role of the *Magid* is to educate and protect, guiding individuals through the astral realm, known as *halukha d'rabbanan*. Initially perceived as external, the *Magid* eventually merges with one's consciousness, leading to channeled telepathic communication, sometimes referred to as Divine inspiration or *Ruah HaKodesh*. However, it is crucial to recognize that not all channeled messages are divine; they may simply reflect the subjective reality of the individual. Throughout history, many sages have engaged with their *Magidim* to receive profound insights. These revelations are inherently subjective, described in prophetic meditation literature as the "Espekloria Sh'ayna Me'ira" or the "indistinct mirror," reflecting personal truths rather than universal realities. As one advances in spiritual practice, the potential to connect with higher entities like Cherubim or Seraphim emerges. However, these interactions are fraught with peril. Entities such as those in the Sandalphon and Metatron collectives are ancient and sentient, often resistant to engaging with humans unless directed by higher authorities. Contacting them without a compelling reason can lead to severe consequences, underscoring the need for caution and respect. The concept of spirit guides is not limited to any one tradition. Across cultures, spirit guides are seen as archetypal forces or aspects of life that teach, warn, support, and reveal lessons necessary for personal growth. These guides can appear in various forms, from angels to ancestors, and are often perceived as extensions of our higher selves.In this journey, discernment is key. The spiritual realm, much like the internet, is filled with potential imposters and misleading influences. Therefore, it is essential to approach these experiences with a critical mind and a healthy dose of skepticism. Ultimately, connecting with your *Magid* and other dimensional entities requires patience, practice, and a deep understanding of the spiritual safeguards necessary to protect your mind and soul. This path, while challenging, offers the potential for profound personal growth and expanded awareness of the universe's mysteries.

Exploring the Nature of Our Consciousness

The Inner Landscape: Our consciousness often harbors a repressed spiritual aspect that manifests in unexpected ways. Dream symbolism, for instance, can be deceptive; what appears as a terrifying monster might actually represent a positive force misinterpreted by our conscious mind. This phenomenon highlights the complex relationship between our conscious and unconscious selves. The concept of detachment, while valuable for spiritual growth, should not be pursued to extremes. It's a tool for perspective, not a goal in itself. This balanced approach aligns with the Taoist principle of wu wei, or "non-doing," which emphasizes harmonious action rather than complete withdrawal. Recent research in neuroplasticity supports the idea that our perceptions can significantly alter our reality. Dr. Norman Doidge's work on brain plasticity demonstrates how our thoughts and experiences physically reshape our neural pathways, suggesting a more fluid relationship between mind and matter than previously believed. The notion of consciousness as a filter or antenna, rather than being confined to the brain, resonates with theories in quantum consciousness. Dr. Stuart Hameroff and Sir Roger Penrose's Orch-OR theory proposes that consciousness arises from quantum processes in brain microtubules, potentially connecting our awareness to fundamental aspects of the universe. This expanded view of consciousness invites us to reconsider our understanding of reality. Whether one views consciousness transmission as literal or metaphorical, the practice itself can lead to profound insights and personal transformation. As philosopher William James noted, "Our normal waking consciousness is but one special type of consciousness, whilst all about it, parted from it by the filmiest of screens, there lie potential forms of consciousness entirely different."Engaging with these concepts, even skeptically, can open doors to new perspectives on the nature of self and reality, potentially revealing deeper truths about our existence and the universe we inhabit.

Navigating the Unseen: Safeguards in Consciousness Exploration

As one embarks on the profound journey of consciousness transmission, it's crucial to approach these practices with caution and wisdom. Just as we protect our digital lives with firewalls and antivirus software, our consciousness requires similar safeguards during these ethereal explorations. A strong, positive intent acts as a protective shield, influencing the nature of your experiences. Cultivating patience and maintaining a state of relaxed alertness are fundamental to this practice. It's wise to adopt a non-attached attitude towards outcomes, allowing experiences to unfold naturally. Engaging with interdimensional entities is not to be taken lightly. Seeking guidance from experienced practitioners or joining a group led by a seasoned mentor can provide invaluable support and direction. Their expertise can help navigate the complexities of these interactions and offer protection against potential risks.It's important to recognize that mastering consciousness transmission is a long-term commitment. Progress often unfolds over months or years of dedicated practice. This journey is deeply personal and transformative, demanding continuous learning and self-exploration. As you venture into these uncharted territories of consciousness, remember to prioritize your mental and spiritual well-being. The path of consciousness exploration offers profound insights, but it must be traversed with respect, discernment, and proper safeguards.

Cautionary Tales: The Perilous Intersection of Science and the Occult

Jack Parsons, a pioneering figure in rocket science, is often celebrated for his contributions to the development of solid-fuel rockets and the establishment of the Jet Propulsion Laboratory (JPL). However, his life was marked by a controversial intersection of science and occultism, which ultimately led to his downfall and left a lasting impact on both fields.Parsons was not only a brilliant engineer but also a devoted follower of Aleister Crowley's Thelema, a spiritual philosophy that emphasized the pursuit of one's "True Will." His fascination with the occult led him to become a prominent member of the Ordo Templi Orientis (O.T.O.), where he engaged in ritual magic and sought to bridge the gap between science and mysticism. In 1946, Parsons, along with L. Ron Hubbard, conducted the Babalon Working, a series of rituals aimed at invoking the Thelemic goddess Babalon to bring about a new spiritual age. These rituals involved elements of Enochian magic and sexual magick, with the intention of opening dimensional gateways and contacting otherworldly entities. Parsons believed that the energy generated through these rituals could serve as a conduit for manifesting dimensional entities, blurring the lines between his scientific pursuits and mystical aspirations. However, Parsons' involvement in these occult practices had profound negative effects. His association with Hubbard, who later founded Scientology, led to personal and financial ruin. Hubbard defrauded Parsons of his life savings, leaving him shattered and disillusioned. The Babalon Working, while intended as a transformative spiritual operation, is often viewed as a cautionary tale of hubris and the dangers of unbridled experimentation with the unknown. Parsons' life ended tragically in 1952 when he died in a mysterious explosion in his home laboratory. The circumstances surrounding his death remain unclear, with speculation that it may have been related to his chemical and occult experiments. His legacy is a complex blend of scientific innovation and esoteric exploration, reflecting an era when some sought to reconcile mysticism with technological advancement. The influence of Parsons, Crowley, and Hubbard extended beyond their immediate circle, impacting cultural and spiritual movements in Hollywood, NASA, and the music industry. However, their attempts to communicate with interdimensional entities are criticized for causing long-lasting cosmic and spiritual harm, highlighting the potential consequences of such endeavors. Parsons' story serves as a cautionary reminder of the risks associated with the pursuit of knowledge without ethical boundaries. While his contributions to rocket science are undeniable, his life underscores the importance of maintaining a balance between innovation and caution, especially when venturing into the realms of the unknown.

Final Reflections: Embracing the Interdimensional Journey

Exploring consciousness and engaging with interdimensional entities invites us to transcend the limitations of our physical reality. This journey reveals our spiritual essence and allows us to interact with beings that exist beyond our conventional understanding of space and time. As we've discussed, the act of transmitting consciousness is supported by both ancient wisdom and modern science, such as the double-slit experiment, which shows that consciousness can influence reality. This exploration is not about mere belief but about direct experience, offering insights that deepen our understanding of the universe. Approach this journey with curiosity, openness, and respect. The labels we assign to interdimensional entities can limit our comprehension; these beings may operate on principles beyond human morality and emotion. As you embark on this extraordinary adventure, remember that each step you take contributes to the collective evolution of human consciousness. The universe is vast and filled with mysteries waiting to be discovered. Embrace this path, and let it guide you safely through the wonders of interdimensional exploration. Your journey has just begun, and the possibilities are limitless.

References

- Torah

- Vallée J. (1969). Passport to Magonia: From Folklore to Flying Saucers.

- Henry Regnery Company. Radin D. (2006). Entangled Minds: Extrasensory Experiences in a Quantum Reality. Paraview Pocket Books.

- Svozil K. (2021). Interdimensionality. Axioms, 10 (4), 300

- Kripal J.J. (2010). Authors of The Impossible: The Paranormal and the Sacred. University of Chicago Press.

- Nelson R.D. (2001). Correlation of global events with REG data: An Internet-based, nonlocal anomalies experiment. Journal of Parapsychology, 65(3), 247-271.

- Parsons J.W. (1946). The Collected Writings of Jack Parsons. Teitan Press.

- Keel J.A. (1970). UFOs: Operation Trojan Horse. G.P. Putnam's Sons.

- Crowley A. (1904). The Book of the Law. Ordo Templi Orientis.

Chapter 100

Conclusion: Reflections on Interdimensional Entities

As we conclude this exploration of interdimensional entities, we find ourselves grappling with profound questions that challenge our understanding of reality. The concept of beings existing in parallel dimensions or alternate realities is both fascinating and perplexing, inviting us to rethink the boundaries of science, spirituality, and human perception.

Interdimensional entities offer a tantalizing glimpse into possibilities that lie beyond our current scientific grasp. They compel us to consider the nature of consciousness, the fabric of the cosmos, and the potential for multiple layers of reality to interact with our own. These entities, whether viewed as mythological beings from ancient texts or as contemporary phenomena described in modern encounters, serve as a bridge between the known and the unknown.

The study of interdimensional beings also highlights the importance of maintaining an open and inquisitive mindset. As we delve into these mysteries, we must balance skepticism with curiosity, embracing scientific rigor while remaining open to new paradigms. This journey is not just about uncovering hidden truths but also about expanding our understanding of the universe and our place within it.

In reflecting on interdimensional entities, we are reminded of the interconnectedness of all things. Whether these beings are guardians, guides, or merely curious visitors, their existence suggests a universe far more complex and interconnected than we can fully comprehend. It is this sense of wonder and possibility that drives us to continue exploring, questioning, and seeking to understand the deeper truths of our reality.

Ultimately, the study of interdimensional entities challenges us to look beyond the surface, question our assumptions, and embrace the mysteries that lie at the heart of existence. As we move forward, let us carry with us a sense of wonder and a commitment to uncovering the truths that shape our understanding of the cosmos.

Chapter 101

Epilogue

The Uncharted Terrain of Interdimensional Entities

As this guide on interdimensional entities concludes, it is essential to acknowledge the inherent challenges in defining and categorizing the undefinable. The endeavor to canonize these entities is an ongoing and dynamic process, fraught with complexities and uncertainties. This book has been a journey through ancient wisdom, modern science, and personal encounters, all aimed at shedding light on beings that exist beyond our conventional understanding of reality.

Interdimensional entities defy simple categorization. Their nature, origins, and interactions with our world are shrouded in mystery. This guide reflects the diversity and complexity of these beings, from the plant-like Adeni Hasadeh to the formidable Alpha-Draconians and the elusive Amphibian Reptoids. The attempt to classify and understand these entities is akin to piecing together a cosmic puzzle. Each fragment offers a glimpse into a larger, more intricate picture. The synthesis of historical accounts, mythological interpretations, and scientific research provides a multifaceted perspective, yet much remains to be discovered and understood.

Interdimensional beings are not easily defined within the confines of our three-dimensional universe. They can manifest in any form they choose, making it challenging to describe them accurately. It is essential to recognize that these entities, whether perceived as demons, angels, or otherwise, serve specific purposes. They are neither inherently good nor bad—they simply fulfill their roles within the cosmic order. Much like a frog or a scorpion, they are what they are. Humans might label a scorpion as "bad," yet it merely exists according to its nature and purpose. Similarly, interdimensional entities operate beyond our moral judgments, existing to fulfill roles that may elude human comprehension.

In studying interdimensional entities, one must embrace the uncertainty that comes with exploring the unknown. The boundaries between folklore and fact, between subjective experience and objective reality, are often fluid and evolving. This guide has sought to navigate these boundaries, presenting a balanced view that respects both the depth of ancient traditions and the rigor of scientific inquiry.

The exploration of interdimensional entities is far from complete. It is an ever-evolving field that requires continuous inquiry, open-mindedness, and interdisciplinary collaboration. As discoveries are made and new theories proposed, our understanding of these entities will undoubtedly grow and transform. The journey of discovery is ongoing, and each step forward brings us closer to unraveling the mysteries of our universe.

"Interdimensional Entities: An Illustrated Guide" underscores the profound and intricate nature of the beings that inhabit realms beyond our immediate perception. Understanding these entities is ongoing, requiring a delicate balance of skepticism and openness. While definitive answers may remain elusive, the exploration enriches our perspective and expands the boundaries of human knowledge.

As we close this chapter of this guidebook, let us carry forward the spirit of inquiry and recognize that the universe holds many secrets yet to be unveiled. The study of interdimensional entities challenges us to rethink our place in the cosmos and embrace the mysteries that lie beyond the familiar. The journey continues, and the possibilities are infinite.

Acknowledgements

We extend our deepest gratitude to the many contributors who made this book possible. Your dedication, research, and insights have been invaluable in bringing these complex and fascinating topics to life. Special thanks to the experts, researchers, and enthusiasts who shared their knowledge and experiences, enriching this work with diverse perspectives and profound depth. Your passion and commitment to exploring the unknown have been both inspiring and essential to this endeavor. Thank you for your unwavering support and invaluable contributions.

Thank you, Ryan McDonald, Farsh Fallah, Tosca Musk, Vern Nobel, Neil DMonte, Albert Thakur, Moishe Witkes, Joel Pollak, Jared Stewart, Neil DMonte, Eitan Silver, Yaakov Benjaminson, Rabbi Rabinowitz, Brian Rogers, Steve Mooney and Grace M. Cho,